Entanglements

It takes two to tangle.

Entanglements

Marking Place in the Field of Religion

Russell T. McCutcheon

SHEFFIELD UK   BRISTOL CT

Published by Equinox Publishing Ltd.

UK: Office 415, The Workstation, 15 Paternoster Row, Sheffield S1 2BX
USA: ISD, 70 Enterprise Drive, Bristol, CT 06010

www.equinoxpub.com

First published 2014

ISBN-13 978 1 78179 076 2   (hardback)
         978 1 78179 077 9   (paperback)

British Library Cataloguing-in-Publication Data

A catalogue record for this book is available from the British Library.

Library of Congress Cataloging-in-Publication Data

McCutcheon, Russell T., 1961-
  Entanglements : marking place in the field of religion / Russell T. McCutcheon.
     pages cm
  Includes bibliographical references and index.
  ISBN 978-1-78179-076-2 (hb) -- ISBN 978-1-78179-077-9 (pb)
  1. Religion. 2. Religions. I. Title.
  BL41.M3493 2014
  200.7--dc23
                              2013040854

Typeset by ISB Typesetting, Sheffield, UK

Printed and bound by Lightning Source Inc. (La Vergne, TN), Lighting Source UK Ltd. (Milton Keynes), Lightning Source AU Pty. (Scoresby, Victoria)

To my father,

Russell Wyman John McCutcheon,

going strong, in his 90th year.

A youth to fortune and to fame unknown…

Contents

Preface

This book, a collection of responses that I've written over the years, tries to make evident that scholarship is situated and comes with implications—in a word, tangled. None of us researches, writes, or teaches in a vacuum. Because the chapters that follow were all originally written for a variety of different occasions, some dating from very early in my career and yet others being part of still ongoing scholarly disputes, I have decided to reproduce them here as they were originally published (though Chapters 6 and 7 have not been published at all until this volume), but to add an introduction to each chapter, in which I describe both the earlier occasion for the publication and try to identify the larger topics of which I then thought, or perhaps now think, the response comprises an "e.g." While the book is by no means to be confused with a memoir, the newly written introductory material freely uses anecdotes from my career to illustrate topics that, in my opinion, have relevance to the chapter, not to mention the field at large as I have understood it (i.e., the situation from which the response emerged or some occasion that illustrates its point)—for like all of us, I speak from where I stand ("we're all stuck somewhere," as I think I once phrased it [2001a: ch. 5]), and so readers have a right to know a little about that spot instead of assuming that a writer's judgments are disengaged, ahistorical referents. While there are those who disparage the use of an anecdote in an academic essay, I have frequently used them in the past for I am unsure how long and just how detailed an *anecdote* has to be before it earns the right to be called an *ethnography* or *evidence*, and is thereby judged as credible and very important. It is for this reason that I feel quite comfortable employing what we might call tactically succinct ethnographies (a.k.a. anecdotes) in my writings on the study of religion—but they are always offered in the service of an argument, as mere background commentary to contextualize a piece of academic writing.

In writing these new introductions I have therefore tried to bear in mind a comment recently made by Bruce Lincoln: "no one ever theorizes for the first time, much as no one claims originality while narrating a myth, although in both cases one's relation to predecessors—and contemporaries—is always more fraught than one knows or admits" (2012: 53); recognizing this, it is my hope that the brief chapter introductions, written as honestly as I dare while also recognizing that much not only remains unremembered and perhaps even unknown of by me, but also that some things certainly (perhaps necessarily?) remain unsaid, will at least help to address a critique of an earlier collection of my essays, inasmuch as I was faulted for failing to provide the full and proper provenance of some of the essays (Wiebe 2004: 3). That each of these replies inevitably are but a piece of a far larger but, in this book at least, unreproduced conversation will, I hope, motivate interested readers to chase down the citations that I provide so that the full exchange can be read and considered. But I have at least taken the liberty of inserting background notes in places throughout the following chapters where I think readers will benefit from, for example, the actual quotation from an author to whom I am replying (in cases where my original chapter does not provide the quote). These notes (either in the endnotes or main text) are identified as Editorial Notes (i.e., "Ed. Note:…"), with myself being the "editor," in distinction from notes that are reproduced here because they also appeared in the original text. But having said this, I should say that I do not see the absence of the full exchange as a shortcoming of this volume; after all, by their very nature texts always start abruptly, in the midst of innumerable prior (often lost or perhaps unacknowledged, even unknown) exchanges, thereby always relying on interested (or imaginative) readers to fill in the gaps for themselves. That this is all the more apparent in this book should, I hope, not be seen as a limitation but, instead, serve to remind us that it is *always* this way, for no text is definitive, exhaustive, or all-inclusively total, for (yes, as Derrida taught us long ago), they gain significance by referral; thus they always rely on the unstated that came before and the as-yet-to-be-unconceived (let alone written), that will more than likely come after. The introductions that I have provided, all written with the benefit (or impediment?) of hindsight, therefore attempt to state (or should I say "invent"?) both.

The chapters are arranged in chronological order for a specific reason: to offer readers an opportunity to judge for themselves whether authors are unchanging, ahistorical referents. (This also provided a rationale for not rewriting and updating the main chapters themselves.) I specifically recall a colleague at another school, not so very long ago, who told me about using a newer essay of mine in her graduate class. When, later in the semester, her students read another scholar's recently published comments on my work, she let me know that the students recognized on their own that the author in question was describing my position as it had been articulated in the mid-1990s, as if my argument was lodged in amber. While it is heartening that people have read some of my early work, and, for whatever reason, continue to think it worth reading (if only to disagree with it, perhaps—for of such things are discourses made), that I am sometimes solely understood as the author of a book that was a revision of my doctoral dissertation, that I am sometimes known as a scholar who criticizes people for being religious, or that I am said never to offer constructive alternatives to the critiques that have occupied some of my time, is (at least to me) all very unfortunate and lamentable. While my own personal sense of self—perhaps conjured into existence by writing these very lines—might be premised on the assumption that there are discernible continuities across the various pieces that follow (and, as a good mythmaker, my task in each chapter's introduction, just as writing this preface, not to mention creating an index to the book, is probably to highlight the similarities that strike me *now* as important, thereby creating a particular sense of continuity), I expect readers will find gaps, for that will signify change, accident, and happenstance, and that's what makes people interesting as historical subjects.

So my hope is that readers—especially my intended audience: someone much like myself, but about twenty-five years ago, long before I knew some of the things at stake in what I wanted to do as a scholar and thus before I was able to recognize the chess moves that would be made in response to the novelty that I tried to bring to the debate—will treat this collection seriously as a series of field notes or dispatches from the front, as I once characterized an essay of mine (2003b), resulting from my living and working among the people whom I study, carrying out a detailed ethnography of scholarly practice for the past twenty years. What readers do with these communiqués is, of course, entirely up to them—if they wish to pathologize me and my scholarly interests (as discussed in my introduction), then I applaud the triumphant and long overdue return of rigorous explanatory theorizing to the academic study of religion! My only hope is that, in seeking to explain away the fact of my interests, such critics are at least equal opportunity reductionists, willing to find their own usual objects of study and scholarly choices just as curious and just as easily reduced. Should they not, then I look forward to learning why their curiosities are protected as natural while mine are not.

Because these essays arise from across my career to date (dating from 1990 to 2013), there are far too many people to name, to whom I am indebted when thinking through the position that I have come to hold. The chapters therefore retain their original acknowledgments in the notes, and I can do no better than repeat them here to re-affirm the important influence that a variety of people have had on my thinking over the years. For reading drafts of the introductory material that is published here for the first time, and for offering helpful feedback that invariably made them better, I would like to thank: William Arnal, Willi Braun, Aaron Hughes, Merinda Simmons, and Vaia Touna. I am also indebted to Andie Alexander, when she was a senior undergraduate student in our Department, for scanning some of the oldest of the following chapters, those that I no longer had in computer files, and formatting them for publication, and also for reading some of the introductions to provide me with feedback from the point of view of a member of my intended audience.

I also appreciate Janet Joyce's continued interest in publishing my work and am therefore pleased to see this volume appearing in her newly reinvented Equinox list dedicated to the academic study of religion. My thanks therefore also go to Val Hall for helping once again to facilitate the publication of my work.

Finally, I have dedicated this book to my father, after whom I am named (while he was named after his own father, who drowned while building a bridge across the Rouge River in Quebec, in 1923, back when my grandmother was just a young women still pregnant with her second child—my father). My father did not go very far in school—only to about grade five, as I recall the story—because his step-father also drowned, when my farther was eleven, while working on the river as a lumberjack (we sometimes forget, today, just how dangerous rivers once were and can still be); as the oldest son, my father then went to work himself. And he worked for the next sixty years, interrupted only by volunteering to serve in Europe as part of the Canadian Armed Forces during World War II. Yet despite his limited schooling, he helped to instill in me a work ethic and a curiosity for practical explanations to account for seemingly miraculous things—a curiosity that made him a jack-of-all-trades and a problem-solver who built and flew his own airplane, who drove dump trucks beneath the city of Niagara Falls when the hydroelectric project was being developed, who was a milkman with horse and wagon, who was a high school janitor, who made his own lamps and sold them door-to-door during tough times, who—along with my late mother—built a successful business in a little gas station that helped to put me through university, and who, many years before, built, by himself, the first house in which I ever lived. I owe more than I can name to his labor, his sense of humor, his love of science, and his patient determination in the face of life's sometimes disheartening obstacles and absurdity. My life is entwined in his and so I dedicate these entangled essays to him.

Sources

The following publishers and journals are thanked for allowing these chapters to be reproduced in this volume:

1. "Naming the Unnameable: Theological Language and the Academic Study of Religion." *Method & Theory in the Study of Religion* 2/2 (1990): 213–29. Leiden: E. J. Brill.
2. "Ideology and the Problem of Naming: A Response to Clarkson and Milne." *Method & Theory in the Study of Religion* 3/2 (1991): 245–56. Leiden: E. J. Brill.
3. "Returning the Volley to William E. Arnal." *Studies in Religion/Sciences Religieuses* 27/1 (1998): 67–68. London: Sage.
4. "Of Strawmen and Humanists: A Reply to Bryan Rennie." *Religion* 29 (1999): 91–92. Amsterdam: Elsevier.
5. "A Brief Response form a Fortunate Man." *Culture & Religion* 1/1 (2000): 131–39. London: Taylor & Francis).
8. "Filling in the Cracks with Resin: A Reply to John Burris's, 'Text and Context in the Study of Religion'." *Method & Theory in the Study of Religion* 15/3 (2004): 284–303. Leiden: E.J. Brill.
9. "A Few Words on the Temptation to Defend the Honor of a Text." *Bulletin of the Council of Societies for the Study of Religion* 33/3 and 33/4 (2004): 90-91. Sheffield: Equinox Publishing Ltd.
10. "Theorizing 'Religion': Rejoinder to Robert A. Segal." *Journal of the American Academy of Religion* 73/1 (2005): 215–17. Oxford: Oxford University Press.
11. "The Perils of Having Ones Cake and Eating it Too: Some Thoughts in Reply," *Religious Studies Review* 31/1 and 31/2 (2005): 32–36. Houston, TX: Rice University.
12. "Theses on Professionalization." In Mathieu E. Courville (ed.), *Next Step in Studying Religion: A Graduate's Guide*, 41–45. London: Continuum, 2007.
13. "A Response to Prof. Robert Campany's 'Chinese Religious History and its Implications for Writing 'Religion(s)'." In Volkhard Krech and Marion Steinicke (eds.), *Dynamics in the History of Religions between Asia and Europe: Encounters, Notions, and Comparative Perspectives*, 295–305. Leiden: Brill, 2012.
14. "'As it Was in the Beginning...': The Modern Problem of the Ancient Self." *Bulletin for the Study of Religion* 39/2 (2010): 37–39. Sheffield: Equinox Publishing Ltd.
15. "A Direct Question Deserves a Direct Answer: A Reply to Atalia Omer's 'Can a Critic Be a Caretaker too?'" *Journal of the American Academy of Religion* 80/4 (2012): 1077–82. Oxford: Oxford University Press. The Appendix was

originally posted as an online interview originally posted at Georgetown University's Berkeley Center http://berkleycenter.georgetown.edu/posts/religion-scholar-versus-advocate (accessed April 6, 2014).

16. "Recovering the Human: A Tale of Nouns and Verbs: A Rejoinder to Ann Taves." *Journal of the American Academy of Religion* 80/1 (2012): 236–40. Oxford: Oxford University Press.

17. "Three Dots and a Dash" originally appeared as a blog posted at *The Immanent Frame*, http://blogs.ssrc.org/tif/2012/05/01/three-dots-and-a-dash/.

18. "The Sacred *is* the Profane," originally appeared as a two part blog posted at: http://www.politicaltheology.com/blog/the-sacred-is-the-profane-part-1-russell-mccutcheon/ and http://www.politicaltheology.com/blog/the-sacred-is-the-profane-part-2-russell-mccutcheon/.

Introduction: Apologia for an Obsession

> it has not yet been possible to demonstrate the essential feature
> which probably lies at the root of the obsessional neurosis. (Freud
> 1964: 117)

Although most of the following pieces have previously appeared in print
separately, I have decided to collect them together as a set of discrete examples of the scholarly back-and-forth that constitutes an academic field. I am
publishing this volume now—guided by the assumption that, together, with
new introductions for each chapter, they make a collective statement that is
worth making—because of two recent experiences, both of which relate to
complaints that I have heard before; in fact, I wrote about both in a preface to a previous book, *The Discipline of Religion* (2003a). That such complaints still persist, more than decade later, and that I now sometimes hear
them being directed at younger scholars who have come to share some of
my interests in the practical implications of category formation, is among
the motivations for publishing this collection now.

    The first is a comment said to me not too long ago about the fact that my
work is not on actual data, so-called real things, but, instead, is on scholars—a comment premised on the apparent fact that I do not work on *primary*
sources (i.e., so-called religious texts, rituals, institutions, etc.—that many
of these so-called primary sources [e.g., those texts that we commonly call
scriptures] are the products of long past scholars and textual elites is, somehow, lost on those who complain about my scholarly focus). I have been
told that, inasmuch as I am interested in the scholarly use of the category
religion itself, I merely offer commentary on derivative *secondary* sources
(i.e., I study the scholars who themselves study the supposedly actual data).
Thus, as interesting as my work's focus on the category "religion" may or
may not be, it is obviously not of real significance or enduring importance to
the study of religion; in fact, it has even been suggested (and not simply by
so-called theological or humanistic colleagues but also those inclined toward
the social sciences) that I should instead be working in, say, a Department
of Sociology. I have a suspicion that this critique, what amounts to discursive border patrols, was never made of, say, the late Catherine Bell when she
turned her attention to the very category ritual (e.g., 1992 and 1997) and that
Bruce Lincoln's study of the history and the politics of the category myth

(1999) still strikes scholars of myth as a book worth reading.[1] That similar work, but on the category religion instead, warrants such responses is the first indication of the category's protected, and thus curious, status—for seemingly rigorous, historically-inclined scholars no less than for so-called religious people. To press it further, I was clearly given the impression, on another occasion not so very long ago, that anyone who follows me in this set of interests, adopting this particular focus for their own scholarship, was somehow *not* doing original scholarship or, even worse, was failing to think for themselves. In the so-called hard sciences I know that doctoral students are often given their dissertation topic by their supervisor and that it can amount to nothing but a sub-project of the supervisor's own research (making it debatable who will get the coveted place of first author on the eventual publication)—curiously, this is understood as a legitimate credentialing strategy and not seen as illegitimate fakery. Or consider how we call it a school of thought (as in "the Chicago school of thought" in our own field, or the "Frankfurt school") when a group, across generations, develops a similar style and focus for their work—those in its subsequent generations are never characterized as doing unoriginal, derivative work. Instead, we reverentially talk about such people's intellectual predecessors and identify their *Doktor Vater*—saying it in German, as many English speakers whom I've met tend to do, makes this imprimatur seem all the more profound and thus legitimate (as does the Latin term imprimatur, no?).

Given that my career has, almost from the start, been characterized by an interest with categories and the scholars who use them (as evidenced in the opening chapter to this collection, first published in 1990), rather than with the supposedly real things that, in the opinions of others, these categories unproblematically name, this is a critique that is rather familiar to me, reminiscent of having my work referred to as mere journalism or literary pieces and not scholarship or science (something on which I comment in the earlier preface to which I referred above [2003a]). Such accusations of illegitimacy, of course, are a sensible way to grapple with anyone who calls into question what Pierre Bourdieu once termed the "monopoly of legitimate thought" (1988: 68) that is evident in any epistemological and institutional field. For as the epigraph from Bourdieu in part read, as it appeared at the start of my first book, *Manufacturing Religion* (whose use there signaled my anticipation that I might be spanked for giving away trade secrets): "The same people who would not hesitate to acclaim the work of objectification as 'courageous' or 'lucid' if it is applied to alien, hostile groups will be likely to question the credentials of the special lucidity claimed by anyone who seeks to analyze his own group" (Boudieu 1988: 5).

As a brief example, consider how the recent work of Aaron Hughes—which critiques the manner in which Religious Studies scholars who study

Islam often function as caretakers for a specific type of Islam (which is politically and theologically liberal, and thus complementary to these scholars' own liberal democratic/capitalist interests)—is understood by some in our field as highly controversial, perhaps even inflammatory (e.g., Hughes 2008; 2012a; 2012b). As someone who is himself interested in the history of our field and the ways in which scholars go about doing their work, Hughes's thesis strikes me as relatively uncontroversial; for (and this is the important point) he is simply arguing in a way comparable to that of, say, the much respected scholar of Islam, Omid Safi, in his impressive volume, *The Politics of Knowledge in Premodern Islam* (2006). From the publisher's website for Safi's book we read the following description of its argument:

> In order to legitimize their political power, Saljuq rulers presented themselves as champions of what they alleged was an orthodox and normative view of Islam. Their notion of religious orthodoxy was constructed by administrators in state-sponsored arenas such as madrasas and khanaqahs. Thus orthodoxy was linked to political loyalty, and disloyalty to the state was articulated in terms of religious heresy.

With regard to *method*, this strikes me as a remarkably apt description of what Hughes is also up to in his work. The difference, of course, is at the level of *data*, since Hughes is not simply using a sociology of knowledge critique to understand how contests over religious orthodoxy were once waged by long departed social actors; instead, he applies the same method to understand the shape of modern *scholarly* orthodoxies and their wider socio-political ramifications—examining how they are policed and the discursive objects that their methods make it possible (or impossible) to study. As Bourdieu noted, doing this work on "them" can enhance one's career, whereas applying this same method to question the legitimacy of accepted academic practices—applying it to "us"—prompts one's colleagues to try to explain why one would ever be interested in such an odd thing.[2]

For instance, consider a summer seminar for early career faculty, sponsored by the National Endowment for the Humanities (NEH), that I had the good fortune to participate in during the summer of 2011, at the University of Virginia (organized by Chuck Matthewes and Kurtis Schaeffer). Having read some of my work as part of their workshop, as an example of a certain critique of the field, I was kindly invited to join the group on Thomas Jefferson's campus, in Charlottesville, for a day's worth of discussion. It was clear that a variety of the participants found my focus on category formation to be somewhat frustrating—likely wanting to just get on with the real work of studying religious people because, apparently, we all just know that there is something distinct in the world called religion, or spirituality, or belief, or whatever else one calls this "it." That such scholars cannot understand their own in-group to be no less interesting than any other group of human beings, all of whom are presumably engaged in meaning/identity-making through category formation and use, is fairly easy to understand—after all, who among us wants to give up our taken-for-granted subjectivity, presumed autonomy, and thus our first person interpretive authority over self-representations and understandings (e.g., the ability to say "When I say this I mean that…" and not be questioned on it), only to become someone else's object of study?[3] One rather early career participant in the seminar, seated at the far end of the room, and trained in anthropology (but, as it turned out, no less resistant than many others are to using ethnography to study scholars themselves), surfed the web on a laptop while the discussion went on; it soon turned out that she had found my CV online and was looking it over, for she exclaimed (the correct word to characterize her behavior, I would say), "You're *obsessed* with the category 'religion'!" The verb was key, I think, for—at least as I heard it—it connoted illegitimacy and a troubling, almost clinically diagnosable, preoccupation that required explanation and, in fact, justification on my part. My reply to what I heard as a direct challenge to the legitimacy of my work was simple and forthright: "In other fields we call that *expertise*." My point was to try to prompt this young scholar to consider why she would never even consider saying that to a scholar who spent his or her professional life studying, say, the bacterial flagellum in Biology or the Q document in Christian origins or whatever it was that she had written her dissertation on. For I know plenty of people who spend their entire careers studying very specific things—such as a colleague who has been writing on Eliade's life and work for twenty years and is therefore considered an authority on the Historian of Religions—and they are called specialists and are never accused of being "obsessed" with this or that object.

It should be evident that such dismissive critiques—I could tell you other stories, such as the seemingly well-meaning scholar who, not very long ago and in front of his grad students, called my interests "passé" and "common," as if these were mere descriptions of self-evidencies and not partisan judgments that, at least when made in a classroom, required argumentation and defense—make apparent a person's presumed norm not only of what gets to count as interesting but also concerning what scholarship *ought* to be; normally, it is simply a study of some obviously curious "them" that is carried out by a set-apart and privileged "us," using specific tools that some "we" know to be in lock-step with the real world—tools, for example, like the category "religion." (We apparently use our real language to study what are, for them, merely metaphors.) Sadly, this norm is usually asserted and therefore undefended (as is the case with all so-called common sense). Perhaps it is simply asserted because the rhetoric of legitimate/illegitimate data and primary/secondary source breaks down rather easily upon closer scrutiny, which makes responding to this sort of critique in any real detail somewhat uninteresting, I admit. After all, apart from a body of scholarly commentary, that one surveys as its own object of study in the first chapter of virtually any dissertation (what we call a survey of the literature), how did this pottery shard or that scrap of parchment, this group's narrative or that person's claims, ever become an object of interest in the first place? Answer: Someone found it, or better put, someone found some thing *useful* for some purpose *alien to the object itself*, some interest that pre-existed the material artifact itself—for otherwise, why/how would just this object have "stood out" (as if objects stand on their own, by which we mean that they present themselves of their own accord) for this person to begin with, from what I take to be the hectic background noise of the world?[4] I do not think that randomly arranged sticks and branches on the ground, with crooked angles and gnarls, proclaim themselves to be "guns" for little boys intent on playing army or twinkling lights in the sky, all at wildly different distances from some star-gazing observer, necessarily arrange themselves into meaningfully shaped constellations. Someone then used this newly constituted "it" as a way to secure an argument they were making or a set of interests they were seeking to realize—"For example, consider the…" they said to someone else. Then, someone else read this or heard that and was persuaded—someone with interests of his or her own, of course. This someone else then put to use the "it," that was constituted by others, for who knows what new purposes…. To bring it back to the idea of a survey of the literature, without the set of questions brought by the one writing the dissertation, how did these and just these particular authors and texts comprise the appendages of this particular "body of literature"? (Many of us know to look through the reference section to any book first, to figure out what authors are arguing, by determining with whom they associate their ideas.) That is, writers constitute the tradition into which they place their own work. I therefore start from the position that the world is filled with too many sources (quite literally, every single thing is a potential source of interest, no? *Including that very assertion itself.* What would Borges have done with *that* self-referential insight?) and I understand scholarly attention and scholarly focus (in a word, discourse, whose iceberg tips are categories arranged in systems of order that we call taxonomies) necessarily to constitute the mere stuff of the world as so-called primary sources.

Flatly stated, despite what I read as the overly confident claims of some of our colleagues, none of us study pristine, primary sources. Instead, so-called primary sources are the artifacts of prior dis/agreements among

stock
of
knowledge

scholars—a claim that hints at the reason for my choice of title for this book; for we all inherit an already sorted and catalogued (but continually malleable, inasmuch as we bring new choices and interests to it, each time we enter it) archive of past conversations, choices, and controversies. For instance, without a lengthy thing that we commonly call a scholarly tradition or discipline (for example, the one represented by the names of Watson and Crick), no one would be studying deoxyribonucleic acid, for if it proclaimed its own significance then we would have known all about it long before their 1953 article in *Nature*; without a long history of research that includes the work of such people as Comte and Durkheim, no one would be walking around studying some thing called society. My friends in Christian origins likely know this better than anyone, for they so clearly sit atop a few hundred years' worth of historical-critical work (so-called "higher criticism"—a term whose valence is hardly innocent), scholarship that is itself the beneficiary of prior, careful hermeneutical work (though, admittedly, motivated by different goals than how many of my friends do their own work today) that has accrued over more than a millennia and a half, all of which makes, say, some particular thing called "the Synoptic Problem," a topic worth talking about and, for at least some of them, trying to solve.

The problem, of course, is that many of us fail to see the processes and procedures (to suggest both the structural and the agential) that produced the particular products to which we lay claim, thereby making them our into primary, seemingly originary sources; to stick with the Christian origins example, we just take the text as a given, a naturally-occurring fact (i.e., a natural kind), that demands study rather than examine the history of choices that made just these and not those parchment fragments part of a collection that is "interesting"—namely worth translating, reading, preserving, and interpreting. Thereby, we, as scholars, transform mere accidental artifacts left over from those who came before us into enduring relics to be preserved in amber and revered. I would argue that this is a failure *required* by the social worlds in which we live inasmuch as overlooking the messy processing work is how *these* and not *those* operations, and the interests they help to realize, are authorized as natural, inevitable, and common sense. This is nothing but an instance of what Marxists might refer to as reification, (German: *Verdinglichung*), whereby the contingent relations between the producers are mistaken for necessary objects that exist independently of people. Somewhat like children who are incapable of imaging their parents as existing prior to being *their* parents (an ahistorical identity attributed to historical beings—I think here of Maurice Bloch essay from not so long ago [2008]), scholars are often incapable of imagining a time before their datum constituted an object of interest and thus value—reimagining those data-producing practices, decisions, and what was at stake in those choices (in a word, studying the work of scholars themselves), strikes me as an important step in that exercise that we call writing history, for in historicizing scholarship itself we see it as no less of a human practice as any.

As a corollary to this, understanding "actual data" and "primary sources" as self-evidently existing and obviously interesting strikes me as extremely sloppy scholarship, inasmuch as it takes so-called tradition or consensus as naturally occurring facts, thereby efficiently erasing the human agency—the choices, the debates, the battles, and the accidents—from the narrative. If, after asking a question concerning why people do this or that, we are *un*satisfied with answers that take the form of "It's tradition!" (inasmuch as such an answer is simply a restatement of the question—"Why do we always do it? Because we always do it!"), then accepting claims that some objects are primary (and thus self-evidently valuable) and that others are secondary (i.e., commentary that is of mere derivative value) should strike us as equally problematic—as a coded way of saying, "We study important things because they are important!" For those who refuse to entertain why and how something came to be seen and treated as primary, original, authentic, legitimate, interesting, etc., also fail to see how their own work on supposed self-evidencies (e.g., patterns in the world that pre-exist our choices and categorizations) indicts themselves *qua* scholars, because they reveal themselves to be anti-historical historians who refuse to study change and circumstance and happenstance when it comes too close to their own doorstep. To put it crisply, while I have no trouble calling the early twentieth century European conflict "the First World War" for a variety of handy reasons, I would be a pretty poor scholar if I did not also understand that the thing known as the Great War, or the War to End all Wars, did not *become* "the First World War" until looked back upon with the benefit of hindsight and previously unforeseen subsequent events a generation later, implying that the name, the label, the category, is but a part of a contingent narrative that did not exist when young men were dying in the trenches in France. One does not have to go as far as Jean Baudrillard's 1991 set of essays that argued that the Gulf War as experienced by the US public did not actually take place (1995), to understand that the thing named as "the First World War" is not the same as "the Great War."

I therefore offer the following chapters, all of which are focused on scholars doing their work on religion, as one more nudge in the direction of encouraging colleagues to consider the constitutive role they themselves play—their assumptions, interests, the way they teach and organize themselves, and so on—in making this thing called religion a primary source in the world that is worth talking about.

The second reason for offering this collection now was occasioned by a couple of unrelated conversations I have had over the past year or two with earlier career scholars who sought me out at conferences to tell me that they (somewhat like that professor mentioned earlier) *used to* think that my work was *passé*—a judgment of my brand of critique of the field that I also addressed in that earlier preface (2003a). "No one reads Eliade anymore," I'm often told, as if having published two chapters in my first book that used Eliade's work as an example (McCutcheon 1997b: chs. 1 and 2), and also one standalone essay in a multi-authored collection, on those who still defend Eliade's work (McCutcheon 2001b: 11–23), somehow constituted my entire writing career. The implication of this claim is that no one thinks that religion is unique or special anymore and that I'm just tilting at windmills, as we say, when I critique this sort of position. Why…, just look at all that emphasis on what we now commonly term material religion, religion on the ground, lived religion, embodied religion—I'm told that this work is empirically grounded (what's more material than material religion?) and therefore lacks the metaphysical and sweeping, generalizing tone that characterized work in our field just a generation or two ago (it's on the always shifting ground, after all, and thus not in the rarified, essentialist ether). I'm not satisfied with such supposed gains in our field, however, for this work fails to ask what it is that is being put into the body (i.e., this is precisely what "to embody" something means, no?)—as if what we're studying is not bodies, the actions of bodies (i.e., ritual, narrative, etc.), collections of bodies (i.e., groups), and the assorted artifacts left over after those bodies have gone (e.g., texts, architecture, etc.), *to begin with*! We no longer talk about souls, of course, but this immaterial thing now called meaning has simply replaced our onetime ethereal objects of study, for it too is generally assumed to be moving outside of bodies, lurking in objects, moving across historical periods via those untheorized things called traditions (referred to above) which carry with them that ill-defined thing we call heritage or identity. Beneath the veneer of lived religion's empiricism there still lurks the same old idealism—what we might call a rebooted theory of animism. The more things change…

But what made these conversations among onetime critics stand out, however, was, as I wrote above, that my interlocutors *used to* think that my critique was no longer relevant; they now both wished to tell me in person that they no longer thought this. What occasioned the change in their thinking? They both had come to moments in their careers when the judgments of their colleagues took on a new and significant material consequence in their own professional lives, and suddenly the freedoms and the boundaries that these younger scholars once took for granted—concerning how they studied, wrote, and taught about religion—were called into question and undermined rather dramatically. Those were serious situations, no doubt, inasmuch as professional critiques can adversely impact employment and thus throw our personal lives into turmoil; but they were sobering for them inasmuch as the limits of the acceptable in our field suddenly became apparent in a way that they had never been before. I'm not sure that this means that my critique of how the field works is correct—after all, I only spoke with two people and we all know about the inductive fallacy—but it does comprise some evidence to continue working with this model until such a time that it does not work.

So I decided to gather together a selection of my writings that I've not previously collected in a volume, essays that each exemplify how scholarship is an ongoing series of conversations—entanglements, to put a finer edge on it, that are sometimes spirited, no doubt, and always with something practical at stake, regardless how seemingly esoteric the so-called primary source may seem—between members of a discourse, conversations that are sometimes aimed at discerning if the interlocutors even share enough in common to be said to participate in the same discourse. The volume presses forward concerns evident in my previous work, but does so this time with an eye more explicitly toward those coming behind me in the career, hoping that, before putting their own neck out, they'll at least pause and take stock of how this writer thinks power within this one academic discipline—let alone society at large—functions to ensure that certain ways of patterning social relations, and the social interests as well as the intellectual curiosities that they help to realize and make possible, continue over time. Having considered this, I'd hope they'd be strategic about when, where, and how to intervene with their own work.

That the various (often dismissive) critiques leveled at my work over a decade ago persist and have not found any more substantive way to register disapproval, and that others who perceive themselves to be ostracized from the profession have been able to use my work to better understand their own situation, tells me that I am doing something right. For if the best someone can do is to call me a fake or to accuse me of not reading their text correctly..., well, then that's a pretty sad commentary for how they employ argumentation and evidence in their own work—the usual tools of our scholarly trade. And if my work is of further assistance to those making a place for themselves in this one corner of academia, then that's rather gratifying—I think here, most recently, of Teemu Taira's important essay on the discursive study of religion, notably the manner in which he uses a debate, published in Finland, between Don Wiebe and myself, as a way to tease out various traditions within the modern field (2012). Because of uses such as this, I am pulling together various of these jousting matches. For what else is a scholarly career but a series of discrete moments and situations, taking place in a space made by those who came before us and leaving some raw material to those who might follow us—a series of moments and situations, agreements and disagreements, evidence of what Lincoln once called affinities and estrangements (1989: 9)?

When collected and then seen with the luxury of hindsight, a career is the name that we give to the place that we've marked—and if readers see in my subtitle evidence of having watched my dog, Izzy, repeatedly mark her turf while we walk every morning at 6:00 am, then so be it—where one has interacted in a thoughtful and rigorous way with others who are equally curious about something and up to the task, those who also use the same tools to make the world an interesting place to be. These are the conversations and disputes in which we are all tangled. What follows are a selection of my own, accompanied by introductions that try to disentangle things, just a little.

Notes

1.   Catherine Bell: "Neither am I concerned to make any pronouncements on the intrinsic value of studying ritual per se. Rather, I am launching an analytic exploration of the social existence of the concept of ritual, the values ascribed to it, and the ramifications of these perspectives for scholarship" (1992: ix) and "In continuity with the earlier book, however, this study brings a particular perspective to these discussions, namely, the position that 'ritual' is not an intrinsic, universal category or feature of human behavior—not yet anyway. It is a cultural and historical construction that has been heavily used to help differentiate various styles and degrees of religiosity, rationality, and cultural determinism" (1997: ix). Bruce Lincoln: "For in the pages that follow I will not attempt to identify the thing myth 'is'; rather, I hope to elucidate some of the ways this word, concept, and category have been used and to identify the most dramatic shifts that occurred in their status and usage" (1999: ix).
2.   This paragraph is adapted from my own introduction to a 2012 special issue of *Method & Theory in the Study of Religion* (24/4-5) in which several Islam scholars were invited to comment on an essay of Hughes's, critiquing the work of a representative group of scholars of Islam, that (presumably because of its seemingly controversial nature) had been rejected by the *Journal of the American Academy of Religion*. See the Introduction for the full background on the controversy over this article and the reason it was published in *MTSR*.
3.   It is interesting to me how scholars of religion resist this no less than the people whom they study—even those scholars who openly theorize and thus redescribe people's behavior as opposed to scholars who try to describe it in terms acceptable to those whom they study. Case in point, in November of

2012, a research group in which I am participating recorded a discussion for the UK's The Religious Studies Project (http://www.religiousstudiesproject. com) on how scholars of religion ought to study identification practices. The entrée into the discussion concerned how students often seek to identify *us* (i.e., their authorized professors) by asking what religion we are. Many of the group's members noted how they resist answering the question, in part out of a concern for how the students will then "box them into" certain pre-conceptions they bring with them to the class. This strikes me as pretty much the same concern voiced by those who critique the place of theory (a.k.a reductionism) in the study of religion.

4. It should be clear that I take classification to be a thoroughly human action, driven by human interests—social as well as intellectual—and thus a proactive and not reactive response to the passive recognition of extra-subjective patterns operating in the world around us. Whether such extra-subjective patterns do indeed exist is, of course, a speculation that I leave to those more confident than I in either their intuitive or predictive capabilities.

Chapter 1

Introduction

I was lucky enough to have been a graduate student at the University of Toronto when two other students—Ann Baranowski and John Morgan—founded *Method & Theory in the Study of Religion* in 1989, a journal that eventually moved from being completely produced by students (publishing only two issues per year) to being edited by graduate students and published first by Mouton de Gruyter of Berlin (volumes 5 through 9, going quarterly in volume 6) and then Brill of the Netherlands (volume 10 to the present). The journal is now (as of 2013) in its twenty-sixth year, produces five hundred pages per volume, is among the widely respected scholarly periodicals in the international study of religion, and long ago ceased being edited by people necessarily associated with the University of Toronto. The journal grew wings and didn't just fly the coop but changed the coop a little too. I'd like to think that, by providing a place for a certain sort of discussion in our field, one not necessarily found in other periodicals, *MTSR* helped to bring about a bit of a revolution in the study of religion, inasmuch as the terms "method and theory" (in whichever order) are now commonly found when you search course titles or CVs for the specialties scholars claim to have. I say "claim to have" because the debate surrounding what gets to count as a theory and what constitutes a focus on methodology means that it is never entirely clear what "method and theory" signifies. But at least almost everyone now assumes that they'd better at least be aware of this (admittedly somewhat amorphous) body of literature.

I got involved with *MTSR* when the issue in which the following article appeared, in 1990, was entering production. Along with Willi Braun, I joined Ann, with my name first appearing on the masthead of issue 3/1 (1991); we managed subscriptions, edited and formatted articles in WordPerfect, used scissors and glue to make paste-ups on blue-lined grid paper (some of which are still in a filing cabinet in my office), we then took it all to a copying service that worked with a book binder and, voila, issues were ready to be packaged up and mailed out. Because it was a journal produced by fellow students (with funding assistance from a small number of units at the university; we were also joined by Darlene Juschka and Arthur McCalla) and I was trying to make the move from philosophy of religion (having already written two Masters theses on work related to the philosophy of Alfred North White-head and having then studied the pre-Socratics, Plato, Aristotle, Kant, etc.) to what our program, under the leadership of Neil McMullin and Donald Wiebe, was calling method and theory, it seemed natural to try my hand at writing an essay *not* for class (a novel thing that all doctoral students sooner or later must try) and submitting it to the journal. The stakes did not seem as high, of course, as mailing it off to *Studies in Religion* (*SR*, the main journal in Canada) or the *Journal of the American Academy of Religion* (*JAAR*, the main US journal, thought by some to be the main international journal as well, perhaps much as *The New York Times* is both a city newspaper and also understands itself as one of the preeminent international newspapers of record as well). I was in part prompted to do this by a story Donald Wiebe, one of my professors, told me, of his own graduate days at Lancaster, when someone he knew had an article of his own accepted for publication. "If his work could get published, then so could my own" was the conclusion that he told me he drew from the experience. I took him seriously; my article was accepted and became my first peer reviewed publication.

This article, which bears no explicit link to the dissertation I was then beginning to work on, was written three years before I started fulltime work as an Instructor at the University of Tennessee (1993–96) and five years before my dissertation was defended in January of 1995 (eventually published in 1997 as *Manufacturing Religion*). The essay—which responded to two articles previously published in *SR*—obviously reflects a number of concerns I had at the time; but despite being very early in my career, I do find interesting how issues of demarcating an object of study from its analysis, on the one hand, and the implications of category formation, on the other, have persisted throughout much of my work since that time. However, reading it now, for the first time since it was published, it strikes me that, despite the similarities, there are important differences between it and my current interests. For example, my current focus on the category religion, the very manner in which we name something *as* religion, is nowhere represented in this early work, focused as it is on advocating for a way to study religion more "objectively" and thus in a non-theological manner. These certainly were my concerns at the time; that this very way of talking, this very way of thinking about the topic, eventually came to occupy my attention as data, was certainly unforeseen when writing this essay.

It is precisely because, in this essay, I do not necessarily recognize my current self that I have decided to include it here, to keep ever present the fact that authors are themselves historical subjects occupying a contingent position. I can't help but feel that some are a little disappointed when they invite me to lecture since the person who shows up to talk is not necessarily the person who wrote the book they read that was published fifteen years ago—which brings to mind the quotation attributed to Rita Hayworth, concerning the sensuous character she played in the film "Gilda" (1946): "Men fell in love with Gilda, but they wake up with me." That this essay does and does not sound like me, at least to my ear now, is good, I think. It seemed worth including also because it picks up on some themes that stuck with me; for example, the ease with which theologically and politically liberal scholars import into their work sets of unargued, extra-scholarly concerns—in this case, the presumption that it is natural and proper to avoid gender-exclusive language when referring to "God" (i.e., avoiding using male pronouns, whether bearing the uppercase honorific "H" or not) even though many of the people whom we might study strongly resist doing anything of the sort, that is, they would argue vehemently that God *is* a man, a father, has a beard (aking to Charlton Heston playing Moses, perhaps), whatever. In this way, scholars routinely take sides in what are in fact local identity debates, picking winners and losers—but doing so in a way that fails to identify the stake that they themselves have in these debates (on this point, see Ramey's important statement in his regional AAR Presidential Address [2013]). The manner in which we employ categories like "Christianity" or "Hinduism" or "Islam" makes this evident rather nicely, inasmuch as scholars routinely subsume within these categories subgroups whose members sometime claim for themselves sole and exclusive membership within the category. What do we do with someone in our classes who, for example, says that Roman Catholics are not Christians (to pick but one example)? Do we correct such claims and thus ignore this position while retaining both the speaker's group and Catholics' membership in the common family we know as Christianity? While scholars would likely never consider taking the side of the so-called conservative exclusivist (and instead, trouble themselves with adjudicating so-called boundary cases, trying to determine whether, for instance, Jews for Jesus ought to be included in a survey of modern Judaism or whether the members of the Nation of Islam count as Muslims), we routinely take the side of the liberal inclusivist. Sadly, we generally don't make the shift from studying some eternally stable object in the world, say Islam, to studying the identification or signification practices that constitute the object *as* object (and the ways in which competing practices, creating competing objects, are adjudicated)—moving from wishing to know what Islam *really is* and who is or is not *really* a Muslim, to examining who *claims* to be Muslim and how they make these claims and how they try to give them a competitive advantage in the hectic economy of signification (a term I routinely borrow from Jonathan Z. Smith [1982: 56]). Making this move frees us from ever worrying about the supposedly tough call over so-called borderline cases, since we, as scholars, are not involved in patrolling or mending other people's fences—we've got no investment in just where the border ought to be.

But phrasing it in this way gets the cart well ahead of the horse, at least as exemplified in the following essay. For while reflecting early concerns in my career that no longer occupy me, I think it also points us in the right direction.[1]

Note

1. See Hughes (2013b) where, after selecting the following chapter for inclusion in this volume, it was also selected for a "best of" volume of *MTSR*, as part of its twenty-fifth anniversary celebration. Rebekkah King (a graduate of the University of Toronto and professor at Middle Tennessee State University) responds to the essay in that volume.

Naming the Unnameable? Theological Language and the Academic Study of Religion (1990)

Introduction: The Problem of Naming

While marking undergraduate Religious Studies papers written on early Christian scriptures, I noted in many margins that it would be wise for the students to consider incorporating general inclusive language into their essay writing. As is commonly the case, "man" and "he" were often used as generic references to people. Later, I found myself thinking once again of inclusive language when various students referred to "God" as "He" or "Father." But it seemed to me that somehow these uses of "he" and "He" were two different cases.

Not long after this I came across two articles on inclusive language in a recent issue of *Studies in Religion* (Milne 1989 and Clarkson 1989). While the first was on the general use of gender inclusive terminology within the academy, the second promoted the use of gender-neutral god-language. That these two articles appear back-to-back made me question whether the Canadian academic community sees any difference between the subject areas of the two articles. Is gender-neutral god-language simply a more specific application of general inclusive language? I have decided that the two applications of gender-neutral language are remarkably different. As a result I offer this reflection on the wider problem of naming and the use of theological language within the context of Religious Studies.[1]

My question simply is this, By what name shall we, as academic students of religion, know the unknowable?[2] As well as being an issue of some importance to religious devotees, naming can present a problem for students in Religious Studies as well. Specifically, the problem of naming arises in two related instances, both of which lie within the sphere of the academic study of religion. First, as noted above, one must take account of the feminist movement. As a result of their critique of language and behavior, a variety of traditional terms, such as "Father," or "King," no longer are acceptable in many contemporary Christian theological circles. The justification for the diminishing usage of such names—and their inventive replacement by such words as, "Comforter," or "Redeemer"—arises from a conception of the changing relevance of language to its historical context.

The second instance arises when one works within a number of religious traditions simultaneously, as in the many world religion courses taught at both secondary and postsecondary schools. When confronted with a variety of deities all originating from within culturally and historically distinct contexts, an instructor might refer to them all through the use of one general term. Within North America, this term often is "God."[3]

I believe that I understand the temptation to refer to the object of religious discourse in general as "God," or to the idea of deity within the Christian religion as "Father." The assumption made in each case is that the conventional term is plastic enough to take on a purely generic sense. However, there are several difficulties with such reasoning. First, one no longer has any choice but to acknowledge that one's terminology has a unique cultural and historical background which, at best, would have to be stretched to a significant extent to integrate divergent conceptions. Such an integration risks overlooking and de-emphasizing characteristics which do not blend nicely into a synthesis of deity. Christian feminists have convincingly demonstrated that due to particular contemporary social facts, the term "Father" is inadequate and inelastic, and actually distorts and limits the full meaning of the Christian experience. Likewise, many would argue that the concept "God" also lacks the elasticity necessary for generic uses.

But suppose we grant that "God" possesses the necessary conceptual elasticity. A second problem then arises: how is one to interpret non-theistic conceptions within religious discourse? Third—and here is the specific problem for students of religion—is one not somehow to identify and, in the very least, bracket any form of Christian or other religious influence? Are not we, as scholars of religion, to be theologically impartial in our judgments and uses of concepts? And so my question seems relevant. By what name are we to know the unknowable?

Gender-Neutral God-Language

For an insider to Christianity, the language debate over which feminists and traditionalists have fought is of extreme importance. But is this a debate to which Religious Studies has anything to add? I say no. We can study it but cannot participate within it.

I say no because the role of the student of religion is not to contribute to the content of theological debates. Here we must understand "theological" not just as Christian theology but, in a wider sense not suggested by the word's origins, as the intellectual formulation or rational expression and description of religious experience. Although such a definition is far from exhaustive—since it emphasizes certain theoretical rather than practical (i.e., praxis) or mystical aspects—I believe it is sufficient for the purposes of this paper. Since this study is concerned with the potential conflict between the religious devotee's articulate self-expression and the rational understanding and possibly explanation of the devotee's position, then confusion will only arise insofar as theological terminology bears some resemblance to the language of the academy.

Simply put, the academic study of religion, as outside the circle of the faithful, has little use for specifically theological terminology and ought not take sides in the disputes or expressions of the faithful. We can chronicle them, speculate as to their origins and effects and even determine their logical consistency. But for the student of religion to take a stand on the side of inclusive Christian theological language is a theological stand outside the parameters of the study of religion. While we may, for example, make note of a student's or peer's use of general inclusive language, to attempt to correct or influence their use of inclusive theological language is something best left to theologians and theological institutions. To paraphrase Hans Penner, whether theologians agree or disagree with the use of gender-inclusive god-language is of no concern to the academy. This is an affair for theologians to settle amongst themselves (Penner 1986a: 169).

The distinction between these two areas—general gender-inclusive language and gender-neutral god-language—is both identified and clouded in a recent issue of *Studies in Religion*. While arguing for the use of gender-inclusive language in a general sense, Milne notes that "the arguments to be made for gender-inclusive god-language are significantly different from those…for general language," (Milne 1989: 26). Unfortunately, Milne does not go on to inform her reader just what this difference is. Rather, she states simply that the case to be made for the latter requires a "separate analysis." Immediately following Milne's essay appears Clarkson's appeal for gender-neutral god-language. Due to the physical proximity and thematic similarity of the two articles, the reader, it seems to me, must wonder if in fact Clarkson's work qualifies as a "separate analysis."

From Milne's point of view I would hope that Clarkson's analysis, however well argued, qualifies not only as separate but, more importantly, as "significantly different." Since Milne chooses only to identify and not elaborate upon this difference I offer this distinction: the first belongs within the academy, the second within a theological institution.[4] In the case of the former, "persons" rather than "man" is a more convenient linguistic symbol representative of a particular set of socio-historical circumstances. In the case of the latter, the use of "God" instead of "Father" or "King" attempts to express and represent more adequately the very essence of the object of religious discourse and devotion in itself. To assert that "God" is not male entails making a claim to religious knowledge and not a claim to knowledge about religion.[5] It is the difference between concepts used for explanation and concepts which are "tools for the engineering of meaning and for sustaining a meaningful existence" (Wiebe 1989: 180). The analysis of each has little, if any, bearing on the other.

Moreover, within the context of the first Christian texts, what some scholars have labeled as gender-exclusive language is actually a socio-historical phenomenon worthy of our attention. Therefore, the accurate representation of the text partly will depend upon the presence of the original "patriarchal" elements. While such passages may be examined as examples of male domination in the first-century CE society, or as images of the deity relevant to the writers and redactors, their concepts must not be replaced by language more appealing to twentieth-century palates. Judging historical events by contemporary criteria is a mistake of the historicist who sees a fluid and necessary evolutionary link between past, present, and future. This may be acceptable within theological circles which posit an ahistorical referent for all history, but it is far from acceptable within the academy. Within an ahistorical framework, the fluidity of time can allow, possibly require, a continual reinterpretation or reembodiment of what one holds to be the essentials of the tradition in light of novel historical developments. This is Clarkson's aim: "the recovery of a fuller sense of God" (Clarkson 1989: 42). Such re-expression can be termed hermeneutical in a wide sense. This tendency to reinterpret, when seen from within the strictly historical perspective of the academy, can be termed revisionist. The two cannot be confused.[6]

One final difference between these two positions remains to be made explicit. Changing relationships in our society between men and women have been reflected in the identification of sexist practices and terminology. As women's spheres of influence have altered, so too has the language of our society. Therefore, gender-inclusive language represents an altered political relationship, ensuring that the use of "man" in a generic sense, and its inclusive alternate "humanity," are both political statements. However, the context of feminist theological scholarship, which necessitates the use of gender-neutral terms for the divine, represents something other than mere political realities. "He," used for the divine, as well as its inclusive alternates, are theological statements.[7] I suggest that the "significant difference" between the two positions is that one is primarily political and the other is primarily theological.[8]

Generic Uses of "God"

Returning to the second and wider issue of the use of "God" in non-Christian contexts, it should be made clear that such usage demonstrates either a basic oversight on the part of the researcher or a fundamental assumption regarding the relationship between the variety of conceptions of deity present in the world. I shall deal with each in turn. The kind of oversight which causes some scholars of religion to use "God" indiscriminately may be traceable to their own Christian origins. Although the domination by theologically-minded individuals in our departments and centers for Religious Studies may be gradually coming to an end, it cannot be denied that a great number of North American and European scholars of religion and graduate students have deep Christian roots, be they explicit or implicit in the cultural ethos of their physical, emotional and intellectual development. It is far from novel to assert that we must always be aware of this.

What one must also be aware of is that all such theological forms are out of place in the academy. It is as improper to use "God" in a generic academic sense as it is to use "Alla," "Yhwh" or even "Nirvana." To Christian-conditioned ears, only the last three concepts are clearly awkward when used in a general sense. We must be careful not to exclude "God" from the class of theological concepts whose meaningful employment lies outside our field.[9]

The second reason why lecturers or writers would use "God" in a cross-traditional setting is due to their implicit (or explicit) theological assumptions concerning the relationship between the variety of deities. The meaningful employment of the Christian concept of "God," with its attendant belief in the absolute authority and relevance of "God" to all contingent life, is quite capable of encompassing all other theistic and non-theistic ideas of absoluteness. This is why some Christian pluralists readily accept the validity of a variety of seemingly incompatible and even competing conceptions of deity—all fit nicely under the one umbrella concept of "God." Accordingly, the use of "God" outside the context of Christianity easily can carry with it a theological message of unity amidst an apparent diversity—whether intended or not.

As adumbrated above, this theological identification of the Many with a One, which can be termed oceanic or religious monism, can occur from within other traditions as well (Gellner 1974: 22).[10] Where the believer posits a theistic or non-theistic absolute he or she quite easily can subjugate the experiences, categories, and ultimately the meanings of outsiders to the categories and meanings of their own tradition, understood as absolute and normative. With specific relevance to Religious Studies, the adherent of a religious tradition which relies upon a belief in an absolute power likewise can appropriate for their own theological use the academic research carried out from within the strict methodologies of the field.

In other words, any ahistorical enterprise easily can encompass the work of: (i) a "lesser" or "flawed" understanding of its own ahistorical "Truth";

and (ii) data which results from an historical enterprise such as sociology, archaeology or anthropology. For this reason, Christian pluralism, Hindu belief, as well as the non-theistic concept of Nirvana are wide enough to be able to contain within them any other experience or category of transcendence/immanence. For instance, many twentieth-century Christians find little difficulty in identifying soteriological elements in the basic assumptions of evolutionism—an acceptance which differs greatly from the positions of their nineteenth-century predecessors. Boundariless situations easily can transform boundaried data to their own purposes. How wise it is for essentially theological systems of thought to appropriate scientific methods and rely upon empirical data has yet to be determined (see Wiebe 1991)

Be it from oversight or implicit theological assumptions, identifying "God" with the traditional terms for deity of other belief systems is a theological endeavor not appropriate for the academic study of religion. Simple carelessness in the use of terminology does not excuse us from the implications for our study of depicting "God" as present in other traditions. Also, to become involved in debates within Christian theology over the proper use of gender-neutral terms for "God" is not the task of the student of religion.

Note, however, that I do not question the honesty of such scholars who attempt to incorporate inclusive god-language into their work, nor those who employ "God" in a generic, universal sense. I can only believe their motivations are noble. However, noble motivations do not necessarily make for reliable methods and legitimate conclusions. Insofar as we assume our research to be intrinsically worthwhile we clearly are contributing to what we believe to be a better society. But to attempt to reshape that society based upon an ideology derivative from what is essentially a theological commitment is beyond the scope of the scholar of religion. More properly, our role as scholars of religion is to describe and account for certain types of human phenomena and not to save the world. Therefore, it is the perspicacity of such theologically-minded scholars, and not their honesty, which I criticize. Students of religion will gain much more if they study those who do these things rather than join them in their enterprises.

But suppose we grant that the modification and salvation of persons and social situations were the "ultimate aims" of the study. This granted, there is no guarantee that such modification would serve to promote what some hold to be the positive aspects of the religious mentality. What in one person inspires awe or reverence can just as directly prompt disillusionment in another; and awe can itself inspire commitment to the most brutal causes. Bruce Alton has recently noted that as a result of studying religion within the university, "many students suffer loss rather than transformation of faith, and…for others, the horror of the discovery of religious dysfunctionality in the social milieu leads them to reject religion as a viable social transformer… More generally, while it may be true that all knowledge changes the knower and the known it is not self-evident that this is 'for the better,'" (Alton 1989: 417). To enter upon the academic study of religion with the goal of personal transformation or religious enlightenment can result in either the loss of one's objectivity and the development of an ineffective methodology or ironically enough, the loss of one's faith and disillusionment with religion as a personal commitment. The academic study of religion is therefore not the province of personal faith.

Critical Pluralism

However, I have not yet answered my original question, By what name shall we know the unknowable? If you have pointed out my own theistic assumptions, identified by my use of "unknowable," you are on the right track. I admit the basic difficulty in finding any term plastic enough to encompass all varieties of religious deities and states of being. After proposing and rejecting a variety of terms such as the One, the Transcendent and the Eternal, John Hick has decided upon "the Real *an sich*" as a term general enough for his purpose (Hick 1989: 9–11). But Hick fully admits that his purpose is to elucidate a religious interpretation of religion. He is an insider and so the name of this Real is of great importance not only phenomenologically but personally, experientially and ontologically. This existential value accounts for the difference between Hick's generic term, the Real *an sich*, and Ninian Smart's more descriptive and functional term, the Focus (e.g., Smart 1973).[11]

Hick proceeds to contrast the Real *an sich* with what he terms the various historically and psycho-socially conditioned *personae* and *impersonae* of the Real, providing him with a method of reducing apparent religious diversity and incompatibility to religious unity and harmony. Hick is searching for a religious theory capable of interpreting the variety of religions populating the earth in terms of their shared essentials. He must name the unnameable for that is what his theology does. But is this what Religious Studies does? Do our questions arise from within the same context?As a suggestion to get us out of this thorny problem of naming I propose that it would be profitable for scholars of religion to employ a methodological assumption I term critical pluralism as opposed to the oceanic monism of religious institutions and traditions. By "pluralism" I mean a methodology whereby the variety is assumed to be a diversity and its components are therefore isolatable and can be examined individually and characterized in terms of their relationships to their historical, sociological, and psychological contexts. Comparing and contrasting these various components is possible but a religious reduction to one essential form is not since their historical and chronological contexts are strictly separate. Only through a leap of ahistorical insight could such a reduction occur—such a leap simply is improper within the academy. By "critical" I mean to guard against too strictly identifying with what I refer to as ontological pluralism. To assert that the world actually is a Many and not a One, that there are many gods and not one God is itself as dogmatic and unprofitable a position for Religious Studies as the very stance this paper seeks to circumvent—namely religious (oceanic) monism. To espouse such a form of pluralism places one in the middle of a philosophical debate regarding the One and the Many. It is not in this dogmatic, or ontological, sense that I use the term pluralism.

Contrary to this I suggest maintaining only a critical pluralism where such questions as, By what name shall we know the unknowable?, are not even posed, since the question itself presupposes that it is sensible to believe that a name exists—whether we can determine it now or not—and that it is important for us to know it. Such a question is monistic and theological. It is an appropriate question for Hick's religious interpretation of religion but not for students of religion.

The methodology proposed in this paper attempts to leave certain questions unasked, questions only relevant within a theological/monistic framework. I can foresee at least three objections to such an exclusion. Some scholars such as Wilfred Cantwell Smith or Mircea Eliade, might believe that such a method is fundamentally flawed since it excludes from understanding the beliefs which are of primary interest and importance to the study of religion. Ursula King appears to speak for such a position when she writes: "One wonders how far the emphasis on 'bracketing' in the search for objectivity has not led to a 'bracketing out' of some of the most central and decisive questions of religious existence, namely those of ultimate truth and value, of the focus of the transcendent and the place of its revelation," (King 1984: 41). Hans Küng echoes such a view: "...more and more scholars of religion, with the Americans in the lead, are acknowledging that in the long run they mustn't dodge the normative question of truth and values" (Küng 1986: xv).

Discerning ultimate truth and value, the assumption of the existence of a transcendent and how and whether it has revealed anything to anyone are not properly the concern of the academic study of religion. The search for ultimate truth is a religious quest at best chronicled, and whose motives can be explained, by the student of religion. To rely upon the assumption that there in fact is such a Truth, that there is Knowledge, is to place oneself firmly within the theological camp. Scholars of religion must be satisfied with the incremental gains in knowledge which result from the application of their methods, gains which themselves produce further unforeseen problems to be solved. The assumptions of our field are clear to the outsider and perhaps wholly inadequate to the religious devotee. But ours is not a quest for Knowledge but for knowledge. The context of our field is historical and critical, not ahistorical (even antihistorical) and confessional. Therefore, I criticize not those who attempt religious reductions from within theological settings, but those who attempt them within Religious Studies. Each community has its own presuppositions and will best do its work within its own world. A global theology and not a course in world religions is more properly the place to speak of "God" in other traditions.

A second objection might arise from a very different perspective. Some might argue that by the apparent invocation of the phenomenologist's *epoché*, the method proposed here—by excluding from judgment and thus protecting concepts of theological value—reveals its own hidden theological agenda. Penner has convincingly made this point regarding the work of Van der Leeuw and Bleeker. According to Penner, it is in the "cloak of the *epoché*" that the theological enterprise has always been with, the scientific study of religion (Penner 1986a: 172).[12] As correct as I believe such an observation to be I do not think it is relevant to critical pluralism. Critical pluralism does not restrict investigations nor exclude concepts from critical examination for fear of their reduction to naturalistic factors. Such a naturalistic reduction must be entertained as a definite possibility within our field. Rather, critical pluralism recognizes the meaninglessness of certain claims and/or concepts once the monistic framework of an absolute, ahistorical referent is not assumed—which by necessity excludes any metaphysical reduction of religion. It is not so much that this method dodges questions of truth and value, but rather it admits that, once such valuations are placed within a critical, historical context, they are merely descriptive and not meaningful. Thus, the religious quest is no more a quest but a datum for examination alongside a variety of other data.

Finally, some might further question why such a methodology entertains only reductions to naturalistic rather than metaphysical, factors. In assuming that both options are open for the scholar of religion, such persons appear to be confusing the difference between these two types of reductions. This point is made by Robert Segal and Donald Wiebe in their response to Daniel Pals' assumption of the basic similarity between the research programs of Freud and Eliade.[13] For Segal and Wiebe, "the difference between Freud and Eliade is that what for Eliade is the explanation of religion is for Freud part of the enterprise to be explained" (Segal and Wiebe 1989: 603).

The division between naturalistic and metaphysical reductions, as noted above, represents the difference between Religious Studies and Theology; the former is based upon empirical considerations such as the effects of economic or sociological influences on persons while the latter utilizes an ahistorical referent—be it a deity, a yearning for deity or principle of some sort—of non-empirical value.

The benefit of such a methodological presupposition is that while it can support substantive pluralism, which grounds any profitable scientific methodology, it does not succumb to dogmatism.[14] Such a position is in many respects very similar to what phenomenology was originally thought to be. It is important to keep in mind that much of the recent criticism of phenomenology has been more concerned with the faulty application of its methods than the methodology itself. In emphasizing the need for our descriptions to employ only those names for absoluteness relevant to those communities or individuals under our scrutiny, critical pluralism simply reiterates the need for the detached observer so important to the eventual development of scientific theories of religion (Goodenough 1959: 80).

Conclusion

The student of the academic study of religion will find no need to search for the proper name for the object of religious worship or reflection. As an outsider, the name utilized by the insider under discussion will suffice, be it Alla, Yhwh, Nirvana, Manitou, Father, the Sacred, the Real *an sich* or Logos. Whether or not the believer maintains his or her concept to be inclusive of other conceptions of absoluteness, the researcher puts all alike on a level with one another—for critical pluralism entails substantive relativity. Each represents, in Smart's terminology, the Focus of the person or community. However, we must note that language as symbol has power and that the abuse of this power can have devastating results for some individuals and groups. Accordingly, we must be respectful in our uses of these terms. This said, anyone in our midst should know what we are about and attend our conversations or lectures and read our papers with this in mind. Opening lectures may well be the occasion to inform new students of the assumptions of the field.

To promote the growth of knowledge in our area of study we must be careful not to overstep our own self-created and maintained boundaries for in so doing we enter me realm of we theologian and, although perhaps unknowingly, undermine our own endeavors. To name the unnameable is to participate in a theological enterprise inappropriate for Religious Studies.

But to assume that the object of religious worship or reflection is unknowable is itself a necessary methodological assumption of critical pluralism. At best we can only name names and identify objects or states relevant to religious devotees. Whether such terms actually name something or not and whether they are all simply aliases for something else is a question of faith best left up to adherents to decide.[15]

Notes

1. By Religious Studies I mean the social scientific pursuit, carried out from within an historical-critical framework and sometimes termed the academic study of religion.
2. By referring to the object of religious discourse and worship as "unknowable" or even an "object" (not to be confused, of course, with the objective of religious discourse) I appear to be taking a theological stand, I return to this issue at the close of this paper.
3. Although "gods" solves some of the problems of the theological assumptions behind our terminology, strictly speaking, it is unable to represent the conceptions of absolute which lie at the heart of the non-theistic religions.
4. Clarkson maintains that, "We use 'Father' to address God although we assert that God is neither male nor female. We use 'he' to refer to God in a sentence in which we are assuring ourselves and others that God has no gender" (37). Certainly this "we" does not refer to the student of religion since "we" do not speak in this way. Clarkson must be referring to a believer. However, are there not believers who quite literally hold that God is male, that God has a gender? Clarkson's paper, while arguing for a normative use of god-language assumes a unanimity among Christians concerning deeper theological questions which in practice does not exist. Her proposal for non-native god-language must first rest upon a normative Christian theology; without this her proposals are well meant but empty.
5. On the distinction between religious knowledge and knowledge about religion see Wiebe (1990: 33).
6. *Studies in Religion*, which in 1971 replaced the *Canadian Journal of Theology*, represents both theological and Religious Studies bodies united best to serve their own individual academic needs in light of their monetary and membership limitations. Hence, Milne and Clarkson approach inclusive language within the same volume but from radically different perspectives. While for some scholars such a collaboration is beneficial, for others, it is more confusing than constructive. For a useful history of the theology-religious studies debate which has taken place in *Studies in Religion* consult the article by Philip Boo Riley, "Theology and/or Religious Studies: A Case Study of *Studies in Religion/Sciences Religieuses*, 1971–1981" (1984: 423–44).

7. I thank Michel Desjardins for suggesting this political-theological distinction.
8. If one presumes religion to be a human projection then the use of gender-neutral god-language can also be examined as indicative of changing political realities. This would entail a non-religious interpretation of such god-language. In this case both Milne's and Clarkson's arguments could be understood in terms of power relationships within society. However, I am sure that Clarkson is not simply talking about a non-religious interpretation of god-language. The force of her argument undoubtedly relies upon the assumption that gender-neutral god-language more adequately reflects or "honors" (46) the true aspects of an ontological reality and not merely a psychological projection. As a religious interpretation which posits the existence of, and attempts to describe, deity, Clarkson's work is hardly sociological.
9. It has been suggested to me that "God," being less contextually centered, is at least a more adequate generic term than, say, Alla. I find such a position highly problematic. I assume that by "less contextually centered" one means to imply that "God" is a term which in our differentiated society has lost some (or a great) degree of its strictly religious connotations and therefore it can be employed objectively. Such a view sets criteria for terminological adequacy which can only be met by what one believes to be the positive features of one's own tradition or culture. This strikes me as imperialistic at best.
10. I take the term oceanic monism from Ernest Gellner's *The Legitimation of Belief* (1974: 22).
11. The difference in terminology results from Hick's affirmation of the reality of the referent (nothing can be more real than the Real *an sich*) and Smart's affirmation of the reality of the referent for the believer, not necessarily for the scholar.
12. For further comments on the suspect neutrality of the phenomenology of religion see Penner (1986b and 1989).
13. See Pals (1987: 259–82) and Segal and Wiebe (1989: 591–605).
14. Here I must clarify two separate levels of the argument. Substantively, there must be a plurality in order that description and explanation can take place in a non-religious manner. However, epistemologically we must espouse critical monism, that is, assume a common rationality among participants in our discussions and studies. The substantive level and the epistemological level of the argument must not be confused, since epistemological pluralism would admit to a variety of types of knowledge, one of which being the privileged knowledge of the religious insider.
15. This paper arises in large part from my conversations with Bruce MacKay and is influenced throughout by some of the work of Sir Karl Popper. I thank Donald Wiebe and Michel Desjardins for their comments on an earlier draft of this paper.

Chapter 2

Introduction

I'm not exactly sure why responses were solicited to my *MTSR* essay—reprinted here as the chapter that opened this collection. An unsolicited reply or two came into the editorial office back then—most notably, I think of the exchange between Neil McMullin (who was my doctoral supervisor) and Gary Ebersole, concerning McMullin's biting critique of *The Encyclopedia of Religion* (see McMullin 1989a and 1989b; Ebersole 1989; Aaron Hughes, the current editor of *MTSR*, has reprinted this early, and likely little read, exchange in a volume celebrating the journal's twenty-fifth anniversary [see Hughes 2013b]. Re-reading that exchange now I am reminded of how influential McMullin's comments were of the dissertation that I was only then beginning to conceptualize—e.g., as I wrote in the Preface to my first book, "It is clear to me now that this book is in large part an effort, whether conscious or not, to further substantiate and elaborate on what I find to be McMullin's insightful criticism—a criticism that extends far beyond what has commonly been termed the Chicago school" [1997b: viii].) And, some years later, the late Hans Penner would periodically write a long, engaging letter to the editors, tackling an entire issue—letters that we would publish (e.g., see Penner 1998, in response to *MTSR* 9/2 [1997]; see also the brief replies by three authors to Penner's letter, which are all published in *MTSR* 10/4 [1998]: 388–90). But back in the days of its first few volumes the journal was still new and largely unknown; *MTSR*'s editors therefore decided that soliciting replies might be a useful way to link the work published in the journal to wider and ongoing conversations throughout the field, helping to set *MTSR* apart as a place where real time, scholarly debate took place on a regular basis. Perhaps it was natural, given that my essay tackled the work of two current writers whose own works had recently appeared in print, that it be used as a springboard into a conversation among authors. Whatever the reason, this set of papers constituted the first exchange I ever had in print with other scholars. As made evident in many of the chapters to follow, it would not be the last time that my work constituted colleagues' work as data.

Looking back on these two papers—Chapter 1 in this volume and the response that follows—it is not difficult to see the possible tension that is addressed in some of the chapters in this collection: a tension between, on the one hand, an interest to demarcate an object of analysis from its analysis (e.g., distinguishing the study of religion from the practice of religion), and an interest to historicize the very effort to demarcate a subject from an object, on the other (i.e., seeing the very distinction between the study of religion and the practice of religion itself as one's object of study). I would now say that these two interests were represented by the influence of Donald Wiebe (a member of my doctoral committee and career-long conversation partner), in whose work the sharp divide between theology and the science of religion is obvious and well known, and McMullin (although a scholar of Buddhism, my doctoral supervisor nonetheless), the person who moved my reading in the direction of literary theory and ideology critique. Whereas the previous chapter makes evident Wiebe's influence on my thinking (when I wrote this paper I had either just taken, or was enrolled in, a graduate course with Wiebe on the topic of the book he was soon to publish, *The Irony of Theology and the Nature of Religious Thought* [1991] and, eventually, I worked for him as a research assistant, helping to scan and format essays that predated computers and which became chapters in his essay collection, *Beyond Legitimation* [1994], a book concerned to chronicle his own move from seeing religious belief and science as compatible to incommensurable), the response that follows, written a year or so later, shows the clear influence of McMullin on my thinking. Gone is the reference to such authors as Ernest Gellner and, instead, we find literary critics being cited, for example Terry Eagleton, Fredric Jameson, Frank Lentricchia, and so on, along with Marx and Althusser. The effect is that the very distinction that I worked to establish in the first chapter, and thus the basis for its critique, becomes the object of study in the response, inasmuch as it is now characterized as an artificial divide that is itself of practical (read: political) utility. While I would no longer use the term "artificial," inasmuch as it suggests that some divides are more real or natural than others, my current sympathies are certainly with the reply over the what appears in the previous chapter as a rather obvious disciplinary distinction. While that distinction is one I'd like to work with, my desire for it does not mean that the distinction does not have a history, have interests driving it, or practical implications to it.

The topic of the following paper, then, is on how any divide is portrayed and what can be accomplished when the world is arranged in a certain way. Despite the fact that, when applied to the category religion itself, some see this as not being a legitimate interest for a scholar of religion to pursue, it strikes me as directly in line with the work of Emile Durkheim, such as his interest in studying not the identity of the sacred but, instead, the rule systems we devise and deploy to manage human space, the systems whereby so-called sacrality results from things being, as he famously wrote, "set apart and forbidden"—prompting us to ask "By whom?" and "How?" or "Why?" What's more, if we make allowances for the now problematic social evolutionary presumptions that characterized much late nineteenth- and early twentieth-century scholarship in what we might now call the human sciences, I do not think that this move is all that far from Durkheim and Marcel Mauss's co-written classic, *Primitive Classification*; for if we begin from their starting point—"the classification of things reproduces *the classification of men*" (1963: 11)—then we no longer study identities but, following someone like Jean-François Bayart (2005), we instead study ongoing identification practices whose arrangements of items in the world is directly linked to the way in which we relate ourselves to others.

This shift toward seeing as our object of study the means by which classification systems are created, authorized, and implemented is important, I think, and, despite criticisms form those who think this is not appropriate work for scholars of religion to be doing, it is the means by which some scholars today approach their work. Most recently, I think of Dennis LoRusso's blog post for the *Bulletin for the Study of Religion*, on the recent controversies over "who owns yoga" (in this case, whether such a supposedly spiritual technique ought to be included in a US public school curriculum, where the so-called separation of church and state is the law of the land). Rather than focus on yoga as an actually existing thing that needs to be classified properly as either religious or not (i.e., as spiritual or as exercise), LoRusso makes the following important observation:

> Categories like "religion" and "culture" serve us better when seen as concepts embedded in discourse that point to particular social processes. The question is not "is yoga religious?" but rather "what is at stake in defining something *as* a religious practice?" This can reveal a much more robust picture of the controversy over yoga in public schools.[1]

Whether the effort to demarcate the supposedly disinterested study of something from its interested practice is undermined by the examination of this very act of demarcation is, of course, the recurring theme for those who characterize the so-called postmodern focus on knowledge/power as something that undermines the hard won gains of the scientific study of religion. While I have argued in a variety of papers—some of which are included in this collection—that the only truly historical study of religion is one that is willing to historicize the category religion itself—one in which we, as scholars, are willing to find our own group's native practices as curious as those of the other people we routinely study—the following paper comes long before the contours of such arguments had become apparent to me. But I include it here because I think that it points in the direction of some of the issues that such a move requires one to make.

Ideology and the Problem of Naming: A Reply (1991)

"His thought is redneck, yours is doctrinal and mine is deliciously supple." (Eagleton 1991: 4)

In the essay to which Shannon Clarkson (1991) and Pamela Milne (1991) respond, I attempt to make clear what I see to be the difference between gender-inclusive Christian god-language (such as replacing masculine pronouns and metaphors with inclusive alternates), whose motives I termed theological, and generic inclusive language (such as substituting *persons* for *men*) which I termed political. Having distinguished between these two, I proposed that the scholar of religion *qua* scholar had no business entering the first debate over whether the Christian, or any other, conception of deity for that matter, had a gender, let alone existed, for that would constitute disputing the characteristics of a deity—a dispute which compromises such a scholar's role. Along a similar line, I suggested that using *God* as a generic term for the *focus* (Ninian Smart's term) of a non-Christian religious community was improper and reflected either academic sloppiness or, more likely, an implicit Christian bias toward some sort of theology of religious pluralism.

Some might wonder what these two issues have in common. I asserted that both betray an agenda which attempts to privilege one among many interpretations of just what this deity may be. I held that it was not the task of the scholar of religion to make or debate such ontological claims, but rather should be an issue over which theologians may argue if they wish.

I am in agreement with many of the comments made by Milne, and especially find interesting her remarks on the poor flow-through rate of female Masters and Doctoral students in the study of religion.[2] However, it is Clarkson's response which once again raises the thorny issue of naming. In my reply I will concentrate mainly upon issues raised by Clarkson, first commenting on the strategies by which she authorizes the use of inclusive god-language within the academy by privileging one reading of text over tradition, seemingly separating meaning from interpretation. Once identified, the use of these strategies—indicating the presence of an ideology—weakens Clarkson's appeal for the normative status of her interpretation. Following this portion of the reply, I take seriously her charge that the academic belief in purely descriptive language simply protects, or even promotes, in this case, sexist attitudes and practices. But first I have some brief reflections on the theology/religious studies distinction.

Theology and Religious Studies

After reading Clarkson's response I am left wondering just what she sees as the difference between the scholarly pursuits of theology and the academic study of religion. Frankly, whether a deity exists or not, and just what are the characteristics of said deity, are not the concern of the academic study of religion. In asserting that gender-neutral god-language more accurately represents a deity, Clarkson is making a judgment that the deity exists, is a unity and is gender-neutral. Such judgments are outside the scope of my area of expertise. If Clarkson wishes to debate the social significance or the political ramifications of exclusively male pronouns in what we generally refer to as religious texts, then we have something to talk about. But if we are talking about a deity, a *sacred* (as noun) of some sort, then we are engaging in theology—talk of god(s)—and I have nothing to add.

Within our field, language about deity tells something about the relations of people within a society, rather than about the deity itself, since, as I have already noted, the assumption of a deity is itself problematic in our field. Here I follow Durkheim in maintaining that *the classification of things reproduces the classification of men*. The distinction in my original essay between theology and politics was not an attempt to guarantee the *sui generis* character of religion nor was it aimed at depoliticizing religion. Rather I tried to emphasize what I understood at the time to be the different motivations behind these two instances of inclusive language. With this in mind, I now make it clear that the distinction between general-language and god-language is highly artificial. They are in fact one and the same—language which in large part reflects and attempts to entrench the interests of various groups in society. In the case of gender-exclusive god-talk, the interests are most often those of males. This makes Durkheim's use of *men* all the more appropriate.

Therefore, I agree wholeheartedly with Clarkson when she writes that the theological is political. We must be aware that theological language is a method for making claims to power and authority in society, encoded in appeals to universality, otherness, and absoluteness. The example Clarkson provides is useful: American religion and currency. Is the imprinting of *In God We Trust* evidence of the influence religion plays in American civil life, as Clarkson believes, or evidence of the attempt to legitimize the interests of those who possess and benefit from capital? Since coins are no longer even worth the metal from which they are made, their artificially inflated exchange value must somehow be guaranteed. Coinage, then, is only as strong as the user's trust in its guarantor, the one whose image is imprinted. What then is the message of American coinage which has on its obverse the profile of the patriarch George Washington accompanied by the phrase *In God We Trust*? Is its value guaranteed by Washington the man, or by association, Washington the city/political power or (since gods have often adorned coins) perhaps some interpretation of the Christian deity? And, if the latter, something tells me it is not the deity of the cotton-picking black slave who we are dealing with here. Rather it is a deity which legitimizes the rules of American capitalism. The irony of imprinting *In God We Trust* on money, which is itself an abstract representation of human labor accumulated only by an elite segment of society, is apparently lost on Clarkson.

The difference between us, I suspect, is that while I am interested in explaining the theological in terms of the political, Clarkson wishes to speak of the political implications of the theological, assuming an essentially religious and autonomous dimension to exist. For, as Clarkson notes in her original essay, "as we change and alter God's name our understanding of ourselves changes as well" (1989: 39). With regards to Feuerbach, I would phrase it slightly differently: our changing relations with other humans is writ large in the very concept *God*.

Texts and Tradition

In both her earlier article and her response, Clarkson's appeal for gender inclusive god-language is founded upon a distinction between what she has most recently termed "current linguistic biases" and what could be called accurate or close readings. In turn, this is grounded in the distinction she draws between text and tradition, that is, original and subsequent. Repeatedly, Clarkson promotes a closer reading of the Jewish and Christian texts so that one might either *recover* or *retrieve* the original elements of gender-inclusive terminology, few or many as they may be, which have been obscured by repeated interpretation, translation, and manipulation by patriarchal societies.[3]

In Clarkson's emphasis on correct reading and translation I find three related problems: (i) the assumption that text takes priority over tradition; (ii) the value placed on origins; and (iii) her failure to recognize that her own interpretation arises from a particular historically grounded tradition.

The prioritizing of text over tradition devalues the role tradition has played in forming a particular religion or interpretive framework. Such religious complexes are far more than what some might see as, say, a homogenous text, or tradition for that matter. "Faithfulness to the text" is one thing, faithfulness to the complex modern heterogeneity known as Buddhism, Christianity, or Hinduism is quite another.

It is at this point that texts and origins overlap, since Clarkson seems to be appealing to some purer form of insight housed in the original documents which, for whatever reason, has been obscured by subsequent (read *patriarchal*) interpretation. Only in this way can she repeatedly stress the need to get back to origins. Here I am reminded of Eliade's unfounded appeal to the priority of the sacred as archaic over its devolution, the profane, which he associated with modernity. Surely Clarkson's theory of textual meaning is somewhat problematic. Her appeal for a *gospel-behind-the-gospel* appears to have something in common with what Jonathan Z. Smith has recently characterized as "the Protestant model of a pristine originary moment followed by corruption" (1990: 39). In the history of the scholarship of early Christian origins examined by Smith, he finds an influential anti-Catholic apologetic operating, one which attempts to illustrate how degenerative later Catholic influences were (i.e., the doctrine of transubstantiation) while at the same time professing to uncover the original or *sui generis* moment (as interpreted by Protestants) within the texts. Although Clarkson is by no means involved in the same enterprise as those scholars scrutinized by Smith, she too searches for the essential heart of documents buried deep in redaction and commentary (an inclusive heart encased by patriarchy). In so doing, she confuses origin for essence. I do not wish to repeat a rather lengthy history of literary criticism, but suffice it to say that the *belief* that some authoritative meaning actually resides within a text, if only it were to be read and interpreted carefully and objectively enough, has been hotly contested.[4]

Let me draw attention to two ways in which Clarkson's language demonstrates her assumption of the hidden meaning of the texts. First, her use of the term *scripture* creates a privileged genre of writing, not unrelated to *sacred* or *holy scripture*, along with all that these imply (i.e., immutability, revelation, etc.). To refer to such documents simply as *texts* (as, I realize, she sometimes does) avoids the assumption that they somehow differ from other pieces of writing, such as those of the editors of the tradition. Accordingly, to deprivilege *scriptures* is the first step to deconstructing the text/tradition distinction. For what is a text but the etched symbols, habits, and connotations of one particular tradition—possibly an elite, skilled, and powerful segment of a society, or maybe a marginalized, revolutionary group. In spite of its use in sharing information, writing, far from a neutral human exercise, at times has been an effective technology employed to silence. To prioritize texts is to support the interests and possibly the hegemony of one group not only over its historical contemporaries, of which we know nothing since they did not write, but also over all who follow them.

A second example of Clarkson's search for original meanings arises when she notes how gender-specific language "shrouds deity with the overtones of a particular gender" (1991: 122). Her choice of *shroud* and *overtones* is very instructive in that it implies that, once such misreadings are corrected by proper translation, the hidden image of deity will be uncovered and revealed, an exercise she earlier referred to as the "recovery of a fuller sense of God" (1989: 42). Further, not only is this evidence of a theory of meaning, but contains a theological claim concerning the existence and characteristics of deity. How, if not by already knowing what in fact the deity is, could one judge a certain interpretation to be cloaked or, for that matter, sexist? In her response Clarkson takes issue with my claim that this aim to *recover a fuller sense of God*—what she in her latest paper rephrases as the "intent…to retrieve a fuller sense of God"—is ahistorical. If by *recovery* and *retrieval* she means to examine the layers of textual interpretation as found in a variety of translations, to disentangle the various premises or commitments—both theoretical and practical—of interpreters, then I have no difficulty with this. This I would refer to as the recovery of a fuller sense of the text's history. Such a task need not assume that the untangling of agendas will lead to the discovery of the proper or essential interpretation. Rather, it simply seeks to unweave a complex tapestry so as to sort out the story of its construction. However, once one admits that the aim of such archaeology is to find a grail—a fuller sense of *God*—then indeed one has leapt off of the cliff of history into ahistory, making unfounded normative claims for the value of origins and the appropriateness of a certain notion of deity. I understand Clarkson to be concerned more with theology than archaeology.

Ideology and Language

Like the word "religion," "ideology" has many meanings, not all of which are compatible with one another. Definitions of the term vary from the widely applicable notion of thoughts characteristic of a social group to the classical Marxist usage of a false-consciousness in support of the ruling class. While the former is of little use, since it is applicable to virtually all situations and as such is simply a tool for sociological description, the latter is limited to examining the covert and deceptive practices of dominant systems of thought (patriarchy or capitalism), leaving alone subordinate and oppositional groups (environmentalism, feminism). Further, the notion of false-consciousness is problematic since it presumes the critic to be making judgments from an ultimate, or at least neutral, epistemological position. Since no one's ideas are "deliciously supple," least of all my own, I avoid making judgments on false-consciousness. To avoid these difficulties, I

ideology
define.

define ideology as: the set of ideas and practices the use of which portrays the particular as universal, to legitimate the interests of one social group. In this way ideology can be used as a tool for investigating specific uses of ideas rather than all socially conditioned thoughts, as well as to study the ideologies of subordinate groups in conflict with dominant ones.

To identify the ideology operating in Clarkson's work challenges the normative status of her appeals, demonstrating that inclusive language, like its patriarchal predecessor, is a phenomenon relevant to a particular historical period and class and therefore is not representative of ahistorical truth. As others have suggested, the claim to represent truth is itself an ideological strategy. However, I do not propose that something is false simply because it is ideological. Rather, because an idea is ideological it is disqualified from claiming normative status since by definition it portrays only a segment as the whole.

Earlier I noted some strategies whereby *text* is prioritized. I would now like to make explicit the ideological strategies which were in operation.[5] Note that there are a variety of strategies whereby the particular is portrayed as the universal, not all of which will be operating at the same time. Further, many of these strategies are interrelated. They are: unification, rationalization, legitimation, universalization, and naturalization.

As noted above, to prioritize text over tradition can absolutize the interests of one social group, even one element of a social group, portraying those interests as universal. One does not have to assume a revelatory status for a text to universalize its meaning; but it certainly can help. One simply must present one abstract interpretation of it, one honored by a tradition either in or seeking power, as not just the only, but also the common and intuitive, interpretation—this I take to be *naturalization*. Now, this in effect is what Clarkson is arguing *against*—the naturalized status of patriarchal language and practices—and I join her in this criticism. Unfortunately, she has chosen to employ the same questionable methods for legitimizing her competing vision, and this is why I think it important to undertake ideology critiques of subordinated groups. Simply put, Clarkson presents the heterogenous text of the Christian Bible as a self-evident homogeneity (unification). She identifies as central in that supposedly unified text meanings which coincide with previously held political beliefs on the equality of men and women (rationalization); she asserts that her interpretation of these portions comprises an authoritative reading (unification and universalization); and she does so all in the service of a set of political beliefs and practices (legitimization).[6] In the words of Smith, Clarkson displays an "archaic locative ideology" whereby a centre is created and protected while the periphery, or in her case, tradition, is seen as threatening (1990: 143).

To put it another way, Clarkson reifies one interpretation in the service of a set of political beliefs. I happen to agree that men and women are politically equal, that social institutions *ought* to reflect and promote this equality, and that patriarchal institutions and paradigms have dominated our discourse. This, however, is not what I am questioning. What I am attempting to emphasize is the realization that all of our deeply held beliefs are historically and socially relative and that they are perpetuated at the expense of other beliefs through, among others, the rhetorical strategies mentioned above. To topple the dominance of patriarchy, inclusive commentators can fall into the same trap of ideological justifications if they portray their beliefs as normative and absolute. The fact that we find such justifications palatable is no reason to exempt them from critical scrutiny. The danger arises when the means of rhetoric, which are themselves neither good nor bad but simply the ways by which we daily articulate thoughts and attempt to persuade our neighbors, masquerade as neutral and self-evident common sense.[7]

Descriptive Language and the Academy

Clarkson does cause me to question the relationship between the perpetuation of the status quo (in this case the exclusion of women from positions of power and influence in Western society) and the scholar's belief in the reality of disinterested description. To assert that what is commonly believed to be disinterested language actually serves to promote or at least protect the ruling patriarchy, is to observe that the academy is itself ideological, since it either consciously or unconsciously deludes itself, and the society which supports it, into believing itself to be neutral. Althusser asserted as much in *Lenin and Philosophy* (2001) when he argued that intellectuals—or, according to Chomsky, the ideological managers—act as the unknowing proponents of ruling ideologies.

Even though the idea that academics possess some neutral descriptive power has in the past several decades come under severe attack—notably in the philosophy of science—it still dominates the academy, as is evidenced by its pivotal role in sustaining the distinctions between theology and religions studies, politics and political science, and ultimately between the insider and the outsider. Such dichotomies are based upon the assumed neutrality, or critical reflective ability, of the disinterested observer. In the academic study of religion much work has been done to distance *our* methods and language from the ways of the religious devotee, especially the Christian theologian, since our field is highly influenced by the legacy of European Christianity. An example of this attempt at distancing (or should I say *purifying*?) is provided by the latter portion of my original paper which argued for the use of descriptive terminology which did not bring with it some implied theological agenda.

But now I question just what assumptions our language still houses. To put it another way, what social interests are being served by the presumed neutrality of our language? What is the significance of my critique of Clarkson's quest for origins and purity when I myself am involved in a similar quest for, if not pure then at least purer language? Clarkson challenges me to decide whether the researcher perpetuates a certain social order if s/he naively repeals, rather than challenges, the devotee's words. From what struggles is the researcher exempt when s/he holds that the academy is neutral and not involved? How, for what reasons, and for whom is academic neutrality beneficial?

Whose purposes does it serve to have a group of human beings sitting alone in offices attempting to describe the dynamics of texts, for example? This group is among a rather small class of people in our society who are highly trained to read and write and by virtue of that they are routinely authorized to make pronouncements only within a strictly circumscribed arena and, as well, to teach students to do the same. Such people could otherwise be involved in countless activities, but for the time being they (*we*) are content to write to each other as I am doing now.[8] According to Lentricchia, they (we) are a group of people whose beliefs have been "invaded by the enviscerating notion that politics is something that somehow goes on somewhere else, in the 'outside' world…" (1985: 7).

The Marxist critique of deconstruction as an elite group of international scholars incestuously reading each other's work while oblivious to the world around them has wider applications. Marx and Engels understood this when, in *The German Ideology*, they accused idealist philosophies of tacitly supporting the status quo by reflecting on the order of some other world: theoretical struggles distract people from other practical activities.[9] I take it that Clarkson may have something like this in mind when she accuses the academy of housing patriarchy in what she suspects to be its uncritical repetition of the gender-exclusive language of the devotee.

Now, I am enough of a believer in the difference between theology and religious studies to say here that I still do not think that scholars of religion ought to go around correcting the language of their subjects. However, Clarkson draws our attention to the need for scholars to examine critically both their own language as well as that of their subjects. Being a multi-disciplinary field, the academic study of religion is quite capable of generating sociological and psychological, even ideological critiques of religious claims to knowledge and therefore power.[10] If studying a group which uses

Father or *Mother* for their deity, I will not edit their words into some neutral alternate, but in reproducing the term, my responsibility is to question why such a metaphor is relevant to devotees and their experience. I will not ask questions about the deity, nor about the devotees' relationship with deity; rather, I will ask what it is about their social organization, the distributions of power, and their habits which privileges certain humans as suggested by their selective use of certain pronouns and images.

If all I was doing as a scholar was repeating devotee accounts while under the spell of neutrality, as in the case of the epoché of classical phenomenology of religion, then indeed I would be guilty of tacit approval of the ruling powers. The dangers of naive description have been identified by Willard Oxtoby in his well-known essay on *Religionswissenschaft*. According to Oxtoby,

> Phenomenologists, in conferring approval in principle on the faith [i.e., the metaphors, symbols, and accounts] of others, preserves it for their own traditions as well... In phenomenology, the science of religion has in effect become a religious exercise itself. (1968: 589–89)

However, there is a difference between the mere descriptive repetition espoused by those who believe it possible to study religion exclusively on its own terms (whatever that means) and those theorists whose initial descriptions are followed by critique. To paraphrase Eagleton, the critical aspect of our field is not to purify obscurities either in texts, "it is rather a matter of explaining the forces at work of which these textual obscurities are a necessary effect" (1991: 133). To ask such questions as to whose benefit is such an image, or what influences are reflected or promoted by such language, is not an attempt to remake the world in a manner more appealing to the political views of the contemporary scholar, but rather it is to take seriously the observation that ideas do not fall from out of the sky, but are socially determined and mediated. Thoughts and actions are never neutral. Along with Lentricchia and Frederic Jameson, such an attitude can be characterized as a critical consciousness whereby one recognizes that not only the subject of study (a text, a drawing, etc.), but the critic as well, is a product of history.

Unlike Clarkson, I do not think that as a scholar I am perpetuating patriarchy if I *descriptively* use the gender-exclusive language of my subject. Ironically, I actually will be de-legitimating the language of the dominant group since to investigate the social, political, and economic interests encoded in its symbols (the conflicts embedded within the text, its *political unconscious*, to tip my hat toward Jameson) is to go beyond mere description. It de-naturalizes their rhetoric, and calls their common sense—their ideology—into question. To map the historical path of language-thought-practice in what some may believe to be a static, inert text (society) is to challenge its (their) claim to ahistorical authority and privilege. To put it into explicit political language, it is to struggle against the presumed norm and the power it gathers/exerts. This, I believe, is what Foucault saw as the role of the intellectual. As well, it is the role of Gramsci's organic and Chomsky's combative intellectuals. To fail to make explicit the social and political motivations/benefits behind what the apparent majority of "religionists" yet think to be the *sui generis* quality of religion, its texts, and its language—of course including, but not limited to, gender-exclusive language—is to fall considerably short of what the academic study of religion could be.

To conclude, I agree with Milne's assessment when she writes that Clarkson "assumes, without reflection, that the god-talk issue is raised only within the community of belief" (1991: 126). As useful as it may be for Clarkson to recognize the difficulty—perhaps even the impossibility—of asking a "fish to analyze the water in which it swims" (1991: 126), she fails to realize that, as much as we are all immersed within a framework, we are not all swimming in the same conceptual pond.[11]

Notes

1. https://www.equinoxpub.com/blog/2013/01/yoga-and-the-boundaries-of-religion-in-the-public-square/ [accessed on January 23, 2013].
2. Ed. Note: according to a 2008 study published by the Council on Graduate Schools (CGS; see http://www.phdcompletion.org/information/) from the early 1990s to the early 2000s, the completion rate (within ten years) for doctoral students from across the disciplines was 55% for female candidates and 58% for males, though in the Humanities it was higher for females than males (52% to 47%). As the report goes on to describe: "The analysis of gender data shows an important difference in late completion (after year seven) as a function of gender. Twenty-five percent of the women who complete in ten years do so after year seven, compared with 18% of men." See the executive summary of the report at: http://www.phdcompletion.org/information/Executive_Summary_Demographics_Book_II.pdf (accessed April 6, 2013).
3. For two succinct and convincing rejoinders to Clarkson's earlier assertion concerning the great degree to which patriarchal societies have misread the original texts, see Milne's remarks in her reply and Francis Landy (1990: 485–87). Citing a variety of feminist scholars, Milne notes how "most feminist reformist interpreters of the bible today concede it is a patriarchal document" (131). Landy's response is brief and to the point: as much as contemporary feminist theologians wish to recapture gender-neutral references to their deity, "there is abundant evidence that the Israelites did conceive of Yhwh as a male" (485).

4.   As an aside, it has always struck me as incredible that, in spite of the rather harsh criticisms post-modernist literary critics have leveled at traditional forms of textual interpretation, scholars of religion continue to draw an analogy between the essentially *literary* aspect of literature and the autonomous *religious* aspect of sacred texts, rituals, and symbols. If one presumes, along with Eliade, that literary criticism never moved beyond I. A. Richards or F. R. Leavis then I guess this is understandable.

5.   Here I rely upon the strategies outlined by Terry Eagleton (1991: 45).

6.   A good example of the strategy of unification is found in the use of such terms as "feminist," "men" and "women." Recently, non-western women and women of color have voiced some concern that the feminist agenda is more properly a movement of white middle class Western women than one of woman *qua* woman. All three of the above terms gloss over significant differences between class and political status of persons who, for physiological reasons, are categorized under one seemingly generic heading.

7.   I take this final point from Frank Lentricchia (1985: 36).

8.   For a useful study of the role of the scholar in society see Jim Merod (1987). Also, see the diverse essays collected in Robbins (1990).

9.   I do not mean to underestimate the role reading and writing play in influencing social change. What I am suggesting is that we may sometimes confuse their role in social *maintenance* with their potential impact for social *critique* (and along with them the roles of readers and writers).

10.   It is sadly unfortunate that the longstanding controversy over the role of reductionistic or naturalistic explanations yet plagues our field and, at least in part, has led to the relatively low profile of modern ideology critiques of religious practices and doctrines.

11.   I would like to thank Stephen Heathorn, Ann Baranowski, and Neil McMullin for their helpful advice on the issues contained therein.

Chapter 3

Introduction

While a doctoral student at the University of Toronto, the bilingual Canadian journal, *Studies in Religion/Sciences Religieuses*, represented one of the places where I hoped that my work would someday appear. Like *JAAR*, *Numen*, and *Religion*, to mention three others, *SR* impressed me then as one of *the* places where important exchanges in the field were taking place. More than likely this was because of a spirited and extended exchange that had taken place in the pages of *SR*, mainly from the mid-1980s onward, between the late Charles Davis (d. 1999; former priest and British Roman Catholic theologian, he came to North America to establish Religious Studies at the University of Alberta, was editor of *SR* [1977–85], and then a longtime faculty member at Concordia University in Montreal) and one of my own professors at the time, Donald Wiebe—an exchange that very much came to life in the conversations that were then taking place in my classes and during coffee breaks on the fourteenth floor of Robarts Library, then the home of what was at the time known as the Centre for Religious Studies (an autonomous, completely cross-disciplinary unit that, since then, has simply become the graduate division of what was once the exclusively undergraduate Department of Religious Studies). It began with Davis's 1974 essay, "The Reconvergence of Theology and Religious Studies," which had been presented earlier that year at the annual meeting of the Canadian Society for the Study of Religion (CSSR—not to be confused with the Council of Societies for the Study of Religion) and, subsequently, solicited by the editors of *SR*. In the editorial that introduced the issue in which they published it, along with invited responses by Gregory Baum, Kenneth Hamilton, William O. Fennell, Paul Younger, and William Hordern (see *SR* 4/3 [1974]: 222–36), the then editor, J. C. McLelland, wrote (not so thinly veiling not only where he stood on the matter of religious studies' relationship to theology but also his apparent appreciation for alluring metaphors):

> The topic [of Davis's essay] has general significance, since today's academic scene has shifted dramatically within the last decade, introducing new departments of religion and altering the orientation of theological studies. The two poles of the new campus

dialectic are still unsure of their relationship, still wary and poised for debate. This may be partly a reflection of what Margaret Atwood has posited as the essential Canadian stance: defensive against the enormities of our environment, seeking only *survival*.[1] In our case it is a matter of irony that we seem threatened by our inner environment, by the nature of the quest which is the very subject matter of both theology and religious studies. In our little nation and in our modern secular culture it is perhaps *tragic* irony that we remain uncertain of whether the field can be shared or the quest examined by more than one approach.

SR itself was born some four years ago from the womb of the former *Canadian Journal of Theology* thanks to the fertilization of the new CSSR. At first, indeed, a second journal was proposed by the religionists, with rivalry inevitable. Then followed a brief and nervous courtship, resulting in agreement to launch a new journal serving the interests of both parties. Differing identities, a pluralism of methods or approaches, yet one organ of expression and dialogue: whatever element of mere survival was present, the decision about *SR* contained seeds of larger vision and more abundant life (like Teilhard's *sur-vivre*).

As with the 1964 reinvention of the National Association of Bible Instructors (NABI—born in 1922 from what had previously been established [in 1909] as the Association of Biblical Instructors in American Colleges and Secondary Schools—a rather blue collar association if compared to the higher criticism credentials of the Society of Biblical Literature [SBL] at the time) as the American Academy of Religion, and the 1966 name change of its *Journal of the National Association of Bible Instructors* to the *Journal of the American Academy of Religion* (for the full history see Wiebe 1999: chs. 14 and 15), so too the Canadian scene provides ample evidence of the liberal theological roots of the modern academic study of religion. That Canada was able, eventually, to support only one academic journal—despite the fact that there were plenty of voices advocating a sharp distinction between the study of religion from a theology of world religions, and that there was sufficient interest, some years later, in founding *Method & Theory in the Study of Religion* in Canada—meant that its national periodical has always needed to reflect the interests of scholars in such societies as the Canadian Society of Biblical Studies, the Canadian Society of Church History, the Canadian Society of Patristic Studies, the Canadian Society for the Study of Religion, the Canadian Theological Society, and the Société québécoise pour l'étude de la religion. While some might name this grouping a pluralism of methods—as the *SR* editor once did and many since then have as well, surely reflecting what

McLelland then characterized as the apparently common "quest" of those studying theology and religious studies—others refer to them as a collection of societies whose interests explicitly contradicted, rather than complemented, one another, suggesting that any so-called dialogue between their members was bound to fail since some of the parties were necessarily talking past each other, engaging in entirely different conversations.

And thus entered Wiebe into the debate, advancing just such an alternative (surely radical in some people's estimation) position. Between him (e.g., 1983, 1984, 1986) and Davis (e.g., 1974, 1984, 1986)—as well as several others invited by later *SR* editors to comment on the debate[2]—*SR* became, for a time, very interesting to read for someone like myself, because something of relevance to the entire field was clearly at stake for these writers and their prose made this evident. For while there was Davis, on the one side, advancing the Rudolf Otto-like argument concerning the fact that scholars of religion are "unavoidably concerned with the experience of faith. Those with no taste for the divine are not in a position to analyze the ingredients of religious experience nor to distinguish good religion from bad" (1984: 394), on the other side was Wiebe, arguing relentlessly that the scholar of religion had no place either in discourses sympathetic to religious belief or in doing so-called critical theology (something very much associated with Davis's work), in which religious beliefs and institutions were criticized (from the vantage point of a theologically inflected critical, Marxist theory) for the manner in which they had, for lack of a better phrase, been appropriated and thus deviated from the proper faith. Contrary to this, as Wiebe phrased it, his effort was

> to show that the study of religion as an academically legitimated enterprise stands in danger of dissolution in a crisis of identity created by the recent plethora of calls for its "reconvergence" with theology. Indeed, that study had achieved academic status as a legitimate scholarly undertaking, housed in its own political structure within the academic and university community, precisely on the basis of a clear demarcation between itself and theology. (1986: 198)

Despite being about thirty years old, it is well worth anyone's time to read through the various essays that comprise this Canadian debate, since the issues and the rhetorical moves have not changed all that much since then.

Early on in my graduate studies, such exchanges had therefore seemed to me to be the norm for scholars—though I soon learned that, at least to my way of thinking, too few direct responses are ever written and published (which is one thing that *MTSR* has done from the start, which still distinguishes it). I also learned that respondents often reserved their most aggressive rhetoric for those who questioned the norms of the field itself. But this early in my career it was rather gratifying to find that an article of my own, published in *SR* (McCutcheon 1997c) had sparked a bit of a conversation on the limits of the field on what was then a pretty active listserve for scholars of religion—Andere-L (yes, "Other" in German), administered by Shawn Landres, then a student at the University of Santa Barbara's Department of Religious Studies. William "Bill" Arnal, who was just a few years behind me at the University of Toronto's Centre for Religious Studies and who was then working at NYU's Department of Classics, tackled my argument, on the listserve, concerning the various ways that I thought "theory" could be defined so that a postmodern influence (i.e., theory *qua* critique, as opposed to criticizing it or what Davis terms critical theology) could comfortably fit within a non-theological, naturalistic paradigm that saw theory as causal, explanatory analysis. Arnal pressed me to consider going even further in my argument than I had at the time, specifically my choice of the metaphor of "game" (as in "We are all playing games but not all games are equally at home in the same institutional setting"—or, as Arnal phrased it: "one does not play tennis with golf clubs" [1998: 62]). Soon, he turned his listserve comment (which had already sparked a lively and extended debate on the web) into a published reply (Arnal 1998; see also MacKendrick's later comment on the entire debate [1999]), affording me the following rejoinder. Arnal's main point, as I read him, was that my choice of "the ludic metaphor does not obviate the extra-discursive elements of our work... [G]aming of any sort requires outlay" (1998: 63). And that this outlay (e.g., training to play it, the tools necessary to play it, the groomed field on which it is played, etc.), is not a mere subjective choice, as he understood me to be arguing, but is, instead, often dictated by a prior structure—can one afford the racket, not to mention the membership to the tennis club or taking time off work to enroll in lessons? Accordingly, one does not just *choose* to play tennis—a point that nicely highlights the complex relationship between structure and agency, a relationship that has come to be a recurring focus of my work.

That Arnal, back then, rightly saw issues in my attempt to portray two different non-theological approaches as complementary (i.e., theory-as-critique and theory-as-explanation)—issues that were not as apparent to me until some time later—says something about his critical acumen, I'm sure. That I eventually had the good sense to suggest to him that we co-write a book together (Arnal and McCutcheon 2013) surely says something about my good taste as well.

Returning the Volley to William E. Arnal (1998)

When I first read William Arnal's posting on Andere-L, I was pleased to learn not only that I had written something that prompted someone to offer a rigorous argument in response but also that one of the shortcomings of my article was that *it does not go far enough!* I therefore welcome Arnal's comments for they pretty much agree with positions I have argued elsewhere in print: the rules of the game (i.e., discursive/institutional/social structures and pre-conditions) are not simply given, games do not take place in a vacuum, and the choice of which game to play is hardly innocent—instead, such games derive from and benefit specific groups of socio-historical actors; no one account (either descriptive, interpretive, or even explanatory) of human behavior is more "true" than any other—instead, each account offers a local map or grid by which differing groups of people sort, classify, and negotiate their way through a complex world; and finally, there is a mega-game going on concerning how one *ought* to talk about human data (including behavior commonly labeled religious) in the publicly funded university—a game with high material/social stakes.

In part, my essay in *Studies in Religion* (*SR*) grew out of the last chapter to my book (1997b), where I was attempting to move from a broad critique of the field as it is, to a suggestion for how it might be redescribed in the future. Arnal is therefore correct to detect in this article an uneasy relation between postmodern inspired critique and the modernist attempt to demarcate public from private discourses. To put it another way, despite there being many publics, I have argued that the discourse on religion where people like Arnal and I make our institutional homes should conform to a specific set of discursive/institutional rules whereby some discourses are ruled out of bounds and other in bounds. Despite some people's now fashionable disdain for exclusionary practices, no discourse can be everything to everyone; in my opinion, any discourse that entails such totalizing claims is a good candidate for ideology critique (although firmly rooted in modernism, I have argued elsewhere that "ideology" remains a useful tool). Theologies—discourses concerning ahistoric origins and endtimes, deep meanings, and the existence of non-obvious agents—are among the very best candidates for such critique. So too are humanistic discourses insomuch as they are concerned with ascertaining the core, ahistoric elements to human nature. In making this argument, I attempted to steer a middle course between the "anything goes" of some postmodern theologians (if such a title makes any sense) and the nagging myth of objectivism or neutrality that sadly haunts the rationales used by many of our departments to normalize their place in the university.

Arnal challenges me to come clean on the reasons why any one local discourse ought to be considered as the so-called public discourse; after all, much of my work contests the long held right of the theological/humanistic discourse to be portrayed as normative. Were I a modernist, I might have said it is because one particular local discourse fit the facts better—but we know that this reasoning does not make much sense in a world influenced by postmodern critique. If all discourses are equally embedded in dynamic social worlds, if all data counts as data only in light of pre-existent theories, and if all theories are bold claims about how the world works, then what makes any one discourse more suited to a particular institutional setting? Despite being influenced a great deal by social constructionist critique, I am enough of a realist to presume that a physical world does indeed exist, that is, I occasionally bump into things and rely on pre-existent social conventions to decide what it is I bumped into and whether it is worth doing again. Although I may be terribly mistaken, this is the world I presume we all occupy. Given this presumption, I then find it curious that, despite making elaborate claims concerning such things as fate, destiny, karma, and devotion to gods, so-called religious people generally do not just pray for food, they also plant seeds; they do not just perform rituals for healing, they also incorporate various practical treatments; they do not just hope for a better future but also take practical steps to bring it about. In other words, despite invoking elaborate ideational systems, we all seem to live in a very real, practical world which can be empirically sensed. What we make of these senses, and which senses count, depends on where we live: if we stop eating, we will soon die; however, whether this is a "good" thing or not will depend on whether you are an Irish hunger striker in a British jail, a Jain monk in India, or adrift in a rowboat on the high seas.

The study of religion as I conceive it is warranted as the public discourse on religion because it starts with a basic presumption: that human beings, regardless of their complex ideational systems, occupy and make claims about a physical world, engage in observable behaviors, and work to maintain distinguishable social groupings. In a world of conflicting claims about value and differing beliefs about an extra-physical world, I would argue that we can at least agree with this. Since it is funded by money derived from a form of taxation applied across a complex, social-democratic nation-state, the study of religion seems to have little choice but to be based on these presumptions.

Where Arnal is quite wrong, however, is in assuming that I have unwittingly attempted to manufacture a privileged zone; instead, I offered several arguments for why it is that we should hold to a specific understanding of "theory"; that I am just as implicated in social authorizing when I make this argument is clearly evident—thinking myself exempt from this would be silly, to say the least. After all, I argued for a normative definition of theory as a method for maintaining a specific institutional boundary. Pointing this out is hardly a criticism on his part; it is simply accurate description. My critique is self-referential, it could not be any other way—Arnal's own rationally argued reply is evidence of this for it is only because of our agreement on both the nature of socially constructed institutions as well as the usefulness of rational argumentation that employs empirically observable, public data that he could apply my brand of critique to my own work. Otherwise, he would not have written a reasoned a reply and posted it as part of a public conversation.

Before concluding, I would like to comment on what I might refer to as Arnal's over-reading of my game metaphor and, specifically, my supposed thoughts on the lack of practical consequences to the institutional, intellectual games we play. Frankly, I am surprised by this criticism since I am in print elsewhere as arguing for just the opposite of what he seems to find in my *SR* article. That I have yet to turn my attention in detail to the socio-political consequences of naturalist discourses on religion is something that is due mainly to the practical limitations on my time than to my lack of interest in the topic. Despite this apparent shortcoming, in a 1997 *JAAR* article (McCutcheon 1997a) I made it quite clear that our scholarship—whether dominant or oppositional—occupies a specific socio-political location and, in *Manufacturing Religion*, I even went so far as to identify a troubling insularity that is used to privileges some instances of the naturalist discourse. Therefore, I hardly suggest that our work only has intra-discursive consequences. And as for my image of gaming, I made no attempt to trivialize human enterprises by using this metaphor; it goes without saying that these human games are often deadly serious for what is being contested are socio-political identities, us/them distinctions which at times delineate not just heightened privilege and increased social standing but one's right to live, eat, and work. Having focused on this in detail elsewhere in print (see my analysis of scholarly and media interpretations of Vietnamese "self-immolations" in *Manufacturing Religion*) I saw little need to repeat myself in the pages of *SR*.

Finally, I would like to repeat my commitment to conceptualizing the public university (and, by extension, the public study of religion as an entirely human enterprise) as based on a set of discursive rules that have something to do with publicly stated claims about an observable and therefore testable world. Is the world more than this? (But for the life of me I do

why not "different"?

not know [i] what this more could be; [ii] how I would ever publicly communicate this more to someone else; and [iii] how I would ever persuade
anyone of just this more as opposed to any other.) I leave answering this
question to those who live and work in any of the many publics that comprise our society.

Notes

1.   Just two years prior, Atwood—who went on to become one of the most
       important Canadian authors of the late twentieth-century onward—had pub-
       lished *Survival: A Thematic Guide to Canadian Literature* (1972b), which
       argued that the survival of the protagonist *qua* victim was, for what was
       now being classified as Canadian literature (i.e., Can Lit), the defining motif,
       much as images of the unexplored western frontier functioned in American
       literature. This thesis was very much in keeping with the theme of her own
       early breakthrough novel, *Surfacing* (1972a). That this topic equally preoc-
       cupied the editors of *SR* indicates the manner in which writers from across
       fields were, at that time, equally invested in defining the specific Canadian-
       ness of their intellectual pursuits.
2.   I have in mind Alton (1986), Dawson (1986), Henault (1986), and Penner
       (1986a).

Chapter 4

Introduction

> Question: in what field of academic inquiry can one still get away
> with employing the analytically vacuous noun "mystery"? Answer:
> in the same field which has hitched its institutional, theoretical and
> methodological wagon to an undefinable datum locked within the
> private, interior recesses of human experiences, intuitions and feel-
> ings. Of course, it is none other than the study of religion, at least
> as it is practised by some. (McCutcheon 1998c: 92)

So opened my book review of Bryan Rennie's *Reconstructing Eliade:
Making Sense of Religion* (1996), a book published the year before my own
Manufacturing of Religion appeared. I don't recall when I first met Bryan
in person—likely it was at a conference; we've known each other for many
years, largely through our shared involvement in the North American Association for the Study of Religion (NAASR), but also, my second book, *Critics Not Caretakers* (2001a), appeared in his Issues in the Study of Religion
book series with SUNY Press—but I came across him in print first, as we
often do with the scholars whom we sometimes eventually meet at conferences. As I recall, it was his reply to Adrianna Berger's critique of Eliade's
political past (Berger 1989; see also 1994; Rennie 1992) that first caught my
eye, at a time when I was reading various critiques and defenses of Eliade's
life and work for my dissertation.

I'm not sure if I suggested the book to them or if the editors at *Religion* invited me to review Rennie's book, which appeared just a few years
after reading his carefully researched defense of Eliade's diplomatic career.
Given my own critique of Eliade's work, it made sense for me to tackle
what I read as Rennie's sympathetic reading of Eliade's oeuvre, but given
that my own book was only then being published, there's little reason to
think anyone would much care about what I made of *Reconstructing Eliade*.
That Rennie responded to my book review—in an inaugural feature of what
the journal then called its "Forum"—by means of a critique of my own
newly published book, was flattering; because I was given the last word, it
also provided an opportunity to press home a few points that I felt had been
missed in the exchange.

All throughout my graduate training, one of the recurring debates in the field revolved around the relationship (or lack of) between theology and the academic study of religion; but it soon became apparent how this way of posing the issue—that of religion versus science—failed to capture what I found interesting about (and lacking in) the various ways in which scholars studied religion. I think it was the exchanges between Dan Pals (e.g., 1986, 1987), on the one side, and Robert Segal and Donald Wiebe (e.g., Segal and Wiebe 1989; see in particular the opening exchange between Pals and Wiebe in *Religion* 20/1 [1990]), on the other, all taking place in the late 1980s and early 1990s, that first got me thinking about a different way to slice the pie—a way that would tease out differences within the seemingly homogenous zone known as "Religious Studies" that I took to be significant. For although not involved in a confessional endeavor (e.g., a textual study aimed at interpreting and then living by the Word of God [i.e., eventually asking "What does the text mean for my life?"]), the way in which many scholars of religion went about their work nonetheless seemed problematic to me, inasmuch as they assumed that a transcendental thing called "meaning" or an author's "intention" and "voice" somehow existed within a text or an action (e.g., a ritual, understood as a symbolic or expressive activity that had to be read like a text for its meaning). As if trapped in amber, this thing called meaning was somehow assumed to evade historical change and the successful interpreter, who was able to give "a close reading" could, quite literally, time travel to ascertain the "deeper meaning" of some symbolic activity. Given my understanding of history—or better put, the historicity of human endeavors, *including* scholarship itself along with such activities as reading and meaning-making—such an approach was little different from the so-called theological approaches, despite the fact that such terms as God or salvation or sin or heaven, and so on, made no appearances in these discourses.

Although I clearly had not phrased it yet as I later came to, I think that it was dawning on me then that there was little difference, on the rhetorical level, between so-called theological claims about the Holy Spirit and what most would term the humanistic claims about the Human Spirit or the Human Condition. It was for this reason that the "theology versus religious studies" model struck me as not nearly as useful as the "humanities versus the social sciences"—though, under the influence of Jonathan Z. Smith, I later came to think of the latter more broadly, preferring "the human sciences." And by "science" I've come to prefer to use the English word akin to the German "*Wissenschaft*," inasmuch as it names a wide range of rigorous professional practices that allow a systematic study of some topic. That this practice is always understood to be focused on historical (i.e., contingent) affairs, using an historical (i.e., contingent) method is paramount—what I think Lincoln was trying to get at when, in Thesis 2, he named History (uppercase intended) as "that discourse which speaks of things temporal and terrestrial in a human and fallible voice while staking its claim to authority on rigorous critical practice" (1996: 225; also 2012: 1). One of the things studied in this manner is what he called Religion, which names discourses that *claim* extra-historical focus and authority. But if we see such claims as "We hold these truths to be self-evident…," "Everybody knows that…," "Coz I said so!"—or even the reply I recently got to my pressing a Barthian/Foucaltian reading of authorship, when I was flatly told, not too long ago, by a colleague at another university, and without argumentation or elaboration: "Surely there *must* be a voice behind the text!"—as all basing their authority not on argumentation and persuasion but, instead, on a form of assertion and perhaps even coercion (the proper name, I think for someone with authority over a grade book informing a student that she has read an author incorrectly), then you may see why a narrow understanding of religion fails to get at that which unites these common, even rather mundane sorts of claims with the more traditional and supposedly sacred "In the beginning…" or "Thou shalt not…" that usually occupies the scholar of religion's careful attention.

I think that this widening of our data is what lies in the background of the disagreement between myself and Rennie, at least as represented in the exchange that ended with the following short reply. For although Eliade's work (as well as Rennie's own, I would add) is by no means theological, as we once commonly used that term—thus signaling to many in the twentieth century that Eliade provided a viable model for the cross-cultural academic study of religion—it nonetheless strikes me as presupposing a number of problematic assumptions concerning, for instance, meaning as being an enduring public expression of an inner experience that, once put into words, makes a private world of affect intersubjectively available. Moreover, as Eliade proposed, the careful interpreter, who deciphers the meaning of the myth or ritual properly, will re-experience the existential situations and values that motivated the symbol in the first place, regardless how long ago it first appeared, leading to his view of Historians of Religions as a conservator of human meaning and truth.

And so, with all of this in mind, my review of Rennie's book concluded with the following paragraph:

> Rennie's exhaustively researched and well-written book will no doubt become a standard work on Eliade's admittedly complex corpus. However, in his preoccupation with finding a coherent meaning and a consistent whole in Eliade's fiction, diaries, early

Romanian journalism and mature autobiographical writing, as well as in his scholarship, Rennie betrays that he, too, may be more interested in constructing timeless essences (whether inside or outside the head and heart) rather than studying the historical, social, economic, and political particularities which comprise not only Eliade's, but our own, lives, work, and authority. It turns out that Rennie's reconstruction is, like all scholarship, only a construction which, through rhetoric, is authorized as providing "the whole of Eliade's understanding of religion" and access to "what has actually been written." Had he recognized the full import of the postmodern turn, Rennie would have avoided making such claims to wholeness, authenticity, and authority and would instead have recognized that his work is no less than that of Eliade's critics (and of Eliade himself) an exercise in tactical persuasion which is locked within a specific polemic. (1998c: 97)

Seeing texts as linked to persuasion and not presentation is a big move for many in our field. Asking not "What does it mean?" and thereby naturalizing a set of conditions that allow it to mean this or that (e.g., a grammar, set of class or race relations, etc.), but, rather, "What sort of world, what set of social relations, are made possible by this or that reading?" is the move that strikes me as far more interesting. Although early on in my move toward asking the latter question, the following represents a step in that direction, I think.

Of Strawmen and Humanists: A Reply to Bryan Rennie (1999)

In *Forum* Bryan Rennie (1998) replies to my review of his book, *Reconstructing Eliade* (1996) by tackling my own recent book, *Manufacturing Religion* (1997b).[1] I will reply succinctly to several of the more notable criticisms he raises.

(1) Nowhere do I identify, or even imply I have any interest in developing, conspiracy theories, as Rennie suggests I do by means of his remark on my supposed identification of a "cabal" (Rennie 1998: 413).[2] To identify the socio-rhetorical mechanisms whereby social formations reproduce themselves is simply an instance of institutional analysis—nothing more, nothing less.

(2) By "discourse on *sui generis* religion" I simply mean that group of scholars who presume that their datum—most often termed "religious experience"—is somehow ahistorical, non-social, and apolitical. Despite Rennie's quotation from Eliade saying that "there can be no *purely* religious phenomenon" (413),[3] it is clear to me that Eliade is here referring only to the historical *manifestations* of some prior *experience*, itself asocial and apolitical. Accordingly, for Rennie to imply that Eliade is not an ahistorical essentialist is misleading.

(3) Rennie, like Eliade, labels this prior religious experience an element of human consciousness (414).[4] I simply ask, experience or conscious of what? What is motivating and providing the parameters for this so-called pre-reflective experience?

(4) If Rennie means that this completely undefined (and undefinable?) marker, "the sacred," is actually part of the hard wiring of human brains, part of the biological, cognitive baggage with which we are born, then he needs to provide more reference to the findings of cognitive science. However, those who know most about the application of cognitive science to the study of religion seem to disagree with Rennie's understanding of "the sacred"—for example, Sperber, Lawson, McCauley, Boyer, Guthrie, and Anttonen. Therefore, Rennie's and Eliade's claims concerning the status of "the sacred" as an element of human consciousness are at present nothing other than a rhetorical device in need of theorization.

(5) If I recall correctly, I say quite clearly in my book that I do not think that Eliade is the "chief proponent," "chief patron," or "champion of

the *sui generis* discourse," as Rennie claims I do (413).[5] Instead, I argue that, because of the complexity of analyzing an entire intellectual, academic tradition, I had to start somewhere and I began with the work of Eliade for reasons I state quite explicitly in the opening to the book.[6]

(6) If the issue is to come down to a numbers game—counting the number of players for and against *sui generis* religion—then it is misleading for Rennie to claim that my work suggests that the modern naturalistic tradition is dominant (413–14). Anyone present in the room for the 1997 Presidential Address of the American Academy of Religion will agree that sympathetic scholarship on presumably non-explainable religious experiences still carries the day in our guild.[7] Moreover, to suggest that my analysis is limited to strawmen growing in the field's pre-modern history[8] is equally misleading for the vast majority of my book critically examines contemporary writers including many of the commentators on Eliade's life and scholarship and the authors of many world religions textbooks. Subsequent to *Manufacturing Religion*, I have continued to document the "names and faces" as well as the practical implications of the dominant, anti-reductionistic discourse.

(7) If so-called mundane objects are "elevated" to sacred status by means of what Rennie terms "historical, material, and rhetorical claims and processes" (414), then he and I agree completely. But we part company when he goes on to claim that these "elevations are not accomplished through purely historical and material claims." What else can accomplish them? It helps us little when he goes on to suggest that these "rhetorical devices involved invariably involve non-historical, 'spiritual' or 'transcendent' terms and they are just as important" (414). Of course, they are important, but only as descriptive data in need of theorizing. Rennie here completely misunderstands that, for the scholars in the human sciences, *all* talk of the so-called non-historical *is* purely historical talk. Failing to move from description, understanding, and appreciation of indigenous systems of classification and interpretation to analytic redescription of these same systems amounts to a scholarship comprised of mere reporting and voyeurism.

To conclude, these are four of the premises upon which my work is based:

(1) The natural world (i.e., the world we bump into when we try to cross either a forest or the hotel lobby at the AAR/SBL meeting) is an incredibly complex place and I presume that no human community

knows what is *really* going on in it. Instead, we all have hunches, recall just this or that past event, and anticipate future events—some of us even build explicit theories—all in an effort to talk about and act within this world. I would therefore be the last to champion onto-logical reductionism as an explanatory option; following Don Wiebe, I advocate methodological reductionism.

(2) Because of the utter complexity of the world, a variety of methods is necessary to start talking about it in an academic manner. I therefore support pluralistic methodological reductionism. It would be quite mistaken to think that, once the work of studying social formations is exhausted (as if it could ever be exhausted), *either* there would be nothing left for colleagues using other scales of analysis to study *or* there would remain some refined distillate called experience, con-sciousness, belief, the sacred, or Human Nature, that we could only study by means of some special methodology from outside the human sciences.

(3) Any system of thought and practice that fails to presume 1 and 2 is a candidate for the status of data. Reflection on the deeper truth or meaning of religion (whether that reflection is theological *or* human-istic) attempts to bypass the historically grounded nature of all human attempts to know the world around us, making them instances of mythmaking in need of theorization. It is for this reason that I think it sensible to exclude certain approaches from the pluralistic method-ologically reductionist study of religion as carried out in the public university.

(4) There are no final explanations. Scholars in the human sciences are just as deeply involved in the art of rhetoric, contestation, and social formation as anyone else. It is a useful rule of thumb to say that it is the people we study who typically propose final, universal explanations. *— ironically including Wiebe*

To conclude, I wish simply to make the point that the presumption that there is some self-evidently meaningful experience behind our varied historical and social practices is *precisely* the presumption that my book critiqued; it is *precisely* the presumption that Rennie seems so loath to give up.

Notes

1. Ed. Note: the original review of Rennie's *Reconstructing Eliade* appeared in *Religion* 28/1 (McCutcheon 1998c).

2. Ed. Note: "McCutcheon's position is that there is a nonnaturalist and ahistorical

orthodoxy, the 'sui generis discourse,' which has hegemony in the study of religion and of which Eliade is the chief proponent—others being Rudolf Otto, Joachim Wach, Raffaele Pettazzoni, Gerardus van der Leeuw, William James, Max Müller, Cornelius Tiele, William Brede Kristensen, C. J. Bleeker, Louis Jordan, and Wilfred Cantwell Smith. This cabal has, he insists, prevented the accurate study of human cultural constructions by manufacturing its own ahistorical object—religion 'conceived as sui generis, absolutely unique, separate, and thereby its own cause' (*Manufacturing Religion*, p. 52)" (Rennie 1998: 413).

3.   Ed. Note: "Despite the fact that Eliade is quoted by McCutcheon himself as saying that 'there can be no *purely* religious phenomenon' and that 'every human datum is in the last analysis a historical datum' (*Manufacturing Religion*, pp. 12, 52), McCutcheon presents him as an essentialist who 'perpetuates the assumption that there is a purely religious sphere' (p. 159). *Reconstructing Eliade*, by contrast, presents Eliade as a humanist who attempts to understand the significance of ahistorical narrative creations (see, for example, *Reconstructing Eliade*, ch. 14)."

4.   Ed. Note: "There is no *disjunction* between the sacred as an external agent and the sacred as an internal experience, as he assumes (review, p. 94). Rather, the sacred is 'an element in the structure of (human) consciousness' (Eliade, *The Quest* [Chicago, University of Chicago Press, 1969], p. i). It is neither a 'mysterious', 'subjective, experience, nor an 'objective' entity, but a classification or structuring of experience—a way of responding to entities. It is the conjunction of external and internal."

5.   Ed. Note: for example, "Discard his claim that Eliade is the champion of the *sui generis* discourse and McCutcheon is hard pressed to prove that the discourse is 'regnant'."

6.   Ed. Note: for example, "In this study, Eliade's texts are one, but not the only, example of this type of approach…" (McCutcheon 1997b: 18).

7.   Ed. Note: this address, delivered by Robert Detweiler, was entitled "Literary Echoes of Postmodernism" (1998).

8.   Ed. Note: "But Eliade never says that the nonreligious dimension is to be excluded. Similarly, McCutcheon's reading of van der Leeuw is of an '*unarticulated* and undefended assumption concerning the ahistorical or superhuman nature of religious experience' (p. 13 [emphasis added]), and his analysis of Otto is ''probably not how Otto would have phrased it' (p. 15). In other words, McCutcheon attacks a straw man. In fact, McCutcheon 'manufactures' the *sui generis* discourse" (Rennie 1998: 414).

Chapter 5

Introduction

In November of 1998, about a year after *Manufacturing Religion* was published, Gustavo Benavides kindly organized a review panel on the book, held at the Society for the Scientific Study of Religion's (SSSR) annual meeting, which took place that year in Montreal, Canada. The papers, including the following response and Luther Martin's introduction, were all published about eighteen months later in the inaugural issue of Malory Nye's journal, *Culture and Religion*. The panelists who were kind enough to offer their thoughts on the book and to include their papers in the published review symposium included: Tim Fitzgerald (2000c), Bryan Rennie (2000), Gustavo Benavides (2000), and Tomoko Masuzawa (2000b).

I have had the good fortune to be involved with several review symposia since that time, some on projects with which I have been involved (e.g., in March of 2002 at our regional meeting of the AAR on *Critics Not Caretakers* and, along with my co-editor, Willi Braun, at the 2000 meeting of the Society for the Scientific Study of Religion [SSSR] for the *Guide to the Study of Religion*) or as a participant looking at someone else's work (e.g., on Richard King's *Orientalism and Religion* [1999] and on Jeremy Carrette's two volumes on Foucault [1999, 2000]—both of which took place at the 2000 meeting of the International Association for the History of Religions [IAHR], in Durban, South Africa, and both of which were later published [the King symposium in *MTSR* 14/2 (2002) and the Carrette symposium in *Culture and Religion* 2/1 (2001)]). Apart from book reviews (which appear for only a fraction of the books that are published annually), such review symposia are often the only place where an author hears directly from readers. For, unlike other writers who produce texts, scholars tend not to go on speaking tours promoting their books; our next project is generally not promoting our most recent project. We do sometimes get invited to lecture on other campuses but, unlike fiction authors, it would likely be considered bad form to stand in front of people and read from one of your own already published works—instead, audiences likely prefer learning that the lecture they are about to hear is from a forthcoming work, as if being let in on a secret. For, rightly or wrongly, scholarly texts are thought to communicate information rather than, say, establish a mood or bring back fans' memoires, ensuring that whereas those creators of cultural content whom we call performers might be booed for failing to faithfully reproduce their original version in each of their sub-sequence performances (say, of a live rendition of a song that preserves all of the inflections of the hit recording that receives radio play), scholars are expected always to say something new. (If, as many of us now agree, any cultural product can be read as a text, and if a text-is-a-text-is-a-text, then it fascinates me that orchestras or tribute bands can do nothing but reproduce other people's work, perhaps "interpreting" it somewhat [e.g., an orchestra playing Beethoven or a Rolling Stones tribute band], whereas no scholar could go on the road simply re-reading or doing an interpretive performance of someone else's essays, unless they were "playing" Walt Whitman or Charles Darwin in some off-Broadway tribute. Why does a mythology of correspondence, an ideology of identity, yet lurk within what we call schol-arship, a specter that does not haunt other cultural productions? Question-ing this, however, likely draws our own credibility and social authority into question.) Of course, there are those scholars whose work catches the atten-tion of readers far outside the academy (something that we see more com-monly among those who write on Christian origins or, say, mythology, I think, given the local interest for such topics and the criteria of national "big box" bookstores' purchasers), and for whom selling a few hundred or even "just" a few thousand copies of their books would be a great insult. (Who knows how many copies Huston Smith's 1958 book, *The Religions of Man*, in any of its many different editions and titles, has sold by now; back in 1991 its paperback front cover boasted 1.5 million copies sold, and its many ver-sions are still in print.) But for the vast majority of scholars, just getting a book written and reviewed, maybe even highlighted at a conference or as part of a published review symposium, is a tremendous honor.

Although my first book's thesis was conceived in the late 1980s, in con-versation with a variety of people but especially Neil McMullin and Don Wiebe, and then written while I was a grad student in the early 1990s (i.e., when I began fulltime work at the University of Tennessee in 1993 the dis-sertation was then about three quarters written, and within several months of defending it in January of 1995 it had been contracted by its publisher and my final revisions were completed that summer, though it took almost two years before it was finally published in 1997), I believe that its analysis remains relevant. Perhaps this has nowhere been more apparent than in the rheto-rics that followed the September 11, 2001, attacks in the US, where claims concerning innocence and guilt, tolerance and terror, quickly dominated the headlines. Using a host of strategies found all throughout culture, the pundits had (or should I say still have?) us believing that an historically autonomous and unique culture, burdened by destiny to be a beacon of freedom for the world, was blatantly attacked by an equally timeless, unchanging adversary of utter evil and depravity. "They despise freedom," was the uniform chorus heard on television in North America and throughout much of Europe in the days and weeks following the tragic attacks (echoed most recently in the wake of the April 15, 2013, bombings at the finishing line of the Boston Marathon). While this script plays well with those in dominant positions who fuel their social identities with feelings of embattlement and victimization, it hardly makes for good scholarship. For, as Teriq Ali wrote: "None of the cultures/civilisations spawned by the three monotheistic religions are monolithic or timeless. Despite the differences between them, they are all affected by the world they inhabit" (2002: 281; that I, in agreement with Hughes [2012a], would trouble Ali's notion of the unity and causal force of the so-called Abrahamic faiths doesn't detract from his point). Insomuch as it lifts human artifacts out of the "the world they inhabit"—a world that always comes with economic, political, gendered, racial, generational, and such other differences and contradictions—the *sui generis* strategy and perhaps even the very category of "religion" itself amounts to what Ali calls a display of historical amnesia. For if, as the US essayist, Joan Didion, has phrased it, "history is context" (2001: 63), then the claim that the inner meaning and identity of those human beliefs, behaviors, and institutions we know as religious have no context and must therefore be studied as essentially religious, manifested first here and then there in what amounts to arbitrary settings, is a politically convenient forgetfulness used by those both on the left as well as the right, to authorize their own particular social worlds (inasmuch as they are understood as necessary, obvious, timeless) while deauthorizing those of others (inasmuch as they are portrayed as contingent, ambiguous, derivative). Thus to whom we bestow the designator "religion"—and, along with it, the privileges that attend being called religious in our society—tells us much about the way we try to manage our social worlds.

Looking over these review essays, the thing that mainly stands out for me now is Masuzawa's challenge concerning the possible conflict between studying the discourse on religion, on the one hand, and supporting a naturalistic approach to the study of religion, on the other (as I did in *Manufacturing Religion*'s final chapter). Her question in this regard was prescient (echoing the position of Bill Arnal in his comment on my work [1998]; see Chapter 3 in this volume), for it identified in advance a move that I would come to make in my work, one that has made much scholarship on the category religion written since then all the more frustrating, as it merely reproduces, in my opinion, the work of Wilfred Cantwell Smith, inasmuch as critiques of the category are often motivated by some special insight into how the real things of the world—the so-called raw material from which we build up those things called religions—already somehow naturally arranged (inasmuch as this and that are Buddhist whereas those other things are somehow obviously Christian or Hindu), *ought* to be studied so that they can be understood properly. That all forms of understanding, all systems of classification, are implicated remains unseen in many of these studies. While this of course does not mean that we cease being scholars it *does* imply that we ought to own the curiosities that drive our efforts to arrange and account for the world in this or that way.

A Brief Response from a Fortunate Man[1] (2000)

> The Master said, "I am a fortunate man. Whenever I make a mistake, other people are sure to notice it."
>
> - *The Analects*, Book VII

Manufacturing Religion has elicited diverse reactions from its reviewers, something apparent not only from the differing opinions represented in the preceding collection of reviews but also from some of the reviews that have appeared elsewhere. For example, whereas Theodore Ludwig—a world religion textbook author whose work is briefly discussed in my book—says I have an "ax to grind" in my "aggressive attack" (1998: 36), the anonymous reviewer in the *Christian Century* was incredulous that I could make the arguments that I do (1998). Paul Griffiths outed me as a theologian insomuch as I have presuppositions: "everything is, in the end, and in the beginning, theology," he confidently says (1998a: 48).[2] Ivan Strenski sees my work as part of an "inbred clique" whose work, in his estimation, is "alternatively an exercise in naivete, bad faith, or ignorant mischief, or indeed, all of the above" (Strenski 1998: 118). Given such assessments, I am all the more fortunate that such writers as Armin Geertz (1999), Susan Henking (1999), Hans Penner (1999), Richard Salter (1999), Steven Sutcliffe (1999), and Gene Thursby (1998) have joined the fray by offering far more constructive comments on the book.

What seems to frustrate some reviewers is that much of my work to date has little interest in studying religion, as should be clear from Fitzgerald's description of the book.[3] Perhaps because I have answered, to my own satisfaction, questions concerning *why* people engage in the behavior we name as "religious,"[4] I feel no compulsion to apologize for finding it infinitely more interesting to ask *why* liberal humanist scholars should want to study religion as a cross-cultural human universal. Somewhat akin to Benavides's suggestion that I start getting my hands dirty,[5] I have been asked on a number of occasions when I would finally study the real data of religion rather than study scholars of religion—a question which seems to presume that, sooner or later, I must out-grow my youthful interests and, much like the early Christian apologist Paul, finally get around to acting in a grown-up fashion. Apart from the unflattering paternalism buried in this question, I find it odd for two additional reasons; first, when coming from scholars of religion, it smuggles in a put-down for their own profession, since they seem to be

saying that scholars of religion are not all that interesting. Despite undoubtedly sharing with many of my readers the experience of sitting through my
share of tedious conference panels, I happen to disagree; people who sys-
tematically re-present, classify, and study human behaviors as if certain of
them were informed by or directed toward some unseen power, charisma, or
lure are an absolutely fascinating group. (Given that life is short, people who
politely sit through tedious conference panels are a pretty interesting lot in
their own right.) Second, critics of my particular research interests presume
that, of the many thousands of people worldwide who study religions in an
academic fashion, our profession does not have room for just a handful of
us who study the profession itself. I would hope that the study of religion
is mature enough to allow a historian of the field's classification systems to
claim just a little space among those who study the things we call specific
religions in certain historic periods and geographic regions.[6]

Although my work has moved somewhat since writing this book in the
mid-1990s,[7] *Manufacturing Religion* states quite clearly early on that it
does not comprise an exercise in theorizing religion (making a number of
Rennie's and Benavides's criticisms irrelevant); rather, it examines the use
that groups of people known as historians of religion, scholars of religion,
phenomenologists, even the media, make of a particular classificatory tool
or taxon, "religion." Given its long history as a Latin-based folk category—
a history traced by many before me and in no need of repetition here—it
may strike some as counter-intuitive to study the use scholars make of "religion." But, while reading contemporary literary criticism, culture studies,
and media critiques—by such writers as Terry Eagleton, Pierre Bourdieu,
Raymond Williams, and Noam Chomsky—it struck me that the very existence of the academic study of religion was somehow connected to the presumption that this thing we call religion, like literature, culture, collegiality,
or freedom, was a real, beneficial, thing existing independently in the world
(either in the heart or in the heavens).[8] Since the thing that is presumed to
exist (the thing which comprises our object of study) is never simply understood by our colleagues as a material, historical, or all too human event—
but rather, is understood as a deeply personal experience, profound emotion,
or some such private response to an immaterial or non-historical cause—it
struck me that the particular discursive object variously named *sui generis*
religion, religious experience, the sacred, ultimate concerns, the holy, and
so on, comes with potent political implications. Careful readers of my work
will understand that I do not deny that "religion" is a useful heuristic tool for
classifying certain sorts of human behaviors (despite our many agreements,
this is a point on which Fitzgerald and I differ[9]); the book simply argues that
historical, human behaviors are variously named and categorized and that

often unrecognized, practical implications and effects attend the sorts of names we as practitioners and scholars give to our acts. Simply put, classifying certain of these behaviors *as* "religious"—a classification that generally connotes the essentially spiritual, meaningful, and other-worldly nature of these behaviors—comes with a political price (whether intended or not), for it takes something historical and elevates it above the fray. I take this to be the work of rhetoric *par excellence*.

Manufacturing Religion was therefore my attempt to document the politics of this rhetoric primarily as it has been deployed in North America since the 1950s. As I stated in the book's preface, I aimed to answer three simple questions: "what is the shape of the regnant Religious Studies discourse, why does it have the shape that it does, and what/who is being served by it?" Given that the book proceeds unapologetically to "name names"—surely this alone gets me into trouble with some readers—and then to argue for a link between a particular style of scholarship on religion, on the one hand, and larger geo-political forces operative in both the nineteenth century and the present, on the other, I take many of the attacks on the book as strong evidence that I have struck just the right nerve. Although I am indeed fortunate that the present four writers have taken time to examine my thesis, I hope that readers would judge the book for themselves. I believe that I have presented a persuasive account and, Rennie's criticism not withstanding, have hopefully done more than merely manufacture a career in the process of writing myself.[10]

This having been said, I appreciate what I take to be Fitzgerald's accurate description of the argument. As already suggested, however, I disagree with him concerning the future utility of "religion" as a taxon; not every use of this term need be attended by the kind of ideological mechanisms that both he and I see operating in its *sui generis* versions. If "religion" is merely a descriptive tag placed on certain sorts of human behaviors—a tag that is dropped once the acts become theorized as social or political, for example— then it has no more or less utility than naming an act in any other fashion. Moreover, I am not persuaded that we have advanced any when, as Fitzgerald argues, we come to the study of such social movements as Ambedkar Buddhism in Maharashtra armed, not with "religion," but instead with the categories of ritual, politics, and soteriology (Fitzgerald 1997). For me, this alternative grouping of three offers yet another example of the confusion of description with explanation; for "soteriology" is but another phenomenological, emic category which is in need of theorization, and ritual is a descriptive, untheorized marker for certain sorts of routinized or patterned behaviors. Both of these activities—people's beliefs in liberation from this to that, as well as the motivations and/or effects of their bodies' patterned, symbolic behaviors—require the kind of study that can be provided by the theories of how and why human communities negotiate issues of power and privilege, suggesting that politics can provide an explanation for both soteriology and ritual. That "religion" fails to fit non-Euro/American and non-Christian social movements when it is exclusively defined in a Euro-Christian manner (e.g., belief in God; a deep inner experience of ultimacy, etc.) is well worth pointing out and Fitzgerald's work makes this point hard to deny; but that hardly means that "religion" as a descriptive tool cannot be redescribed as part of a thorough scholarly lexicon that is driven not by presumptions of deep, enduring value but, instead, by theories derived from the human sciences.

There is not sufficient space to adequately respond to Rennie's liberal humanist critique of my work (as already indicated, I have already addressed some of Rennie's criticisms of my work elsewhere) or what I read as his assertions that "understanding" meaning is pretty much the only legitimate basis for our field. But I would like to tackle this topic a bit by addressing what I see as his failure to grasp the full weight of Robert Sharf's (1998) potent critique of the rhetoric of experience.[11] As I read scholars such as Sharf, Joan Wallach Scott (1991) as well as Fitzgerald (2000a), it is not simply that internal, experiential states are externalized, represented, and interpreted in narratives; rather, the very presumption that we have active inner lives that need or receive representation and narrativization is itself the datum deserving of study. As Scott and Sharf phrase it:

> What counts as experience is neither self-evident or straightforward; it is always contested, and always therefore political. The study of experience, therefore, must call into question its originary status in historical explanation. This will happen when historians take as their project *not* the reproduction and transmission of knowledge said to be arrived at through experience, but the analysis of the production of that knowledge itself. (Scott 1991: 797)

> [T]he rhetoric of experience tacitly posits a place where signification comes to an end, variously styled "mind," "consciousness," the "mirror of nature," or what have you. The category experience is, in essence, a mere placeholder that entails a substantive if indeterminate terminus for the relentless deferral of meaning. And this is precisely what makes the term experience so amenable to ideological appropriation. (Sharf 1998: 113)

Fitzgerald agrees: experiences are always public, he suggests, for "the semantic context for having and interpreting an experience is necessarily also a social, institutional context" (Fitzgerald 2000a: 129; Judith Perkins persuasively argues this in the case of early Christian discourses on the self as a site of suffering [1995]).[12] As Scott concludes, "understanding experience" is *not* the goal of our studies; instead, experience is "that which we want to explain"!

I have argued elsewhere (1997a) that to "understand" the meaning of the experience of the other means one must already have tacitly agreed upon and thereby have reproduced the discursive parameters of just one of the many possible "meaning" worlds (on "world" see Paden 1992 and 2000). Since each "experience" and each "world" comes with an active politics that delineates what and who gets to count as meaningful and significant (what J. Z. Smith aptly calls the "economy of signification" policed by ritual behaviors), Rennie's hermeneutical quest smuggles into the academy an indigenous politics that has little to do with any so-called essential features of the phenomena to be explained; after all, these features are recognizable and valuable only when a specific, local economy is accepted as inevitable or beneficial and thereby reproduced. Because, in my estimation, scholars play by their own set of discursive rules, I have little interest in reproducing the politics of the signification systems I study and, therefore, I have little interest in pursuing Rennie's hermeneutical quest. Of course, should one go along with the modernist *Verstehen* school and presuppose that so-called religious experience is an essential feature of human nature or the enduring human spirit (a rhetorically efficacious abstraction that homogenizes historical/material difference), then my warnings will be seen as misguided, since religious experiences are understood to be simply given and in no need of explanation. Perhaps this is what Strenski had in mind when, resurrecting Schleiermacher's reactionary romaniticism, he lumped Gary Lease, Fitzgerald, and myself together as religion's "despisers."[13] All that we as scholars should apparently be doing is an exercise in catalog production: ordering these obviously religious experiences based on their assorted types and then proceeding to understand how their transhistorical meaning can be found amidst their varied historical expressions. That at least two prior generations of phenomenologists have attempted this in the pages of countless comparative religion handbooks—and repeatedly failed—seems not to deter scholars such as Rennie.

I detect a similarly modernist tone to Benavides's dissatisfaction with the way I argue for my thesis. Although *Manufacturing Religion* is clearly influenced by writers such as Foucault and Derrida, I do not wish to play the role of postmodernism's defender to Benavides's critic.[14] It strikes me as if he—like Paul Griffiths before him—has used the opportunity of commenting on my book to vent on a host of issues that are obviously of interest to him but only tangentially related to my work. In fact, upon first reading

Masuzawa's opening comments on the importance of avoiding the temptation of telling me how I should have written my book, I could not help but
think that this temptation was too great for Benavides.

What deserves comment, however, is the relationship Benavides sees
between theorizing religion and theorizing scholars of religion. His chief
complaint against my work seems to be the need for me to study religions
(the supposedly richer soil to which he alludes) as well as scholars of religion. For instance, he suggests that we need to compare the results that different theories of religion generate when they each address the apparently
uniform data of religion: Muhammad's followers, Amazonian shamans,
American devotees of Jesus, and so on. What immediately strikes me is that
Benavides somehow knows that "the many varieties of Buddhism, Christianity, Islam, etc.," are religions worth studying. I am surprised he says this
since, in my understanding, data is a function of theory and different theories
make different things into data. This implies (i) that there is no *Ur*-phenome-
non known as religion which sets religions apart from all other social events
and, therefore, (ii) that there is no common means by which to adjudicate
better from worse accounts of the data.[15] In rushing to label me as a post-
modernist, Benavides has not grasped the full import of my book's thesis.
In a suitably modernist move he seems to presume that a fairly stable, self-
evident body of human behaviors ought to be known as religious and that
differing theories of religion will be more or less adequate in studying these
behaviors. This makes little sense for, as I understand them, scholars such
as Marx, Otto, and Freud have very different interests, approaches (I am not
persuaded that they have theories in the technical sense of the term) and,
because of that, they classify very different human doings under the name
religion.

Finally, I come to Masuzawa's comparison of my work to that of, among
the other influential Smiths, Jonathan. Z. That *Manufacturing Religion*
examines the politics of classification is, I believe, the primary evidence
of his influence on my thinking (see Smith 2000b). Reading my work as a
materialist revision of his book—although *Imagining Religion* is certainly
within the intellectualist tradition in our field, it is neither philosophically
idealist nor politically conservative—is therefore no small compliment to
me. Masuzawa does, however, put her finger on what I now take to be the
main problem in the book: the effort to speak seriously of "religion" as
manufactured while at the same time the effort to argue for the priority of
naturalist/explanatory theories of religion. As she correctly notes, taking
the former thesis seriously seems to imply the pointlessness of the latter
enterprise. Or, to phrase it another way, taking the former thesis seriously
implies that the only topic of interest is theorizing the act of classification

itself, whatever it might be. And perhaps this is the direction in which future research in our field must go.[16] But I still maintain that recognizing that certain construction techniques are appropriate to certain institutional settings is still worth our time and energy.

With this in mind, let me close by offering a classification of my own. The four review essays collected here are clearly grouped into two camps: Rennie and Benavides move within a modernist context (while the former is certainly a liberal humanist influenced by the *Verstehen* tradition, the latter is more influenced by the social sciences and is clearly within a Marxist tradition) and Fitzgerald and Masuzawa move within a more playful, meta-theoretical, culture studies context. Although Rennie and Benavides critique my work differently, they both seem to presume a utility, even common sense, to "religion" that Fitzgerald and Masuzawa are more than willing to call into question. Although I clearly have sympathies for the latter pair, I hope that readers do not come away from this symposium thinking that they have learned how our object of study, religion, really ought to be named or theorized. Rather, I hope that our exchange itself is seen as a datum, as an exercise in tactical, discursive boundary contestation and maintenance. Only by changing our gaze from self-evident external products to the practical impact of contingent, human discourses will we be able to follow Masuzawa's closing suggestion concerning the need for some of us to be "dispatched to inspect the exact date of manufacture, to investigate the history, the process, the mechanism, the circumstances of manufacture." I concur with her completely: "This is no idle navel-gazing of the academy."[17]

Notes

1. Before embarking on my reply, I must thank both Gustavo Benavides, for organizing the review panel at the 1998 meeting of the Society for the Scientific Study of Religion, and Luther Martin, for acting as the chair for that panel and for organizing the submission of these papers for publication.
2. Regarding Griffiths's criticisms of my work, readers should consult his rather spirited response (Griffiths 1998b) to my essay on the scholar of religion as a public intellectual (McCutcheon 1997a; see also my reply [1998d]).
3. Ed. Note: apart from (rightly, I would now say) questioning my siding with Wiebe and Strenski in part of the book, Fitzgerald's description of the project is consistently laudatory, as one might predict given the general agreement we have on some issues.
4. For my thoughts on religion as a rhetorical mechanism in ongoing acts of social formation, see McCutcheon (1998a, 2000). In formulating this approach I am deeply indebted to the provocative work of Bruce Lincoln. For recent related

studies applied to the data of Christian origins, see Braun (1999a, 1999b); Mack (1999, 2000).

5.   Ed. Note: see McCutcheon (1997b: 7) where I mention how I choose to answer such questions as "Where do you get your hands dirty?" The back story here is that this particular question arose at a short job interview, conducted at the annual meeting of the AAR/SBL, in the early 1990s, when Western Michigan University was looking for a specialist in method and theory. Despite the ad specifying a theorist of religion, one senior member from that Department was not satisfied whatsoever with my answers concerning studying scholars (I recall saying that I did my fieldwork at conferences such as the AAR/SBL and in the academic literature of the field), for he consistently pressed to have me name the actual religious tradition, historic period, or region of the world that I studied, all of which was very clearly driven by his apparent grasp of what counted as legitimate data to study *as* a scholar of religion. I admit that the experience was somewhat puzzling inasmuch as their own ad had specified a theorist. As I recall, their search failed that year (perhaps indicating the unresolved internal disagreements that the job interview questions had already suggested to me) and it was re-advertised the next with theory of religion being listed as but one additional sub-competency among others.

6.   As an aside, it is indicative of our field's anti-intellectual tendency that the only group in the American Academy of Religion which is exclusively devoted to studying the history of the study of religion failed just this year to have its status renewed. [Ed. Note: this aside is in reference to a temporary program unit devoted to The History of the Study of Religion that was rejected for renewal by the AAR program committee in the mid-1990s; that, if memory serves, the unit was advised simply to merge with a program unit devoted to pedagogy is evidence of the Academy's sad absence of historical consciousness when it comes to the study of religion as itself constituting a practice of interests. This was, of course, long before such now successful AAR program units as The Cultural History of the Study of Religion or Critical Theory and Discourses on Religion were conceived and proposed for inclusion in the annual meeting.]

7.   Benavides refers to several essays I have written since this book was published; for me, these essays round out and advance the project begun with *Manufacturing Religion* (1997b). They are now collected in a volume entitled, *Critics Not Caretakers* (2001a).

8.   Please note: although I am a social constructionist, I am certainly also a realist; while I agree that there are certain events in the world which we can rather confidently name as nondescript human behaviors, classifying them as religious behaviors is a socio-political act. That distinguishing human from animal behaviors is itself a classification with political import is more than obvious; my work happens not to be interested in this particular politics. Although I more than realize that all classification comes at a price, despite

Benavides's scolding of my tacit approval of the Gregorian calendar, I do not think that I can be expected to scrutinize the politics of all taxons. Like others who are more than aware of the arbitrary nature of our systems of knowledge, I do use many as if they work. My work on "religion" tries to persuade readers that, given certain interests I have, it happens not to work well at all.

9.   For his argument concerning the need to subsume the study of religion within culture studies, interested readers should consult Fitzgerald's *The Ideology of Religious Studies* (2000b; Ed. Note: since this essay was first published, Fitzgerald has extended his critique; see, for example, 2007a and 2007b). Despite an apparent similarity in title, Donald Wiebe's latest collection of essays, *The Politics of Religious Studies* (1999) argues for a reinvigorated, modernist science of religion which is not subsumed under a culture studies rubric whatsoever.

10.   Rennie's comments on the role writing plays in the construction of self strike me as rather odd for they state a truism applicable to any and all writers— Rennie included. For example, after I reviewed Rennie's book, *Reconstructing Eliade* (1996) in the periodical *Religion* (McCutcheon 1998b), Rennie replied with a criticism of my book (Rennie 1998) and I was invited by the editors to respond to his critique (1999; [Ed. Note: reproduced in this volume as Chapter 4]). Given that Benavides is reportedly also reviewing my book in *Religion* and that Rennie has a review of it forthcoming in *Zygon* [Ed. Note: this review was published in issue 35/2 (2000): 455–57], it appears that others are equally implicated in, and therefore benefitting from, my apparently misguided attempts to construct a self through writing.

11.   Ed. Note: see Martin and McCutcheon (2012) for a set of readings on the topic of religious experience, that includes both Sharf's and Scott's essays. For my own approach to the topic, see the volume's introduction.

12.   Although it may at first appear counter-intuitive, even privacy and secrecy are public insomuch as ever changing public standards and values set the bounds concerning what social actors—who are always intent on maintaining/attaining specific social rank—believe they should and should not disclose to their peers. (Ed. Note: see McCutcheon [2003a: 4ff.] for a discussion on the public nature of privacy.)

13.   Ed. Note: See Strenski (1998) and, for my own reply, see McCutcheon (2003a: ch. 11, 2004).

14.   I trust that more careful readers of the article (McCutcheon 1997c) cited by Benavides will see it as a critique of theological uses made of postmodern relativity in the study of religion.

15.   As I have tried to argue in various other places, it is not so much that one theory is a better fit with the data, but, rather, that certain types of theories are better suited to specific institutional contexts (e.g., naturalistic theories in the public university).

16.   I believe this is precisely the move made throughout the thirty essays collected in the *Guide to the Study of Religion* (Braun and McCutcheon 2000),

a volume which moves from William Arnal's opening article on the politics of defining religion to Sam Gill's closing essay on the playfulness of scholarship. The entire volume is concerned with examining both the analytic tools and institutional contexts that enable us to classify and study parts of the world as religious.

17.   Ed. Note: Masuzawa (2000b: 129).

Chapter 6

Introduction

The following brief response, not previously published, was written for a conference panel, entitled "Comparativism Then and Now: Stocktaking and Critical Issues in the Formation of Cross-cultural Knowledge." It was held at the XVIII Congress of the International Association for the History of Religions (IAHR), which took place in August of 2000 in Durban, South Africa. Chaired by William Paden, now retired but the longtime Chair of the Department of Religious Studies at The University of Vermont, the panelists included: Norman Girardot ("Max Müller's *Sacred Books* and the Nineteenth-Century Origins of the 'Comparative Science of Religions'"), Robert Segal ("Robertson Smith's Use of the Comparative Method"), Thomas Ryba ("Comparative Religion, Taxonomies and 19th Century Theories of Science"), and Michael Buchowski ("Is Comparative Study of Belief Systems Possible? Anthropologists' Views from Frazer to Levi-Strauss").

Although I only heard reports, when I was a doctoral student back in Toronto, from people who attended the 1990 meeting in Rome (Don Wiebe brought its thick Proceedings volume to my attention [Bianchi 1994] and I included it in a review essay published in *Numen* [McCutcheon 1995; reprinted as McCutcheon 1997b: ch. 5]), I have been involved with the IAHR since 1995, when I attended its Congress in Mexico City, staying in a hotel directly across from the *Zócalo* (i.e., the large town square bordered by, among other buildings, the Metropolitan Cathedral of the Assumption of Mary, the National Palace and, significantly beneath it all, the ruins of the Aztec Templo Mayor, destroyed by the Spanish in 1521); taking place every five years, I've been lucky enough to attend each of its Congresses since then (Durban in 2000, Tokyo in 2005, and Toronto in 2010) and helped with some of the planning that went into the meeting in Toronto (the Congress Director was Don Wiebe and I served as the Associate Director). Unlike many scholarly organizations, one does not join the IAHR; instead (somewhat akin to the now defunct Council of Societies for the Study of Religion [CSSR] in North America [on the history of the CSSR see Harold Remus's detailed essay in Elliott 2013][1]), it is an umbrella organization of organizations. Founded in 1950 (but claiming lineage with meetings that began as far back as 1900 in Paris), it is now comprised of about fifty national and regional academic societies that one would join, such as the British Association for the Study of Religion, the Japanese Association for Religious Studies, or the North American and the European Associations for the Study of Religion. While each of its member societies likely hold their own annual conferences, perhaps even publishing their own academic journals, the IAHR Congresses take place every five years and, despite the American Academy of Religion's onetime internationalizing imperative, they still provide the only occasion for a truly international meeting of scholars of religion.

Given that my dissertation was on the history of the field, such publications as *Numen* (the IAHR's official journal, long published by Brill of the Netherlands, and now in its fifty-ninth year) were crucial sources of information for me. For example, I clearly recall reading its various reports on earlier IAHR Congresses; especially interesting to me were the disagreements over the shape of the field that resulted after its 1960 meeting in Marburg, Germany, at which the "scientific" tone of the IAHR was, in the eyes of some, in trouble. (For post-Congress debriefings see Bleeker 1960, Schimmel 1960, and Werblowsky 1960.) Commenting on a session entitled "Religion and Thought in East and West, a Century of Cultural Exchange," the well-known Dutch phenomenologist and ancient Egyptologist, C. J. Bleeker (1898–1983) soon after wrote:

> the discussion of this theme cannot be held in the spirit of complete disinterestedness which is normally characteristic of the study of the history of religions. It touches directly the burning issues of the present day. One is therefore involutarily [sic] forced to formulate one's conviction and to determine one's attitude. In this connection I want to declare that in my opinion oriental scholars are equally capable of strictly scientific research as western students of the history of religions. But if I am not mistaken, because they are mainly studying the living religions, their approach and their aim in view is somewhat different. (1960: 225)

R. J. Zwi Werblowsky (b. 1924)—who, like Bleeker, was a longtime executive member of the IAHR—took a rather different view on matters in his report on the meeting:

> To look back on Marburg is, when all is said and done, more than just to report on a Congress. Remembering [the IAHR Congress in] Tokyo two years earlier [i.e., 1958], and taking account of the fact that another congress has been scheduled for 1963 in India [the meeting did not take place], any report on Marburg must include a review of recent developments and trends in the now truly "international" Association for the History of Religions....

It is the particular realization of modern *Religionswissenschaft* which the IAHR has to guard and cultivate. That there are also other ways of being related to religions and of studying them may be readily granted; but there are also other institutions and organizations to take care of these alternative ways. If the IAHR has any *raison d'etre*, it is by reason of a division of labour which makes the Organization the responsible organ and the international meeting ground for those scholars who wish to serve the cause of *Religionswissenschaft* in its strict sense. The coming years will have to show whether the IAHR is capable of assuming and carrying out the task that has devolved upon it. (1960: 216, 220)

Whereas the narrowly European nature of the Association was surely lost once the 1958 meeting took place in Tokyo (and since then its full Congresses have met outside Europe a total of seven times, though five of these were either in Australia or North America), what was also lost, at least as Werblowsky portrayed it, was the taken-for-granted assumptions about just what the science of religion (i.e., *Religionswissenschaft*) was up to. That the Association had long had a major presence within it of phenomenologists who descriptively and empathetically studied the historical layers only to cut through them in order to find the universal core, as well as humanistically, possibly better described as perhaps even theologically, inclined scholars who studied religion either to save themselves or mankind, seems to have been overlooked somewhat in Werbloswky's critical report; the far more optimistic portrait by Bleeker (who, from 1950–70 was the General Secretary of the IAHR) of "the oriental student [who] is inclined to contend that the very heart of religion can best be reached by intuition and that the ultimate result of the study of religious phenomena must be a deeper insight in the actual value of religion" (226) indicates that the scientific was already at risk.

Although I have no idea what I would have made of the pre-internationalizing Congresses of the IAHR that long predated not just my active involvement but also my birth (though, judging from the papers published in the early years in *Numen* I see much that I find problematic about the style of scholarship that characterized much of this era), having by now been to the last four of its World Congresses, I can say that, generally speaking, I have not found them to be so different in tone from the many annual meetings of the AAR that I have attended since my first, in San Francisco, in 1992 (since that time, I believe that I have missed only one, in San Diego, in 2007). While meeting scholars from around the globe who, in one form or another, study religion, can be tremendously rewarding, and while the very real privilege of attending meetings in such places as Tokyo, Durban, and Mexico City cannot go unmentioned, the preoccupation with nurturing mutual understanding, tolerance, and inter-religious dialogue, on the one hand, or portraying religion as somehow in sync with whatever it is that we may consider to characterize either the so-called deeply human or our own contingent political preferences, on the other, is—in my experience—no less evident among scholars from distant lands than it is in the work of North American and European scholars (something I've critiqued in chapter 10 of McCutcheon 2001a). For while it is pleasantly surprising that one's work is known to scholars from what may seem to me to be far away places, what is perhaps less pleasantly surprising is that the same troublesome theoretical and methodological issues yet persist in much of their work. That some of the national members of the IAHR worried over the AAR's recent admission to the Association as a member society—assuming, I gather, that its well-known humanistic/theological brand of scholarship would somehow dilute and undermine the seemingly serious scholarly work carried out within the IAHR—suggests that these members were not paying close enough attention to the work already being done by people in their fellow member associations.

Of course, it was encouraging to a scholar such as myself that the 2010 Congress in Toronto tried to correct this, with an explicit focus for some of its panels on theory and method. But given that humanistic and theological work on religion permeates the field, it inevitably was apparent in the program—evident even in some of the plenary sessions; I think it would therefore be naïve to think that the sort of scholarship lamented by Werblowsky back in 1960 would ever entirely disappear from the scene. For, as the following response tries to argue, even in the work of those who claim to adopt an explicitly historical perspective, a normative, anti-historical tone is sometimes easily detected.

Who Sets the Ground Rules? A Response to "Comparativism, Then and Now"[2] (2000)

To begin my response, let me recount a story found in Karl Popper's *Conjectures and Refutations*: he writes of requesting that his engineering students perform a simple experiment: "Take pencil and paper; carefully observe, and write down what you have observed!" (1962: 46). Soon, he writes, it becomes painfully obvious to his students that, without some clearly articulated set of criteria that assign an *ad hoc* importance to our many diverse and competing experiential events, criteria ranked on some imported grid on which these relative significances can determined, juxtaposed and then assessed—well, without such a grid and such criteria no one really knows precisely *what* to observe, *when* to observe it, with *which* of the five senses, or for how long. Do you observe the feeling of your feet in your shoes, the beating of your heart in your ears, the crease in the professor's pants, the after-taste of coffee in your mouth, or perhaps the smell of a classmate's perfume? Popper concludes that pure induction is an impossibility: "Observation [or, for our purposes, we could add comparison, interpretation, and explanation] is always selective. It needs a chosen object, a definite task, an interest, a point of view, a problem." The moral of the story?: the world does not come pre-packaged for our experiential consumption and, despite the best efforts of phenomenologists to convince us otherwise, nothing merely "presents itself" to our sense. A field of study, then is constituted by its particular problematic, its curiosities, its point of view.

The question before many scholars of religion today is just who gets to determine our field's problematic and its point of view. For scholars in Popper's tradition, such a perspective is provided by our theories of such things as human minds, behaviors, and institutions, but many now generally acknowledge that these theories are hardly innocent; Norman Girardot's thoughts on the generally Protestant, colonialist context of F. Max Müller's work makes this abundantly clear, as does Michal Buchowski's survey of, in his words, anthropological theory's evolution toward a lessening of enthnocentrism in cross-cultural work. Our theories, then, are hardly benign. But, as Robert Segal's paper makes clear, the operations of generalization and comparison are fundamental and unavoidable scholarly exercises, whatever the politics that drives them. Even in the case of Clifford Geertz, whom Segal cites as one of the more vocal critics of these operations, an abstraction called "Morocco" is all too easily compared to another abstraction, "Indonesia." In agreement with Segal, then, we could cite Luther Martin who, introducing a 1994 North American Association for the Study of Religion panel on "the new (as opposed to the old, or Eliadean) comparativism," observed that, according to one of the panelists, Tom Lawson,

> the act of comparing is a fundamental cognitive property of all human beings and, as such, can be neither old nor new. The issue, in Lawson's view, is not *whether* to compare but *how well* we compare. Lawson is concerned, in other words, to address directly the theoretical framework within which comparison proceeds. (Martin 1996: 1)

Accordingly, comparison—the disciplined juxtaposition of two or more things in accordance with a grid or set of criteria—is not merely an important scholarly activity but, it would appear, an essential cognitive component. But my original question still stands: just which (or, better put, whose) grid or criteria will drive our comparisons?

Buchowski and Girardot seem to agree that today we are in the position to make up for a previous era's imperializing tendencies evident in the importation of foreign grids to the study of "their" religions. For instance, Buchowski looks for a framework capable of taking into account what he terms the "actors' humanistic coefficient"; and Girardot, after a detailed study of Müller's writings, concludes his paper by noting that a

> self-reflexive comparative study of religion more aware of its own alien status and the ambiguous strangeness of religion still has an important "humanizing" role to play in the postmodernist academic environment of the 21st century where a kind of arrogant globalism and hyper-secularity increasingly prevails.

Girardot makes this prescription for the field partly on the basis of Richard King's own criticisms of the classic science of religion, contained in his book, *Orientalism and Religion* (1999). Citing King, Girardot notes that this postcolonial field will prevent the "erasure of indigenous perspectives" and will "contest the hegemony of secularism in the Western Academy" (in King 99: 61). Echoing King's thoughts on the so-called "epistemic violence" done to the indigenous perspective by the so-called alien science of religion, Girardot had earlier observed that Müller's emphasis on capturing

> some ancient written-down textuality of the *Rig Veda* in the amber of his "critical" edition really did violence to the Brahamanical insistence on the oral nature of the Vedic tradition.

Quoting Wilfred Cantwell Smith, Girardot concludes that Müller's turning "Hindu *Veda* into a written book is an entrancing instance of nineteenth-century Western cultural imperialism, here quietly imposing the Western sense of 'scripture.'" In a suitably Cantwell Smithian tone, Girardot then concludes that, as a result of the comparative science of religion, "ancient books…count more in the understanding of authentic meaning of a religion than the later corruptive actions of persons… Books thus weigh more than living persons."

So, what we have here is a potent critique of the dehumanizing, ethnocentric roots of comparative religion, an alien form of knowing juxtaposed to the indigenous and, I would presume, more authentic way of knowing. But can these roots be overcome as easily as some suggest? Is it really just a matter of recovering the indigenous perspective and developing what Cantwell Smith described as a humane science of religion? After all, we all know that the very categories "religion," "faith," and "spirit," as well as the "West/East" and "sacred/secular" binaries are part of a taxonomy and worldview dramatically alien to the majority of groups we as scholars study. Therefore, can there even be such a thing as the indigenous religious perspective? In attempting to do justice to the other, are we not but again in the business—and, following Girardot, I use that word purposefully—of concocting objects of study far removed from what they may in fact really be, whatever that is?

At the 1995 Congress in Mexico City, on a panel devoted to examining Benson Saler's important book, *Conceptualizing Religion* (1993), I quoted David Hoy as saying: "the difficulty with ethnocentrism is not so much that we see the world through our own self-understanding, but instead that we expect every other self-understanding to converge with ours" (Hoy 1991: 78). This adds an important nuance to Buchowski's understanding of ethnocentrism, defined by him as the act of perceiving, describing, interpreting, and evaluating with one's own notions and standard patterns found only within one's own culture. The nuance it adds is brought out by another author I cited five years ago, the anthropologist Roy Wagner; as Wagner correctly observes, "the study of culture is in fact *our* culture" (1981: 16). In other words, as Segal, Martin, and Lawson suggested, we have no choice but to classify, sort, and compare, and thereby come to know the other *as* other by means of our own local concepts and patterns. To presume otherwise is either to presume some extra-historical context or god's eye-view to which we and possibly others have access, or to privilege the participant's patterns and grids over those of the academy, as in Girardot's lament for the "Brahmanical" point of view on *Veda*. (As an aside, is it only ritual elites that must concern us or is there an authentic insider voice that rises above those class and gender discontinuities all too apparent to the observer

of a religion?) To presume some god's eye perspective beyond the limitations of context undermines the historical specificity of our field, and to side
with Cantwell Smith in sanctioning this or that participant's point of view
as the benchmark for the field makes the study of religion little more than
a mouthpiece for the insider perspectives with which the scholar happens
to have sympathies.[3] Buchowski's concluding comments on our so-called
awareness of the "actors' humanistic coefficient" suggests that he presumes
just such a common, extra-historical basis, what I'll simply name as Human
Nature, a non-empirical entity that transcends time and space, uniting me
with all people, past, present, and future. Girardot's lament for the indigenous perspective seems to presume that some purer form of religion will
be recovered once we shake off the category religion's colonialist loadings

Given the manner in which we now understand human subjectivity to be
tactically constructed, presupposing the stable existence of this thing we call
a "humanistic coefficient" may very well turn out to be a supremely ethnocentric act; after all, as Hoy notes, expecting "every other self-understanding
to converge with ours" is the nature of ethnocentrism. All I mean to suggest
is that, depending on how you decide what constitutes this human coefficient, I assume very different "things" will get to count as a human being. I
know that in North America—the specific context from which my sense of
self is derived—there is a vigorous and sometimes outright violent debate
on whether a fetus is a person under the law. Given the inability of groups
to come to an easy consensus on this question suggests to me that it is not
entirely self-evident what constitutes this "human coefficient" and that much
is politically at stake for persuading us that there even exists such a thing.
Presuming it to be otherwise, presuming that the history of anthropological
research on the "other" is, in Buchowski's words, evolving toward a lessening in normative standards, is therefore, perhaps, overly optimistic. As I
suggested before, perhaps ethnocentrism by degrees is inevitable, insomuch
as the reproduction of our culture, at least the culture of this room's inhab-
itants at this time and place, depends on studying and renaming the lives of
other people and coming to this place to report on our findings—an activity far removed from simply living the lives of the people we study. As with
many postmodern/postcolonial criticisms that develop from within the study
of religion, I find myself agreeing with Buchowski and Girardot, and even
King—but only to a point. Naming the historically entrenched nature of the
knowledge generated by the science of religion is a much needed corrective;
our comparisons are our's and may well be nobody else's; but, presuming
that some more authentic understanding is out there, awaiting us, seems to
fly in the face of the postmodern critique of all knowledge as being *ad hoc*.
I therefore appreciate the careful analyses of such writers, but I hesitate to

think that the ground rules for our field ought to be set by, or be in sympathy with, the people we seek to study by means of our work. It is a disservice to "the other" to presume that our interest in classifying the world in terms of its diverse "religions" is a classification which is somehow in a one-to-one relationship with their own self-understanding. Because the study of culture is our culture, I have no interest in reproducing anyone else's self-understandings, patterns, or grids; like virtually all other scholars in the human sciences, I feel no compulsion to limit my work to the participant's own view. *— so you can say they are wrong.*

Notes

1. From 2005–2009 I served as the President of the Council of Societies for the Study of Religion (CSSR); after the untimely death of the CSSR's long-time Executive Director, David Truemper (1939–2004), the Council moved from Valparaiso University to Rice University, where it was hosted by the Department of Religious Studies. Working first with Dena Pence, and then Andy Fort, as Truemper's successor, it soon became evident that the CSSR's decline in member societies meant that the Council was no longer needed to provide the sort of member services that it once carried out, which eventually led to the Council dissolving under my leadership. The *CSSR Bulletin* was sold to Equinox Publishers (and renamed the *Bulletin for the Study of Religion*) and *Religious Studies Review* was sold to Rice University, which continues to publish it.

2. Ed. Note: chapter 5 of McCutcheon 2001a drew on portions of this, until now, unpublished response, which itself uses portions of McCutcheon (2000b), delivered originally in 1995 in Mexico City, and which was first published in *MTSR* 12/1 and 12/2 (2000: 294–306).

3. Ed. Note: as Wilfred Cantwell Smith famously wrote: "no statement about a religion is valid unless it can be acknowledged by that religion's believers… [B]y 'religion' here I mean as previously indicated the faith in men's hearts. On the external data about religion, of course, an outsider can by diligent scholarship discover things that an insider does not know and may not be willing to accept. But about the meaning that the system has for those of faith, an outsider cannot in the nature of the case go beyond the believer; for their piety *is* the faith, and if they cannot recognize his portrayal, then it is not their faith that he is portraying… Anything that I say about Islam as a living faith is valid only in so far as Muslims can say 'amen' to it" (1959: 42–43).

Chapter 7

Introduction

As with the previous chapter, the following response, which has also not been published, was presented at the 2000 Congress of the IAHR in Durban, South Africa, in reply to a panel entitled "Missing Links in the Study of Religion." Chaired once again by William Paden, this time the panelists consisted of Jacques Waardenburg ("Cracking the Constructs: Studying Religion as Meanings"), John P. Dourley ("Jung, Mysticism, and a Newer Myth"), and Lieve Orye ("Missing Link in the Study of Religion: Religion as 'Learning Tradition'").[1]

Although my response did not focus on his paper, this was the first and only time that I had the good fortune to be on a panel with Waardenburg, the Dutch Islamicist and the author/editor of, among many other books, the two volume *Classical Approaches to the Study of Religion* (1973, 1974). Along with the important work on the history of the study of religion by such writers as the late Sam Preus (1987)—who, in 1995, served as the outside examiner on my dissertation defense—the late Eric Sharpe (1986)—whose book was recommended to all incoming graduate students during my time at the University of Toronto—and Brian Morris (1987)—whose book was essential to me when I first began teaching a course on theories of myth and ritual, working hard just to stay a day ahead of my students—it was mainly Waardenburg who, when I was a graduate student, provided me with a map to navigate through the history of the field, before I dove into such writers as Müller, Tiele, Söderblom, and van der Leeuw, among others. A new edition of his two volume book, finally available in paperback, was issued by his publisher in 1999. (As an aside, an update to this book would be a tremendous resource to current students—containing not just his broad state-of-the-art survey essays but also the anthology-like excerpts from writers along with extended bibliographies of the field's sub-specialties. Walter Capps's [d. 1997] history of the field aims in that direction, somewhat [2000], but his book is merely an introductory overview, somewhat akin to my own even slimmer introduction [2007], and thus lacks the detailed, authoritative sweep of Waardenburg's book.) Given the importance his work played in helping to orient me to the field, it was an honor to sit on a panel with him.

At the time that I wrote this response—early in the summer of 2000—I was about to enter what turned out to be my last year working at what was then called Southwest Missouri State University, in Springfield, MO. The Department—where I worked for five years as a tenure-track professor, after three consecutive one-year contracts as an Instructor at the University of Tennessee had come to an end[2]—was, and still is, a terminal MA program, inasmuch as it awards only bachelor's and master's degrees. As I recall, apart from attracting local students who wished merely to delve deeper into their studies, regardless what their career aspirations may have been, that program was also appealing for students who wished to reinvent or retrain themselves, as they prepared for applications to major doctoral programs. Having worked for five years with some outstanding students who were aiming toward earning their MA—I maintain a working relationship still with a number of them—I learned that there can be much good about a regional, terminal MA program. I recall one of the MA students in particular, who was himself teaching a course or two in the Department—Joby Taylor, who went on to earn his PhD and is now the Director of the Shriver Peaceworker Program at the Shriver Center at the University of Maryland Baltimore County—talk about what he then called "the Eliade Effect" (something I've also referenced elsewhere [2003a: 207], but without citing him, I believe). As I recall, he described it in class one day as the feeling that resulted from reading Eliade earlier in his life: the comforting impression that resulted concerning how the potentially confusing or even contradictory nature of reality was, if seen in the right way, discernable as a deeper, transcendental unity. For anyone overcome by the complexity of their surroundings, this message of simplification was, he remembered, particularly alluring.

To confirm my memory of him looking back on first coming across Eliade's work, I recently contacted Joby and he indeed confirmed my recollection. He replied (quoted with his permission):

> I distinctly remember my final seminary semester (at Catholic University), just as the hounds of orthodoxy were sounding louder and louder.... Into my hands came a copy of *The Sacred and Profane*! Over the next few years I poured over them all. *The Myth of Eternal Return*, the three volume *History of Religious Ideas, From Primitives to Zen*, then Joseph Campbell too, *Hero, Myths to Live By, Inner Reaches of Outer Space*... The "effect" amounted to a "way out," a means of preserving the sacred while leaving behind the narrowing confines of "a religion." My copy of Huxley's *Perennial Philosophy* was worn to tatters...

We could, of course, rename this the Campbell or the Jung effect, to capture the comfort that equally comes with their god's eye viewpoint. But then again, why not name it the Freud or the Marx effect, or perhaps even the cognitive science effect? That is, isn't a comforting simplification the result of all efforts to understand, inasmuch as they each posit a totalized system into which seemingly discrete parts fit, doing so in a manner only apparent to the trained observer? Might it therefore be unfair to name it "the Eliade Effect" when, for example, anyone who talks about "the human condition" or "nature," let alone "society," "the universe," "language," "the law" or "the free market" may be just as lulled into a soothing sense of security by positing a fictitious system beyond the local and into which their discrete experience simply fits "just right," as a falsely secure Goldilocks might have once phrased it?

Thinking back on a quote I used from Daniel Dennett (1995: 73–80) in the Preface to my first book (see 1997b: x), concerning his metaphor of sky-hooks and cranes—the former floating freely in the air, with no basis for their leverage, as opposed to the latter, which are firmly anchored on the ground—I might now rethink this imagery and suggest that failure to recognize that one's analytic, one's tools, one's questions, *are in fact one's own* (i.e., situationally specific, always interested), amounts to the main problem in our field—whether it is carried out by a social scientist or a humanist. For now I tend to think that the portrait of one's curiosities as universal and self-evident amounts to a skyhook whether you are a cognitive psychologist or a Eliadean. (To put it another way, what persuasive basis do we have to suggest that while *their* metaphors are just metaphors, *ours* are neutral words that name stable facts?) While this is *not* how I saw it back when I was writing my dissertation and supporting a naturalistic approach over a theological one, I have come to be rather critical of all scholarship on religion that fails to see the designator "religion" itself, along with the criteria that allows the researcher to collect together otherwise discrete items in the world as all being "religious" and thus interconnected, as a tool with a history and—like all tools—practical implications and limitations.

Although it was not included in his recent edited collection of writings on pedagogy (Smith 2013), Jonathan Z. Smith's little essay, "The Necessary Lie: Duplicity in the Disciplines" (2007)—originally presented as part of an initiative of University of Chicago's Center for Learning and Teaching, to train graduate teaching assistants—draws attention to this very problem, with a concision that we only find in Smith's writings. "We hide consistently," Smith writes, "the immense editorial efforts that have conjecturally established so many of the texts we routinely present to our students as classics" (2007: 74). He continues: "Then we read them with our students as if each word were directly revelatory, regardless of the fact that the majority of the words are not in the language in which the test was written"

(74–75). Successful education, he goes on to argue, is an initiation process whereby the certainties of earlier schooling—such as the seemingly obvious and therefore commonsense fact that there is such a thing as society and that it does certain things and develops in certain ways—are undermined, demonstrating that, in this case, "society" is merely a useful shorthand that we develop to work with, that allows us to group things together to satisfy specific curiosities that we have. Instead of "convey[ing] to our students a specious perfection of the object [under study] and a specious necessity to the history of the object" (75), Smith argues that scholarship must convey to our students the hard human labor that is required to make things in the world stand out as interesting. The missing link in the field today, I would now argue, is the move Smith recommends.

While I may retain "the Eliade effect" to name this shortcoming of scholarship, I now think that any simplification that fails to empower students to see themselves as agents who, although working within structures not of their making, are nonetheless actively constituting their worlds, is a simplification that amounts to rather poor scholarship. For, as Smith concludes, "in the name of simplification, what we really end up doing is mystifying the objects we teach" (Smith 2007: 76).

Artifacts Not Relics: A Response to "Missing Links in the Study of Religion" (2000)

The two papers that I would like to have us think about, for a few moments, are those by John Dourley on Carl Jung's proposal for a new myth for achieving world unity and psychic wholeness and Lieve Orye's paper on Wilfred Cantwell Smith's interest in developing a *humane* science of religion capable of understanding inner faith as well as outer tradition. The reason I'd like to focus attention on just these two essays is because they are about scholars who shared a common, and still very attractive, assumption concerning this thing we call Human Nature or the Human Condition—an assumption which, I believe, might better constitute data rather than a theoretical option.

Just as indigenous reports on such things as unmediated experiences deserve to be thoroughly historicized and studied as social events—and thereby translated into the explanatory language of a thoroughly social theory of religion—so too Jung's interest in a new myth of (as Dourley phrased it) a "God who frees humanity from a sense of God as other" and Cantwell Smith's interest in recovering some purer, more pristine individual faith overlooked by scholars both count as data for the scholar of religion; both writers are elite native informants within the liberal individualist tradition—nothing more, nothing less. Given the ease with which I draw this distinction between studying these seemingly privatized discourses on invisible beings, inner states and dispositions, as well as non-empirical world unity, on the one hand, and engaging in such discourses, on the other, I find myself continually puzzled as to the surprising resiliency of writers such as Jung and Cantwell Smith. But I have a theory about their tenacity that I would like to propose and I would like to do so by using a recent book as an example: Robert Ellwood's *The Politics of Myth: A Study of C. G. Jung, Mircea Eliade, and Joseph Campbell* (1999). I believe that Ellwood's book sheds considerable, though likely unintended, light on why it is so tempting for contemporary scholars to continually revisit the work of Jung and Cantwell Smith. Briefly put, I am concerned with two items: (i) the ease with which liberal humanist speculations on a non-empirical, universal Human Nature that transcends such specificities as gender, nationality, and class is mistaken for the work of the historically embedded academic study of religion; and (ii) how easily persuaded our colleagues sometimes are by rhetorics of essential unity that supposedly transcend the public, historical, political world.

To return to my example: in his study of myth theorists,[3] Ellwood makes several significant autobiographical asides—asides that provide the attentive reader with clues as to the appeal writers such as Jung and Cantwell Smith (not to mention Eliade and Joseph Campbell) held for students in the 1960s, the Cold War generation that re-established our field in North America and reinvigorated it in Europe. One day, in 1962 while he was a US Marine chaplain stationed in Okinawa, Ellwood writes that he

> came across a review of one of Eliade's books. Something about the account led me to believe it might help. I ordered the slim volume, read it, and suddenly the significance of a wholly new way of looking at religion arose into consciousness: not theological, but in terms of its phenomenological structures... It was one of those books that make one think, "This was really true all the time, but I didn't realize it until now." Soon I left the chaplaincy and enrolled as a graduate student under Mircea Eliade at the University of Chicago Divinity School. (Ellwood 1999: 5)

Just what Ellwood needed "help" with was dealing with what he terms "modernity's pluralism of space and time" (1999: 111), a particular problem for those whose societies are affluent and powerful enough to allow them, for example, to be stationed thousands of miles from their home. In other words, "the problem of modernity's pluralism of space and time" is, strictly speaking, not the result of some intellectual movement we call "modernity," but, rather, the direct result of cultural, political, economic, and military dominance enabling members of one particular local group to freely move across the globe (whether that movement is in the physical world or in cyberspace). "I could not help but believe," Ellwood writes, "that some indefinable spiritual presence lingered in the lovely sylvan shrines of Shinto, or that there was more than mere atmosphere in the great peace that filled temples of the Buddha" (5). This, to me, is a wonderful example of how we overcome our inability to successfully apply local concepts and patterns in our attempt to domesticate and thereby make sense of, novel forms of information. For what conflicts on one level can, of course, be homogenized and thereby "understood" on a higher logical level, so that conflicting social or cognitive patterns are easily resolved by means of an appeal to, in the case just cited, "some undefinable spiritual presence." Utter unity and therefore understanding is purchased at the price of dehistoricization and thus simplification.

I recall a literary example of this used by Edward Said (1994): in the case of Rudyard Kipling's novel *Kim*, Said draws attention to the ways in which the protagonist is represented as having virtually unimpeded access to all of India's geography, languages, religion, and culture. As Said describes him, the character Kim is the lone occupant of the calm center of a Babel-like storm of differing languages and conflicting customs, a privileged position that allows him (much like an omniscient narrator) to pass in and out of various guises and dialects, understanding it all perfectly well. Said concludes that "*Kim* shows how a white Sahib can enjoy life in this lush complexity." He goes on to observe that, in the novel,

> the absence of resistance to European intervention in [India is] symbolized by Kim's abilities to move relatively unscarred through India [all of which] is due to [the novel's] imperialist vision. (1994: 159)

Just as with mid-twentieth-century Americans in Okinawa, so too with nineteenth-century Brits in India: full understanding and unimpeded access results from universalization of merely local concepts, elevated to the level of abstractions, making them capable of organizing and homogenizing new and possibly conflicting information. That all this inevitably comes with a political price is more than obvious—though not to everyone, apparently.

Despite some surface differences between the work of Jung and Cantwell Smith—not to mention Kipling—their efficient projection of what were merely their own local patterns of thought allowed their privileged readers struggling with the new, the exotic, and the strange to depart from their own sectarian perspective and embark on an equally salvific quest for what Ellwood euphemistically calls "benign pluralism," a truly liberal quest in which the "good" of the comparative method is that it "enables one to experience vicariously the passions of other faiths as well as one's own, so leading to the enrichment of total human experience" (1999: 110–11). These writers happened upon a stage in which their imperial societies were desperately in need of tools to domesticate the other and they gladly offered tools to accomplish the task, tools that made possible the smooth transition from local to universal, accomplished by means of their assumption of an inner, private, life of the soul that is shared throughout all human cultures, past and present. What better tool could there be to allow the local to be portrayed as universal?

Simply put, the attraction of our field for those disillusioned with Christian denominationalism was its ability to shift the ground from seemingly incontestible yet inevitably conflicting *Truth* to infinitely variable and personal *meanings*, which Ellwood, like Jung and Cantwell Smith before him, defines as "that which comes from a universal source but is congruous with one's own dreams and deepest significant fantasies" (1999: 177). Armed with what ends up being all things to all people, how could Kipling not win wide readership in his time, and how could the History of Religions fail to win converts during the Cold War, all of whom were grappling with "modernity's pluralism of space and time"? The attraction to studying myth for Jung, and scripture for Cantwell Smith, then, is obvious for, expressing the core assumption of this entire liberal humanist tradition, Ellwood writes: "Myth [and we can add scripture], like all great literature, can become universal, transcending particular cultural settings" (177). And here, I think, we have our answer to the perplexing appeal of such writers: an imperialist transcendence of the local is made possible by their supposed insights into the architecture of the human soul. A powerful rhetoric, indeed.

This liberal humanist refashioning of dogmatic theological truth into elusive meaning, a meaning that, although experienced individually, is yet understood as universal and self-evident, is accomplished by claims concerning our shared moral center—variously called Soul, Human Nature, the Collective Unconscious, the Human Condition, Religious Experience, or simply the Human Spirit. However, despite the best efforts of such rhetorics, the end result of these universalist claims is always a very local picture characteristic of a specific group with specific interests, all dressed up as if it were somehow shared by everyone. Soon, Sydney's 2000 Olympic Games will be broadcast around the globe, providing an obvious instance of this ideology of homogeneity which, thanks to modern communications technology, is no longer the domain only of worldwide dominant cultures; it is an ideology that efficiently supports a rather narrow set of national and economic interests, tailored to suit whichever nation and whichever economy happens to be wielding it. For while the rhetoric of world unity will surely be thickly layered over almost every aspect of the televised Games— regardless of who televises it—based on the actual coverage and all depending where one views it, it will likely be difficult to believe that countries other than the broadcast host's will be competing and winning medals. At least as a Canadian watching past US coverage of this so-called world event, I keep wondering if Canada sent anyone to the Games. In this case, the myth of non-empirical, essential global unity legitimizes national identities that in turn are supported financially by and simultaneously promote consumer loyalty to brand names that corporations manufacture to create profit for share holders (why else do corporations sponsor the games but to gain ever larger advertising markets?). Despite the rhetoric of unity, then, the Games are clearly about promoting some very local loyalties. And so I return to the rhetorics of unity, collective unconscious, and a seemingly more humane science of religion that takes seriously the individual's "faith in transcendence." What are Jung and Cantwell Smith selling with their rhetorics of psychic wholeness and global theology? And in taking these writers as models for our own scholarship, what have we bought into?

I suggest that such universalizing and homogenizing claims are not supported by the ethnographic data that we as scholars study; apart from certain basic shared biological functions common to the group we name as *homo sapiens sapiens*, I am not sure that all human beings take my particular set of meanings as universal or self-evident; I am therefore far too timid to join Jung and Cantwell Smith in triumphantly extending my local meanings to worldwide significance (dare I say hegemony?). And I am hardly prepared to posit that my local meanings, made possible by just this social world that I happen to inhabit, are somehow part of a non-empirical whole—say, the Human Condition. We may therefore continue reading scholars, like Jung or Cantwell Smith, who make such grand and surely heart-warming yet undefendable claims, but I hope that we read them not as exemplars, but, instead, as artifacts—in the sense of curious leftovers from the Cold War, whose original popularity and influence deserves scholarly explanation—rather than as enshrined relics deserving our ritualized veneration through citation and quotation.

Notes

1.   A version of the second paper was published the following year (Dourley 2001).
2.   The faculty member who, while I worked as an Instructor, was a senior administrator on the University of Tennessee's Knoxville campus, moved back into the Department and so the funds that the Department had used to replace him in the classroom (hiring myself and another Instructor [Dan Deffenbaugh, now of Hastings College]) came to an end.
3.   Ed. Note: I re-used this example later in chapter 9 of McCutcheon 2003a, as part of a revision to what was originally published as McCutcheon 2001b.

Chapter 8

Introduction

> Geza Vermes, a religious scholar who argued that Jesus as a histor-
> ical figure could be understood only through the Jewish tradition
> from which he emerged, and who helped expand that understand-
> ing through his widely read English translations of the Dead Sea
> Scrolls, died on May 8 in Oxford, England. He was 88.

So opened the May 16, 2013, obituary in *The New York Times* for the late,
Geza Vermes.[1] I quote this seemingly mundane paragraph—one that many
scholars would say sensibly argues for understanding Jesus in his historical setting, as but an example that, upon closer scrutiny, might not be as
straightforward as it seems. But in order to return to this example, we first
need a long digression.

There was a time when the study of religion seemed to have natural affinities with work carried out in Departments of Philosophy (the many, small,
combined Departments for these two otherwise distinguishable pursuits that
can easily be found around the US, at least, tell you as much). After all,
both were largely concerned with the history of ideas, inasmuch as religion
was generally presumed to be about what people *believed*, something that a
scholar was able to study (e.g., the long history of philosophers of religion
examining the rationality of religious belief) via the analysis of scriptures,
creeds, theologics, and so on. Texts (in a narrow, or traditional, pre-Derrid-
ean sense) were thus the site where those internal, cognitive states called
belief (or, for a slight variant on this philosophically idealist tradition, we
could say those internal, affective states called faith) were somehow externalized or, as the old school phenomenologists would have phrased it, manifested in the intersubjective world. Recovered, transmitted, and translated
texts, available for study by groups far wider than the practitioners who
originally used them, was thus the raw material for such scholarship. Belief,
then, was understood to be the motivating force behind action (like writing
these texts in the first place), much as myth (for many, but of course not all,
nineteenth-century scholars) was once understood as coming prior to, and
thus causing, ritual—with the latter seen as the performative element that
merely acted *out* the substance of former, that lurked *within*.

But today this has changed for many scholars of religion—the title of Manuel Vásquez's recent book, *More than Belief* (2010) indicates as much; the once close, almost taken-for-granted ties with Philosophy and what was once known as the History of Ideas have therefore been replaced with close ties to such a field as Social/Cultural Anthropology—if not that specific discipline then at least to the now widespread judgment that knowing the context of an item of cultural production is the key for accurately understanding its meaning (i.e., doing fieldwork and going to the source, to one extent or another, has become the credentialing instrument in the study of religion and not just anthropology—if you've not "been to India," as I recall a friend putting it [somewhat sarcastically], then how can one talk about Hinduism properly?).[2] No longer does a so-called religious text stand alone, requiring "a close reading" for understanding its meaning but, instead, it can now only be fully understood in the light of its historical, social, political, and economic context (a context often thought somehow to endure over time— call "it" tradition or heritage, perhaps—otherwise, the context-seeking trip to modern India seems somewhat out of place for anyone who is trying to understand productions from ancient India, no?). Oh, and also its contextualization in terms of the gender of both the author and his or her intended audience. And of course their race. Oh, and their sexual orientation. Perhaps their generation and the place they occupy in their family's birth order as well. And what about the ecological situation of the text's origins and the occupation of its author...?

My hope is that readers start to see a bit of a problem here, namely the unregulated economy of competing contexts—for the serious historian, it's contexts all the way down!—that, in coming to some sort of understanding about the world, we must try to manage by identifying which of the virtually limitless circumstances will count as *the* context (i.e., sufficient or definitive), a problem that I further explore in the following response that originally appeared in *Method & Theory in the Study of Religion* in 2003. For despite the seemingly progressive move toward reading texts with greater historical and social nuance by placing them into the broader social world from which they arose, the manner in which we often still use these two terms (i.e., text and context, as if the one is a pearl forming in a discrete, nurturing oyster) suggests to me that little has actually changed despite the apparent progress—somewhat like Vásquez's book, perhaps, which, although described as materialist and "a new way of studying religions," nonetheless seems to rely on a well-known idealist model (despite working to overcome the old dichotomies that once characterized the field), whereby something on the inside is projected outward into the public world, something that already exists (i.e., religion) thereby finding a home in a context (i.e., in bodies and practices), inasmuch as religions are seen "as dynamic material and historical *expressions* of the practices of *embodied individuals* who are *embedded* in social fields and ecological networks" (emphasis added). Put briskly, what more have we said about people when we qualify "individual" with "embodied"? (That is, if it makes no sense to talk about a disembodied individual, then why use the adjective "embodied"? Or do we presume that some thing exists apart from, outside, or prior to the body that is put into it [i.e., em-bodied]...?) Are individuals "embedded" in social fields, are our experiences "*mediated* through our discursive and non-discursive practices" (321; emphasis added), or are individuals and the things our folk psychology calls experiences the *results* of social fields?[3]

Thus, a curious essentialism yet persists despite immersing our work in the apparently non-essentialist specificities of bodies and discrete historical setting—"setting" tells us much about the problem, for just what dynamic item is being put in place, that is, set (as opposed to produced by) within these environs? What's more, in portraying one of the innumerable contexts as *the* context we mask the choices and interests that allow scholars to narrow the field to just what they wish to talk about. That narrowing the all-but-limitless field that we know as the past or as culture is necessary for any sort of conversation to take place is something that I take as so uncontroversial as to happily pass it off as a given; recognizing that this narrowing requires effort, interests, curiosities, and point of view is, however, lost when the context we have created, which allows certain objects to stand out *as* interesting texts to be read (i.e., text, now signifying far more things than just writing on paper, of course, is nothing but concentrated context, context simplified and abstracted), is taken as given. For if gender or race, let alone embodiment, were such obviously important elements of cultural analysis, then why did our intellectual predecessors, bright as they no doubt were, routinely overlook them? Either such scholars are culpable for their gross oversight (a position adopted by many who critique past scholarship's blind spots) or, as I tend to think to be the case, *we* are responsible for dividing the pie up in what, from what I imagine to have been an earlier scholar's point of view, would be an entirely novel manner—and we have good reasons for doing so, of course: because we bring with us a set of novel questions, directing us to single out new items from the limitless background that we regulate and call context.

What's more, from the latter theoretical position, the former is seen to be a particularly troublesome approach, one that universalizes its specific interests and the objects in the world that those interests make it possible to discuss and analyze—misportraying discursive objects created from within virtually limitless context-upon-context as if they were naturally found,

authentic objects merely placed within a vista, a portrait that erases the artist's own hand in multiple ways. I think here of a plenary address delivered by Jonathan Z. Smith at the Atlanta meeting of the American Academy
of Religion (October 31, 2010).[4] Introduced by then AAR President, Ann
Taves, Smith's lecture, entitled "Reading Religion: A Life in Scholarship,"
consistently emphasized reading—whether a text or an artifact—as a medi-
ation between an ambiguous world and an interested reader, rather than
portraying scholarship as an experiential immediacy that passively results
from some self-evidently organized and thus inherently significant object
or domain simply presenting itself to our senses. As an illustration of this
point, consider the following anecdote Smith tells (quoting from the 35:09
point forward):

> Through the years my chief mode of travel has been to go to the
> library or to my bookshelves. Although I've written a good bit
> about place, I've never had the slightest desire to see for myself
> the places I've described. I've relied, rather, on published sources:
> photographs, sketches, verbal descriptions, maps, diagrams. Once,
> with Elaine, by accident, I found myself before an unknown, rather
> confusing, building in the old city in Jerusalem. When told that it
> was in fact the Church of the Holy Sepulcher, a site to which I had
> devoted a chapter of a book, I went no further inside, remarking,
> "I prefer *my* church to *theirs*."

After brief laughter from his audience, Smith drove home his point:

> This is to say—and I'm serious about this—this is to say, as I
> wrote in the conclusion of "When the Chips are Down,"[5] I have
> consistently made a choice of the map over the territory. Although
> you may well disagree, it has been a self-limitation that, for me,
> yields cognitive gain.

What I have most come to appreciate in Smith's work is his constant attention to choice, interest, and the wider situations in which these take place—
summed up in the metaphor of a map that, at all costs, is not to be confused
with being some neutral or disinterested presentation of an actual place
(i.e., territory). Whatever the territory may actually be, we do not know, of
course, since we can't get *there* from *here* but by means of an abstraction
that we call map, that generalizes and translates, opening room for interpretation and ambiguity, all of which allows us to think into existence a
series of relationships in time and space (such as some *here* as opposed to
a *there* that is far beyond eyesight but not imagination). And that there are
many, potentially competing, maps/map-makers out there, each vying for
the right to be understood as representing some definitive territory, is one

of the cognitive gains of this approach, as I see it, for now we can study not just construction but also authorization and competition (i.e., what's at stake for erasing interests), something signaled, I'd like to think, in Smith's choice of the plural possessive pronoun "theirs" (as in "I prefer my church to theirs"), as opposed simply to using a definite article. For, according to this approach, *the* church is always someone's representation of "it," a representation that happens to have been so successfully authorized as to erase the agents who put it front and center in the first place. (Despite routinely talking about this thing we call "the law," anyone who took a civics course knows how laws in a social democracy are made and that they are, in fact, always someone's—*their* law, *our* law, and so on—inasmuch as they are the result of interests, proposals, deals, amendments, votes, and judgments.)

But I find that admitting ownership over our creations ("*my* church…") is not very common, in the study of religion, even when we think we're cognizant of the role played by theory. (It is so uncommon, in fact, that I have no doubt that Smith's frank acknowledgment of it might have caught many in the audience off guard, thus prompting their laughter at that point in his lecture—for I have no doubt that many in attendance knew which of the two churches was the *real* one.) For instance—finally turning my attention toward returning to my opening quotation—consider the changes that have taken place over the past few academic generations in the work of a sub-group of scholars who no longer identify themselves simply as New Testament scholars but, instead, refer to themselves as scholars of Christian origins. For whereas the former study the text, as made evident by their disciplinary name, to determine its meaning, the latter are interested instead in the social world from which the text arose, trying to explain, among other things, the origins of the documents that came to be known as the New Testament, rather than simply studying their meaning. As with all name changes, this revision in nomenclature signals important differences for those involved in these exercises—New Testament scholars are, in my estimation, akin to classical Humanists in many ways, being exegetes and hermeneuts intent on finding meaning in texts (regardless whether they take what might be termed the inevitable theological step to determine "what the text means for my life"), whereas those working in Christian origins generally see themselves as social scientifically-inclined, working not with the vagaries of meaning but on the firmer ground of explanatory theories about the social world. Or so it seems, for despite the shift to the historical (i.e., examining the specificities of the turn-of-the-era Mediterranean world) from the ahistorical (i.e., interpreting the transhistorical meaning of the text that somehow coheres across the ages and across different readers), there is something unsatisfying about this change: a missed opportunity to accept ownership.

The problem (also identified in a number of the other critiques in this volume) is the anachronistic manner in which the past is managed so as to transform it into something that can be studied, a process whereby contemporary understandings are inevitably retrojected backward in time—but not as modern heuristics that scholars must use, or as a result of what are acknowledged to be contemporary curiosities (i.e., the relatively uncontroversial claim that we have no choice but to confront the limitless, the unknown, through the limited and the known). Instead, the trouble is the manner in which scholars ontologize and thereby authorize the contemporary, taking the world-as-it-happens-to-be-now and representing it as the world-as-it-always-was and necessarily-must-be. To stick with my example of Christian origins, despite their apparent difference from their New Testament colleagues, the stable item that stands at the center of both New Testament studies and Christian origins is this thing called Christianity, conceived as a transcendental identity. For despite the apparent priority that *text* takes in the former and *context* takes in the latter, these two pursuits presuppose that each is simply a medium in which some prior thing—Christianity—manifests itself. In the case of New Testament studies this critique may be a little more apparent to some readers, inasmuch as the goal of these studies, determining the *meaning* of the text, is thought somehow to float free of history, as if artful, modern interpreters were time travelling when they made statements about what Saint Paul did or did not mean when he wrote this or that passage—an origins claim all the better supported if we know something about the original setting in which the original claim was made and apparently made sense. The problem here, of course, is the old presumption of the linkage between contemporary readers and past writers, between the meaning we derive from a text and the original intentionality that supposedly propels the text across the ages—for only this linkage allows one to travel to the time of the ancestors simply by reading what they wrote. Making the move that comes with admitting into consideration the importance of context for "properly" understanding the meaning of an ancient text—and thereby learning about, say, this or that Greco-Roman practice or Jewish belief—hardly improves anything since we still find ourselves resurrecting a long lost origin, whether it be an original intention of a long dead author (presumably discerned from some text-read-in-context—whether it be scripture, an inscription, a vase painting, etc.) or the social features of an originary landscape long ago erased from the face of the earth (whose topographical features are no less reconstituted from—yes...,—reading texts-in-context—whether it be scripture, an inscription, a vase painting, etc.). Others have identified the problem of origins—that is, the always contemporary conjuring necessary to seemingly "walk in Jesus's footsteps"—so I will not let that detain me here, but simply note it as being no less relevant in our critique of this model of meaning-making than it is to the way we understand mythologists talking confidently about the dream-time of the ancestors (e.g., in the study of religion see Masuzawa 2000a).

But, despite how progressive some may portray it, when it comes to Christian origins a similar problem remains, for trying to reconstruct the social world from out of which Christianity arose means not only the impossibly circular hermeneutical goal of reading yet more texts-in-context so as to reconstruct the context from out of which the text arose, but also implies taking the presumption of Christianity's existence (as it eventually came to be, at whatever moment the scholar wishes to see it as normative and orthodox—second century? Fifth? Nineteenth? Twenty-first?) for granted as a virtually Hegelian Geist that was somehow there at its own birth. For despite their attempt at far more nuanced and historically-grounded scholarship, a Christian origins scholar's work is possible only if we so naturalize the existence of what we today know as Christianity that we can retroject it backward, confident that, like the British working class in E. P. Thompson's famous line that opened the Preface to his *The Making of the English Working Class* (1991), it was there at its own birth. While the realist in me certainly assumes that there were people in the recent as well as ancient past doing all sorts of things (whether we're talking about London in the nineteenth century, as in the case of Thompson's work, or the first century of the common era in the part of the world we today call Israel or Palestine), the careful historian in me would argue not just that a shared class consciousness came long after those early modern behaviors and economic relationships that eventually were taken by scholars to be its markers but also that the self-designation "Christian" was not present at its supposed origins. What's more, this marker has been used over the years to signify so many different things in so many different situations that generalizing it to be some overarching identity, that had a source and a developmental trajectory, is the sign of either terribly sloppy scholarship or invested scholarship engaged in its own identity formation practices. Put simply, the historian in me would argue strongly that there were no Christians at the origins of Christianity, making "Christian origins" an oxymoron whose contradiction remains unseen only so long as one is untroubled by the practice of self-beneficial anachronism.

Take, for example, debates over "the earliest Christian documents." If, as a number of scholars now think, the self-designation "Christian" was not used (or we at least do not have material evidence of its use) prior to Ignatius of Antioch (sometime around 100 of the common era) then would a document written prior to that time, if read into its "proper" context, rightly be termed an "early Christian document" (e.g., what we commonly call the

Pauline epistles or any of the gospels) without risking the anachronism of retrojecting, say, Ignatius's self-understanding to social occasions and texts written a generation or more before? And given what—to stick with my arbitrary example, but one which is working back toward the opening quotation—Ignatius's self-understanding for what Χριστιανισμός might have signified for him (i.e., Christianity), how is homogenizing such an early appearance of this term with any of its subsequent uses (e.g., the manner in which I just juxtaposed an ancient Greek term with a modern English one by means of the simple Latin translator "id est"), let alone homogenizing both with the appearance of the term Χριστιανός in the Book of Acts (11:26—written perhaps a generation prior to Ignatius), the mark of a careful, situationally-specific historian?

The problem we encounter here is failing to study identifying practices rather than taking for granted the social worlds that result from their successful implementation (i.e., identities). For if we studied the former, then every signifying act involving the designation "Christian" would be a moment when an identity was originating all over again, and we would no longer look toward the time of the ancestors, as I've been calling it, for some definitive big bang that started it all and whose animating momentum somehow yet persists. Making the shift to studying identity as an ongoing, always-in-the-present exercise, focuses our attention on the "i.e." in my previous paragraph, the ease with which one translates and moves between what are otherwise entirely discrete (potentially competing or even contradictory) uses and situations, for the impression of uniform tradition, heritage, and identity is the result of this movement between what are portrayed as correspondences, a move that finds little difficulty in glossing over the many possible gaps between a first century use of "Χριστιανισμός" and a modern use of "Christianity." For despite my use of "id est," in many ways the ancient "that" *is most certainly not* the same as some contemporary "this," which prompts us to ask what scale of value we are choosing to use to manage the competing similarities and differences in the objects that we so casually relate to each other. Where is the trace of those who made these choices and what do we know of their consequences? Who owns it all?

For all their seeming progressivism, I therefore find that scholars studying context-oriented Christian origins are *not* asking such questions of historically specific situation and agency. Akin to those theologically-inclined colleagues from whom they try so hard (but, according to my analysis, fail) to distance themselves, they are instead actively involved in constituting the timeless, essential object that they think they are historicizing—perhaps this is why they must put such effort into their efforts to distinguish themselves. For, as we read in the opening quotation—

Geza Vermes, a religious scholar who argued that Jesus as a historical figure could be understood only through the Jewish tradition from which he emerged, and who helped expand that understanding through his widely read English translations of the Dead Sea Scrolls, died on May 8 in Oxford, England. He was 88.

—the uniform figure of an actually existing Jesus (i.e., the text)—whom, we are now told, subsequent social actors know of *only* if we take as settled and thus authorized a complex writing tradition (i.e., context) filled with its own easily documented internal debates, ambiguities, contradicitons, and controversies—passively *emerged* from out of an apparently uniform thing called "the Jewish tradition" (i.e., yet another context). But I am unsure which of the many Judaisms that we read back on that time will constitute this normative, apparently universal core, just as I am also not clear on why, of all the ways of slicing up the ancient social pie, this is the "only" context capable of providing a proper understanding of this seemingly timeless figure who was somehow already fully formed at the origins of the discourse on him.

Text and context, then, and the method of reading a text back into a prior context to understand it, is not nearly as progressive as many of us think it to be; those seeking to understand the founding and development of ancient Christianity by placing some transcendent "it" into its proper context would therefore be well advised, instead, to study the ever changing and always competing contexts, and those who select from among them, that enable some generic item from the past either to become Christian or not.

Filling in the Cracks with Resin:
A Response to John Burris's "Text and
Context in the Study of Religion" (2003)

> The very opposition between what is inside and what is outside
> texts is rendered problematic, and nothing is seen as being purely
> and simply inside or outside texts. (La Capra 1983: 26)

I am grateful to the editors of *MTSR* for inviting a reply to John Burris's recent
article (2003). Because David Chidester's *Savage Systems* (1996) was published after the manuscript for *Manufacturing Religion* (1997b) had been submitted to the press in late-1995, I am pleased that Burris juxtaposes these two
books, for I think that they have some important things in common, not least
of which is the manner in which both squarely place the study of religion into
a geo-political context. Moreover, I think it sensible to identify the influence
that some of Ivan Strenski's work had on my thinking at a formative stage in
its development, notably his use of the "text in context" method in his *Four
Theories of Myth in Twentieth-Century History* (1987). But at some points
Chidester and I diverge, I think, although not necessarily because I emphasize text whereas he emphasizes context, as Burris argues. And, because of
the rather harsh criticisms that Strenski has leveled at the work of those who
focus on the category "religion"—for example, Gary Lease, Tim Fitzgerald,
and myself—I think it unwise to place too much emphasis on those points
where our works appear to converge, despite both of us being concerned with
contextualizing theories and theorists of religion.[6] And despite being flattered
to find my book placed in a tradition that also contains the work of the late
Eric Sharpe, I see my work as dramatically different from the sort of apolitical history-of-ideas approach that characterizes this way of telling the story
of our field's past.[7] Given that the various similarities and differences that
are crucial to Burris's argument all have something to do either with text or
context, I would like to focus my response on the way in which he uses this
pairing, as well as to examine the view of history, including the task of historical research, that seems to inform his attempt to "imagine the discipline
as a whole" (2003: 39).

Although generally supportive of Burris's interest in moving beyond the
regnant idealist approach to writing the history of an academic field (e.g.,
Burris 2001), I am somewhat suspicious of any attempt to recover "the full
historical context of a field of religion" (2003: 33) by a synthesis that over-
comes that which is characterized as a series of merely partial viewpoints,

each of which is judged, "from a historiographical perspective," to provide "an excessively narrow perspective" (2003: 33). So, despite the fact that he welcomes my critique of "the subject of transcendence and its political implications" (2003: 31) that has acted as a "driving force" throughout the field's history, I find Burris's presumption that there exists some definitive and full historical picture to be informed—ironically, perhaps—by the very same technique I critiqued in *Manufacturing Religion*. For the rhetoric of uniqueness that comes packaged with claims that something is *sui generis* necessarily implies that there is some definitive and final vantage point from which something ought to be seen, a perspective to end all perspectives. This technique is present no less in studies that advocate obtaining a full under-standing of the history of the study of religion than in studies that advocate obtaining a full understanding of religious experiences. Given my view of human history-making as an open-ended, contingent process of hindsight *ad hoc*ery that is responsive to a continually changing present, I would argue that there is no complete, full, or sufficient stance or point of view to be had by any social actor, scholars included. As such, narrative closure, the whole, and a full accounting are the products of wishful thinking. Instead, all we have is a host of competing and inevitably provincial narratives, along with the institutions in which such narratives are judged as either legitimate or illegitimate, sufficient or insufficient.

If one maintains that there is no external standard that determines which narrative is sufficient, then a number of claims that might otherwise pass unnoticed begin to stand out as curious and deserving of further scrutiny. To pick just one example, when we read statements such as "London's Great Exhibition and the international exposition tradition it gave birth to *need to be viewed* as a complex interplay between economic, political, aesthetic, and discursive cultural forces" (Burris 2001: 22; emphasis added), partic-ular attention can now be placed on the use of "need"—a need that, once satisfied, allows one to see the "real significance" of such historical events as the late nineteenth-century exposition movement (2001: 22). Despite his essay's critique of the brand of positivism that still exerts its influence in many of our peers' understanding not only of the field's past but also the field's current object of study (Sharpe's and Strenski's works are cited as examples of this), I nonetheless find many of the same assumptions behind Burris's overly ambitious claims concerning the "real significance" and the "need" to study the past in just this and not that manner. That some things are possible to say when the past is narrativized in a specific manner—such as making linkages between geo-politics, social Darwinism, and the use of the taxon "religion" when studying people's behaviors—is certainly evident and not something I contest. However, that some specific ways of talking about the past are superior, definitive, complete, sufficient, final, or downright better, is not evident at all. Simply put, *why* do we need to study the past in just this manner? Is the answer to this question self-evident or is there a persuasive series of reasons for why this context ought to be included?

Therefore, despite some clear agreements with the direction in which Burris's work is moving, I nonetheless see some important differences between the goals of our critical efforts. For instance, consider an example that has some overlap with Burris's interest in the nineteenth-century exposition movement: my critique of Richard H. Roberts's report on the 1993 revival of the Parliament of World's Religions (reprinted in McCutcheon 2001a: ch. 6). I read Roberts's essay (1995) as highly romanticized and dehistoricized insomuch as its characterization of the Chicago meeting seemed only to repeat the participants' own self-beneficial understandings of this so-called spiritual event (for his reply to my critique, see Roberts 1998). However, in offering a critique of Roberts's 1995 essay my aim was not to argue that a full understanding of the 1993 Parliament will be possible only if it is studied in its economic context (the context I chose to examine in my own essay). Instead, I argued that there are practical political consequences that attend the contexts in which we choose to place events and that the rhetorics we use when doing our studies are not simply descriptive labels we attach to some stable, real world populated by natural kinds. I argued that, despite his understanding of the event as being in opposition to global, consumer ideology, Roberts's portrait of the Parliament as an apolitical, "fecund beehive of religious activity" was at considerable odds with the fact that it was housed in the elite Palmer House Hilton in downtown Chicago. For it was precisely this setting that provided the necessary preconditions for the participants to have the luxury of perceiving themselves and their actions as somehow being above the socio-historical fray. I therefore concluded that despite trying to overcome consumer commodification, his ahistorical representation of human practice "reproduces the very system he proclaims to critique" (2001a: 89). My goal, therefore, was *not* to demonstrate that Roberts's analysis was incorrect or that the context in which he placed the event was partial and thus in need of supplementation in order for us to understand the Parliament's *real* significance. Instead, the aim was to take seriously the Marxist context in which he placed the event and then to demonstrate that his analysis contradicted itself—as one would expect of any account that tries to offer a totalized reading of any historically contingent events. By placing this event in a material, rather than a so-called spiritual, context, I concluded that his essay's internal contradiction was a function of the way in which he conflated what, for the social theorist at least, are two different things: the text provided by a description of participant self-understandings of their own motives and behaviors (understandings that routinely posit the existence of semiotic closure and the social authority that comes from occupying such a superior position) and the socio-political analysis of these self-perceptions. That my own text was hardly privileged, that is, that it could be placed in new, unanticipated contexts, was evident from the criticisms contained in Roberts's own reply.

Just as the text/context distinction had utility in accounting for the internal contradictions of Roberts's article, the rhetoric of sufficiency and completeness that attends Burris's text/context distinction also has utility insomuch as Burris is able to create a synthesis that attempts to collapse the distinctions between two of his interlocutors' efforts to construct their own picture of our field's history. But at this point I must say that I am not entirely sure what Burris means by "history" and "historical method" when, for example, he distinguishes Chidester's "broader historical approach" (Burris 2003: 36) from my work insomuch as the former emphasizes context, whereas my own is more concerned with "the close attention to texts" (Burris 2003: 38). If I am not mistaken, both Chidester and I (like all scholars) are part of a contemporary discourse on "the past" that makes use of things we designate as "texts" that we place within various sorts of contexts, contexts which are themselves open to subsequent scrutiny, in a never-ending series of contexts.

Perhaps this is unintended on Burris's part, but in placing such significance on the distinction between text and context—instead of seeing text and context merely as heuristics whose distinctions disappear upon closer scrutiny—he seems to rely on a realist notion of history as something that is obviously and chronologically "out there" somewhere—or should I say, sometime—which forms the stable backdrop against which isolated items can be read, interpreted, and compared. Or, to rephrase it, despite his reticence to propose a "sharp distinction between text and context" (Burris 2003: 29), he does not take seriously the implications of seeing the two as simply poles along a sliding continuum.[8] Had he thus seen things, then there would no longer be any basis for the opposition he sees between Chidester and myself; and there would be nothing to synthesize. Failing to entertain that "nothing is seen as being purely and simply inside or outside texts," to reiterate La Capra's words in the epigraph, Burris presses on and argues that the more components (or "elements" [2001: 22]) we add to the picture, the more complete our historical jigsaw puzzle will be, and hence the closer we will come to understanding the real significance of historical events. For instance, after the above quotation from *Exhibiting Religion*, Burris goes on to write:

> When all of these elements [e.g., the economic, political, aesthetic, and discursive cultural forces] are understood as being fundamentally interrelated to one another and inseparable, it will become more feasible to understand the extent to which they combined at international expositions to have a decided effect on the formation of the field of religion. (2003: 22)

My difficulty with such an approach lies in determining which elements get to count as necessary for arriving at a full understanding. Should gender be added to the above list? If so, what about ethnic, national, and generational forces? Without some sense of the criteria by which a context gets to count as a legitimate context, how will we know when we have arrived at our much anticipated full understanding? Are astrological or gravitation forces of relevance? To bring it back to earth, let me ask if future readers who attempt the contextualization of this very text itself must take into account my stage of career when I first wrote, then rewrote, the text on which Burris comments (i.e., McCutcheon *qua* graduate student or McCutcheon *qua* Instructor at the University of Tennessee), let alone the stage of my career at which I am now while offering this response?[9] To understand my text sufficiently must readers take into account that I am now elaborating on a book that was largely written a decade ago and whose contents I neither remember nor agree with completely? Are these not some of the fundamentally interrelated and inseparable elements whose recovery forms the necessary contextual precondition for a full understanding of my text (to paraphrase Burris)? Case in point: in his response to my critique, Roberts alluded to my then status as an early-career academic by writing that "he knows as well as I do that his paper is itself a commodity and part of the campaign mounted by any aspirant academic with a view to gaining tenure and promotion in the competition for survival in the relevant job market" (1998: 68–69). Was that a patronizing jab on the part of a senior scholar, meant to minimize my critique of his work, or was he simply making explicit yet one more legitimate—even necessary—context required of the careful reader tackling my 1998 text? That I could easily multiply the virtually limitless elements and contexts *needed* for the so-called complete understanding of any historical event should go without saying, and this is precisely my point.

Having raised the specter of an unregulated semantic growth economy, it would be inaccurate if I suggested that this problem had not dawned on Burris. In fact he worries about just this when he observes that the hermeneutical circle ends up being replaced by the "historiographical circle and the problem of defining historical context" (Burris 2003: 32). As such, "the discourse about context itself becomes the new text with a great deal now at stake in that discussion" (2003: 32). Indeed! How could it be any other way? But instead of scrapping the distinction and, with it, the hope for ever arriving at the final context that contains all required elements, he asks the following rhetorical question: "*can* the discussion about *sui generis* religion and the affiliated discussion about the correct understanding of religion as an academic discourse be conducted effectively within the historical and geographical parameters McCutcheon adopts?" (2003: 32). His answer is obviously no; and this makes evident that the problem here is with his quest for the "correct understanding." Because I do not share this goal, I would never claim that the discussion about *sui generis* religion as laid out in *Manufacturing Religion* could ever be read as sufficient. And because I have not made, and could not make, such a claim, I fail to see how Burris's rhetorical question makes any sense. Without the performance anxiety that comes from having such an unreachable goal—one Burris ironically shares with his phenomenological predecessors—one would never unduly fret about whether one has accumulated all the puzzle pieces. Instead, one would simply define one's parameters and dive into the mix of human behaviors using one's taxa and one's persuasive skills, never fearing the sort of paralysis that threatens those who seek all the opinions prior to pronouncing their own judgment. Due to a host of profoundly practical and mundane reasons, I had no hesitation in explicitly limiting *Manufacturing Religion* largely to the recent North American field.[10] Although he recognizes this to be the focus of the book (Burris 2003: 32), his quest for a complete understanding seems to prompt him to mischaracterize the book by saying that "the study presents itself as an exhaustive survey of recent scholarship on religion as an academic construct." Although I do not recall claiming such an exalted status for a book of only seven chapters written mostly as a doctoral dissertation, he then goes on to observe that "the omission, for the most part, of Europe, the rest of the world beyond the West, and pre-twentieth-century literature pertaining to the field of religion limits the book unduly and paints a restricted and potentially illusory, picture of the central issues of religion as an academic discipline" (2003: 32–33). In other words, the central flaw of my book is that, while it examines texts in context, "the larger historical context in which *it* places *itself*" is "from a historiograhical perspective…excessively narrow" (2003: 33). Of course this judgment—that the work has omissions that make it "excessively narrow"—is meaningful only insomuch as it is juxtaposed to a sense of the complete "big picture," to which my limited perspective might contribute, but only partially. Without this sense of the big picture, I am not sure how one can make judgments regarding omissions.

But, as suggested above, I am at a loss to figure out what this big picture is, or to know how or when it is that we will ever know when it has finally arrived. For example, is it a sad limitation that all of the works in consideration in Burris's essay take no account whatsoever of, say, recent Romanian or Greek scholarship on religion? Is this so-called limitation and omission something to lament, overcome, and thus correct? Or, rather, is it an understandable and, in fact, inevitable result of how all scholarship—even experience itself—is an exercise in focus and exclusion? And I can only guess what our colleagues in Japan might think of premising the full understanding of the field's history on events associated with European colonialism. Although Burris seems to find partial perspectives to be unfortunate limitations, I see them as an inevitable outcome of historical existence. Listening to National Public Radio (NPR) this morning, I heard it phrased as follows by Jack Angstreich, a devoted film-goer about whom a documentary film has just been made: "When you put a frame around things you intensify them; experience without that frame is banal."[11] Or, to repeat a quote from the historian of architecture, Witold Rybczynski: "A recreational vehicle in the rain is just a wet metal box; a screened porch with wide, sheltering eaves is a place to *experience* the rain" (1990: 49; quoted in McCutcheon 2003a: 10). Transposed to the work of the academy, we can say that a theory without explicit definition and parameters is not a theory at all. It is simply a banal, wet metal box indistinguishable from other banal, wet metal boxes. It is for this reason that I do not believe there to be any such thing as the full story, but only parochial tales that are or are not suited to the requirements of various institutional, discursive settings.

Since his analysis of Chidester's *Savage Systems* follows Burris's critique of my text's limitations, and given his above quotation concerning "the West and the rest" along with his 2001 book's emphasis on colonialism, I gather that the undisclosed frame that enables him to settle on a definitive context involves the study of religion's place in the history of European colonialism and social Darwinism's impact on the nascent discipline. Although I would not disagree regarding the importance of this particular historical context—in fact, despite not being about these historical events, the successive colonial, social Darwinist, and Cold War settings of our field have occupied my attention at several points in the book and in some subsequent writing as well (e.g., ch. 4 of Arnal and McCutcheon 2013)[12]—I am not convinced that this frame allows us to answer "the question of how the full historical context of a field of religion, inclusive of its economic context write large, should be constructed" (Burris 2003: 33). I am not convinced because the "full historical context...inclusive of its economic context writ large" will surely have to go back still further, at least to the beginnings of the retooling of the taxon "religion" in various sixteenth- and seventeenth-century European vernaculars to signify a non-empirical inner piety, disposition, and private experience rather than outer social membership and observable ritual action (e.g., see Smith 1998: 271; McCutcheon 2003a: chs. 11, 12; and McCutcheon 2004c). Only then will we understand the true signifi-cance of the taxonomic marker that, within several generations, gets honed into a useful management tool that, along with Europe's second sons, could be productively exported to the colonies. Detailed work on this prior histor-ical period enables us to understand the proto-nationalist context from out of which the modern nation-state emerged, populated by newly constituted atomistic citizens said to be willfully entering into social contracts, each of whom were thought to share certain inner, inalienable rights. Plotting this along side the development of capitalism and the never-ending search for raw materials and markets in which to exchange commodities is thus crucial for understanding the later colonial story.

But in saying this my hope is that readers will understand that I am not trying to trump Burris's laudable focus on the colonial context by bringing up an earlier time period, as if one somehow knows that "the Real" lies just a little beyond the reach of one's critics. All I intend by raising the example of the pre-colonial context of the field is to suggest that seeing his focus on the colonial era as "laudable" hardly constitutes this context as "sufficient" or "complete." Lacking a standard by which to conclude which of the many contexts is definitive in providing the whole picture of the field's history, I therefore would not say that when it comes to exploring the question of the production of capital through idealization in the modern period, the bound-aries provided by the colonial period are simply insufficient (to paraphrase Burris 2003: 33). Dropping his effort to arrive at the total picture of history, and instead moving forward with a series of controlled frameworks that each tell us something different about the object under study, would help things considerably, in my opinion. But then Burris would lose the hook of his essay and the engine that drives both his distinction of my work from Chidester's and the warrant for advocating a synthesis of the two.

Dropping this hook would also require him to reconsider just what he means by "history." Inasmuch as he sees my work as focusing on the activi-ties of reading and interpreting (what he characterizes as my hermeneutical emphasis) he judges it insufficiently historical and thus inadequate for the task at hand, that is, reconstructing the definitive history and politics of the field. Following such a line of thinking, history and historical context are not just "sometime," but sometime long, long ago and in a galaxy far away. Because of this, my work on texts published in North America that, more-over, date only from the 1950s through the early 1990s apparently fails to qualify my work as historical, whereas work on texts that were published in, say, nineteenth-century Europe, and which purport to be about Afri-cans seems to qualify one as a historian.[13] Although I wish not to alienate my friends in the Department of History, and although I wish not to repeat things said much better by many others (e.g., Hayden White and Dominick La Capra), I have for some time been troubled by such a common-sense understanding of history and the historical quest to place things in their proper context. After all, when anyone of us picks up a text, there is no time-travel happening; the text is not old for it is always—inasmuch as one can see and touch it—contemporaneous with the reader. If a text is always in the present, then it is never old but, instead, "old"; its antiquity (and thus the status of authenticity that comes from its apparent age) is always an item of discourse only.[14] No matter how "old" a text may be, it is merely a collection of patterned blotches, or scribbles, or shades of grey, or ink on parchment or vellum, or chiseled marks in stone, all of which are *always in the present*. While not wishing to come off sounding like some stereotypical Zen Buddhist monk, there is simply no other place for this thing and its reader to co-exist *but in the present*, and only through some imaginative leap do we create the fantasy that we are somehow walking in step with our ancestors in the act of carefully reading something that some posited "they" apparently "held in their hands."[15] This is what I would call the "Washington slept here" view of history, whereby scholars *qua* tourists treat sites as if they were fans fawning over autographs thought to hold some enduring presence/essence inscribed onto the perishable paper. While I certainly do not deny that there is a past, it is just that there are too many pasts to justify talking about "*the* past," just as too many contexts prevent us from so easily talking about reading a text "in *its* context."

This commonsense view of a unified or authoritative history that constitutes some definitive context, at which we can arrive if we pay close enough attention to the right details, is easy to find, both in academia and outside of it. For instance, this view was evident in a mid-April, 2003, popular television segment on the National Broadcast Corporation's (NBC) evening news magazine show "Dateline," which was devoted to the so-called "ossuary of James."[16] In this segment Hershel Shanks, editor of the popular magazine *Biblical Archaeology Review* (*BAR*) and one of the people most responsible for the hype that currently surrounds the artefact, said that looking at it, behind its museum glass, one could just "feel the awe coming off of it" (see also LeMaire 2002; Shanks 2003a; Shanks and Witherington 2003).[17] That this artifact was on display in Toronto during the 2002 American Academy of Religion, Society of Biblical Literature, and American Schools of Oriental Research conferences was surely a happy coincidence for all those motivated by the "Washington slept here" view of history who were intent on soaking up some of the awe. Something told me I should go up to Toronto's Royal Ontario Museum just to watch the scholars of religion who made their pilgrimage (by foot, taxi cab, or subway) to bask in the artfully lit glow of the plexiglass display case in which the small limestone box was housed from November 15, 2002, until January 5, 2003. After reading Burris's thoughts on the need for a complete picture of the discipline's past, I wish I had done some fieldwork at that exhibit while I was in Toronto for the annual North American Association for the Study of Religion meeting. Despite the obvious difference between a scholar such as Burris trying to recover the real significance of our collective history, on the one hand, and Shanks basking in the glow of the bone box, there is something oddly similar about how these two scholars go about their discourses on the past.

What makes the story of the "awe-suary"[18] particularly useful to me is not only that the artefact was purchased on the antiquities market—making it "unprovenanced" and thus contextless[19]—but that on its trip to Toronto from its home in Israel, "tragedy struck" in a development that could not have been planned any better by a Hollywood script writer, the bubble-wrapped artifact was damaged and a small crack appeared "directly through the inscription— just before the name of Jesus" (Shanks 2003a: 21). Accordingly,

> [c]onservators at the ROM cleaned the surfaces of the ancient and modern cracks, and bonded them together using plastic resins. The damaged edges of the modern cracks were then filled with resin and calcium carbonate, simulating the hardness and colour of the limestone. The ancient crack was left unfilled to indicate its age. Conservators strive to make their work reversible. If in the future the ossuary requires disassembly, the joints can be released using acetone and water.[20]

According to Shanks, as a result of the conservatory work at the Royal Ontario Museum, "[t]he cracks were barely visible, and the ossuary was structurally sounder than it had been when it left Israel" (2003a: 21). Of particular interest was that *some cracks were deemed authentic while others were not*—despite the fact that all of these cracks were undoubtedly created in precisely the same manner: unexpected degrading things do happen to a breakable material object. As a result of this picking and choosing, the *illegitimate cracks* were filled, thereby showcasing the *real cracks*, that is, those that contributed to the antiquity of the box. Ironically, as a result of the work in Toronto, the box was more authentic than it had been in Israel.

This example illustrates how we routinely make the imaginative leap across the chasm of historical happenstance (that is, the world in which cracks happen and the world in which viewpoints inevitably compete). By picking and choosing among cracks we leave far behind the otherwise unescapable world where, to put it elegantly, "shit happens." Translated to the topic at hand, the prioritizing of specific contexts, followed by ignoring just some of the gaps, seems to have allowed Burris to produce not just a different narrative, but a more complete and thus "structurally sounder" history than either Chidester or myself could have managed on our own. The end result is the impression of a complete and authentic narrative—so long as the fresh resin goes without notice. In Burris's case the resin is akin to his rhetoric of fullness and synthesis whereby the inevitable differences between opposing approaches and partial contexts are subsumed so as to recover an event's real significance.

However, because the "Washington slept here" view of history is necessarily without provenance, there are no extra-discursive constraints that can be used to assess the provenance of his claims. Because virtually any claim about the past can sidle up to the bar—hence the resiliency of conspiracy theories—competitors need considerable shoring up if they are to win the contest. While in some communities claims are authorized by sheer assertion, they can also be authorized by appeals to the age of the speaker, the gender of the speaker, and, as we routinely see on the world stage, by the size of the speaker's bat. Among scholarly pundits legitimacy for their speculations sometimes lies in statistical analysis. Case in point: the above-mentioned limestone bone box with an inscription. Leaving aside debates on the inscription's authenticity—debates that rely on paleographic analysis and studies of the patina's distribution[21]—what is the likelihood that the inscription refers to *the* Jesus? After all, debates on its authenticity are driven by the presumption that the inscription provides hard, irrefutable, empirical evidence of theological claims.[22] In other words, how does one add meat to the bones of the utterly speculative "very likely" and "it seems very probable" that we find peppered throughout Shanks's text (e.g., 2003a: 26, 33)? Well, given that the numbers are against us—after all, "[t]he names of James (Jacob), Joseph and Jesus were all fairly common among Jews at the turn of the era" (2003a: 33)—we had better use numbers to our advantage. And Shanks does just this; according to L. Y. Rahmani's *A Catalogue of Jewish Ossuaries* (1994), there are currently two hundred and thirty-three *known* ossuaries bearing inscriptions, with the name of Joseph appearing in fourteen percent of the inscriptions, Jesus in nine percent, and James/Jacob in two percent. *Assuming* that each male had two brothers he determines that eighteen percent of the men named "James/Jacob sone of Joseph" would have a brother named Jesus. He concludes that, "over two generations, 0.05 percent of the population *would likely* be called 'Jacob son of Joseph brother of Jesus" (2003a: 33; emphasis added). *Although we have no idea if this limestone box was actually associated with Jerusalem* (since it is "unprovenanced"), *assuming*, a population for Jerusalem of about eighty thousand for this time period (and with fifty percent being male), he concludes that "[i]n Jerusalem during the two generations before 70 CE, there were therefore *probably* 20 people who could be called 'James/ Jacob son of Joseph brother of Jesus'" (emphasis added). He then adds a final, cautionary aside: "It is, however, *impossible* to estimate how many of these 20 people were buried in ossuaries and how many of these ossuaries would be inscribed" (emphasis added).

Considerable, though generally undisclosed, work is being done at the site of Shanks's compounded qualifications, work that attempts to harness competing narratives of the past. This is precisely where the resin of wishful thinking—call it conservation, if you will—meets the cracks of historical happenstance. For example, for both Burris's rhetoric of full historical disclosure and for Shanks's mathematics to be persuasive one must completely overlook a whole series of gaps and fissures, such as the point argued above concerning every context being but a new text to be interpreted in light of yet more contexts (if nothing else, the context of a new writer or speaker tackling some tired, old text). In the case of Shanks's statistics, we must overlook the fact that there is no necessary relationship between the number of inscribed ossuaries recorded in Rahmani's 1994 catalogue and some stable historical reality (e.g., the number of inscribed ossuaries that were in use in Jerusalem by 70 CE), making the numerical starting point for all of his calculations a banal number of no particular significance. That there is no necessary link between the unprovenanced artefact under consideration and the city of Jerusalem is equally important to overlook, as is the fact that there is no necessary relation between early recorded Church tradition (coming largely from Book II of Eusebius of Caesarea's early fourth-century CE *Ecclesiastical History*) that places James's death in Jerusalem and the actual fact of his burial in Jerusalem—assuming that there was in fact an actual historical actor named James of the significance that the subsequent tradition places on him and, moreover, assuming that a modern archeological find in Jerusalem indicates that the object was in Jerusalem in 70 CE.

Despite claims to the contrary, I would argue that these judgments, assertions, assumptions, and conclusions are all *items of discourse* and not *items of historical fact*. Such debates as whether or not the colonial era provides the definitive context for understanding our field's history will therefore not be settled by appealing to an ever increasing army of facts but, instead, by means of theory, argumentation, persuasion. Lacking such persuasion, the gap between discourse and history must continually be refilled with rhetorical resin, so that claims regarding the real significance of the past can bypass our recognition that our knowledge of the past is only "fragmentary, uncertain, or nonexistent" (Thompson 1999: 7). For only after the conservator's steady hand has done its task can we leap past the qualifications and empty spaces, as does the Royal Ontario Museum's website when it confidently concludes that "[a]lthough we cannot be certain of the identity of the people named *the James ossuary does put us in contact with an age when there were still people alive who knew Jesus of Nazareth*" (italics added).

Let me repeat, as a concluding remark, that although I share an interest in placing the study of religion into the context of conflict and contest, I do not think—as I suspect both Burris and Chidester do—that employing such a context is morally incumbent upon modern-day scholars. Rather than being a study of the ways in which an other culture was classified and thereby managed by each successive wave of colonial administration, in the background of Chidester's book I find a rather harsh indictment of the European failure or outright refusal to "recognize the existence of indigenous religions in southern Africa" (1996: xv). In other words, instead of seeing "religious"—no less than "superstitious" and "savage"—as a classification tool useful in creating cognitively and socially habitable world, one whose varied uses were handy assists in ranking and managing diverse populations and thereby creating certain types of "civility," Chidester seems to employ a classic humanist set of assumptions regarding the universal presence of religion in human cultures. It is on the basis of this assumption that he indicts our predecessors for the "mistakes of the past" (1996: 259). To avoid their sins he advocates that more things (what Burris might term "elements") must now be entertained as religion (hence Chidester's support for polythetic, open-ended definitions). The failure to recognize indigenous religions for what they really are, and instead seeing them either as savage precursors to or degradations of the normative European world, is therefore the basis of the present's judgment against the sins of the colonial past.

But just as I previously questioned whether having a perspective was evidence of an omission, I now close by asking whether this a *failure* on the part of our intellectual predecessors. Although for a host of reasons I wish not to reproduce their approach, must I conclude that they are culpable for their classification systems? If so, then culpable by what standard? Have we, their latter day judges, finally arrived at the end of history, such that we now know what things really are and how they ought to be studied? Being far more timid in my confidence with our own use of classifications, I think that a different book would *not* have portrayed the discovery that "they" had religions just like "us" to have been a triumph but would have problematized this now taken-for-granted classificatory development—and the current preoccupation with cultivating a type of interreligious dialogue and global cooperation that shores up liberal democracies—by mapping it into the long history of management techniques used to ensure a specific sort of cooperation and organization among potentially competing and conflicting

nation-states. Then we would be serious about engaging in a historicization of our field, for we would cease treating "religion" as a natural kind.
Instead, we would be open to scrutinizing the social worlds it helps to make
possible. Keeping in mind Burris's critique of nineteenth-century scholarship's sadly mistaken presumption to have transcended its own cultural
boundaries (2003: 42–43), it occurs to me that both Burris's and Chidester's
use of "religion" is evidence of the failure of scholars to place themselves
and their own work into a historical context. For when Burris writes that
"[b]ecause of its size and more importantly because of its formidable *religious heritage*...it proved impossible for the West to dominate India in a
religious sense, even if it was able to colonize her through *insidious political maneuvers*" (2003: 43; emphasis added), he seems not to recognize
that his presumption that India quite naturally has a "religious heritage"
that is somehow distinguishable from the messy world of insidious politics
is itself a management technique of tremendous utility (see McCutcheon
2004c). In fact, that people the world over now routinely understand themselves to have an active but inner religious life that is distinguishable from
their outer political activities is evidence, to me, of the very dominance that
Burris somehow thinks did not occur. That the invention and perfection of
the distinction between religion and politics, insomuch as it is related to the
belief/practice, experience/expression, and the private/public distinctions,
was useful in creating a specific type of order in the European world several
centuries ago seems to be of no relevance to us today; instead, like many
before us, we self-confidently export these distinctions to distant shores as
if all groups naturally understand themselves in just this manner, and as if
all groups know what does, and what does not, count as real significance.
Like the current young generation's inability to imagine a world in which
there are no microwaves, no CD players, and no Internet, scholars cannot
imagine "religion" to be an historical invention.[23]

  While I am not trying to suggest that, like a golden egg resting comfortably beneath a fairytale goose, some authentic, indigenous self-understanding awaits the careful conservator who has cleaned all the surfaces of some
exotic artefact, I *am* suggesting that all we have are discourses by means
of which banal stuff becomes artefacts, texts, and contexts. I am therefore
arguing that recognizing this will help to dispel the rush to culpability and
the search for authenticity and complete understanding that drives so much
of our historical work. In place of this quest for closure I suggest that we
retool the field as the study of contesting classifications and the differing
identities and social worlds made possible by the simulation of hardness,
permanence, and finality. That means we must get to work on the ancient
and modern cracks, not with resin but with acetone and water.[24]

Notes

1.   Available at: http://www.nytimes.com/2013/05/17/world/europe/geza-vermes-dead-sea-scrolls-scholar-dies-at-88.html?_r=0 (accessed May 17, 2013).
2.   Going to the supposed source is not specific to judging one's legitimacy in just these two fields, of course; for instance, if you've not spent time "down in the archives," how can one count oneself as a historian?
3.   In part 2 of a July 2011 online interview with Craig Martin, after Martin had used the story of the Tower of Babel as an example of a non-reductive way that some people might understand the existence of different races in opposition to a scholar's reductive understanding of race, Vásquez replies:

> In the example that you give, as a religion scholar, I would definitely approach race as a product of particular discursive and non-discursive practices operating upon and from the body. But I would be interested in understanding the conditions under which the Babel claim comes to be lived as authoritative by those who hold it, as well as the material effects this claim carries in terms of the articulation of subjectivities or forms of social organization. My role here is not to dismiss the claim as wrong from the get go, but to study the conditions of its production, circulation, and reception. In fact, dismissing the Babel claim off-hand may even be an unproductive methodological move, since it may thwart consideration of the effectiveness of the claim, that is, of the real, material effects it may have in the believer's everyday life.

Despite reference to "the conditions of its production...," the "more" of his book's title signals an interest in the material effects of belief, thereby leaving intact an idealist metaphysic. Find this part of the interview at: http://www.equinoxpub.com/blog/2011/07/more-than-belief-an-interview-with-manuel-a-vasquez-part-2/ (accessed March 4, 2013).
4.   For those unable to attend in person, the full lecture can be found at: http://aarweb.org/Meetings/Videos/2010Atlanta/2010_A31-137.asp (accessed May 14, 2013).
5.   This essay—which Smith refers to as a "bio-bibliographical essay" (2004: 1)—opens his collection, *Relating Religion: Essays in the Study of Religion*.
6.   Despite Burris's claim that my work "follows largely in the same vein" as Strenski's, I concur with Chidester's critique of Strenski's emphasis on establishing direct and demonstrable causal links and his aim to ascribe individual culpability; such an approach strikes me as failing to entertain the structural nature of political institutions. For an early formulation of this critique, see McCutcheon (1997b: 96–100; 2003: ch. 11; 2004b). For examples of Strenski's own criticisms of my work, see Strenski (1998 and 2002).
7.   The work of the late Walter Capps also comes to mind as an example of this approach to writing the field's history. In a review of his *Religious Studies: The Making of a Discipline* (1995), I phrased it as follows:

Capps's use of the "great man" heuristic is itself problematic, for he presents the history of the study of religion as essentially an intellectual adventure, a virtual Hegelian narrative unfolding in history, failing to take into account the material and social origins of the field. Indeed the Enlightenment played a considerable role in our history, but today it is rather difficult to talk of the Enlightenment simply as a purely intellectual event, as Capps does. As important as the beliefs and conscious intentions of our field's founders may have been, such things as European colonialism and the more recent advent of American imperialism have played a considerable role as well. (McCutcheon 1999c: 529)

8. For example, immediately after noting that "trends in postmodern scholarship have tried to collapse all distinction between text and context," he adds, "with the former being exalted at the expense of the latter" (Burris 2003: 29). If the distinction is collapsed, I do not see how one can be exalted over the other; after all, there no longer remains either a specifiable "one"nor "the other."

9. Ed. Note: not to mention the fact that this very essay was written a decade prior to its inclusion in this present collection, indicating that what was once text might now be context when attempting to understand the person who is writing this very editorial note.

10. More accurately, the book examines mainly US scholarship, giving only brief attention to Canadian works. For good or ill I do not examine developments in the Mexican field.

11. The eighty-minute documentary film, "Cinemania" is directed by Stephen Kijak and Angela Christlieb (Hanfgarn & Ufer Films, Berlin, 2003), and follows the culture of intense cinephiles in New York City. An audio version of the interview from which I am quoting can be found at Weekend Edition Saturday's site for May 31, 2003, at http://www.npr.org/templates/story/story.php?storyId=1281837 (accessed May 12, 2013).

12. At some points in his essay I suspect that Burris thinks I ought to have written on the nineteenth century instead of the mid-twentieth. For example, consider the following critique: "it is interesting that a broad-minded book which uses the term 'manufacturing' in its title would pay so little attention to actual rather than metaphorical manufacturing in how it conceives the study of religion, because to my mind the phenomenon of manufacturing is very much at the center of the rise of the field. I would argue that global comparative religion did not begin as a religious, philosophical, or aesthetic enterprise, but emerged as a byproduct of an economically-motivated colonialism and at certain points contributed to it" (2003: 44). Had I intended to study the colonial-era beginnings of the field in any detail likely I would have concurred with Burris. Leaving aside for the time being the problem of so easily distinguishing "actual" from "metaphorical" manufacturing (since "actual" is equally a metaphor, this distinction seems driven by the same

commonsense realism that also informs Burris's text/context distinction), all
I can say in reply is that because I was concerned with a period that began
with the field's rebirth in the US in the early 1960s, I am not sure what to
make of Burris's criticism. [Ed. Note: my essay on the cold war setting for
the rebirth of the study of religion in the US, forthcoming when this chapter was first published, was eventually published in *Culture & Religion* 5/1
(2004): 41–69 and reprinted in Arnal and my 2013 book.]

13.   I find in this distinction something of the standard "dirty hands" critique that
       accompanies work on "religion" rather than on religions (see McCutcheon
       1997b: 6–7).

14.   Following a long line of critics and as already suggested in this essay, it
       should go without saying that the very fact that some generic material item
       in one's environment is understood and used as a "text" is equally an item of
       discourse and not of factual history.

15.   See McCutcheon 2003c where I elaborate on this problem of assuming that
       history can somehow be bridged by means of an artful re-construction.

16.   Ed. Note: I revised and used this portion of this paper (concerning the ossu-
       ary of James) in McCutcheon 2005c: 42–45.

17.   The existence of the ossuary was first made public in the US at an October
       21, 2002, news conference in Washington, DC, sponsored by *BAR*. For those
       not up on their recent biblical archeology discoveries, the ossuary of James
       is a limestone box about fifty centimetres long, twenty-five centimetres wide,
       and thirty centimetres high that would have contained a deceased person's
       bones (this form of Jewish re-burial was practiced from around the first cen-
       tury BCE to the destruction of the second temple by the Romans in 70 CE); the
       box bears an Aramaic inscription, about eighteen centimetres long, which,
       in transliteration, reads *Ya'akov bar Yosef akhui di Yeshua* ("James, son of
       Joseph, brother of Jesus").

18.   This highly appropriate pun was invented by a student at the University of
       Alabama, John Parrish, who coined it upon hearing of Hershel Shank's state-
       ment. I thank him for allowing me to use it.

19.   An authenticated artefact, of course, is one that has a certificate that docu-
       ments where it was found, by whom, when, and so on. What this has to do
       with reading the artefact back into some ancient history is, of course, rather
       more troublesome than the notions of a provenanced versus an unprov-
       enanced artefact at first suggests. Also of interest is that the owner, Oded
       Golan, a fifty-one year-old engineer and private collector who lives in Tel
       Aviv, at first was reported to have said he obtained the box fifteen years ago.
       He later corrected this, saying that although he had it in its current place for
       about the last fifteen years, he has owned it since the early- to mid-1970s (in
       one report, he is even said to have purchased it in 1967 when he was 16). If
       the first version is correct—and Israeli Antiquities Authorities are at pres-
       ent looking into the matter—this would put his acquisition of the box well
       after 1978, the Israeli government's cut-off date for those who purchase or
       discover artefacts. According to the Antiquities Law of the State of Israel of

1978 (5738–1978 [1]), if the purchase or discvovery of an antiquity (defined in the Law as anything made by human beings before 1700) was made *prior* to 1978 then owners who have no receipt documenting that their purchase was made from a licenced antiquities dealer are allowed to keep their arte-facts, no matter how they obtained them. However, post-1978 purchases and discoveries that cannot be documented become the property of the state of Israel (see Shanks 2003a: 22).

20.   This is quoted from an brief article entitled "Conservation," which is itself part of the Royal Ontario Museum's web article, "The James ossuary" (www.rom.on.ca). [Ed. Note: this article is no longer posted at the ROM's site.]

21.   Of course the authenticity of the inscription is hotly debated. For example, as melodramatically reported by Shanks, at the 2002 meeting of the Society of Biblical Literature Eric Meyers, of Duke University, "suggested that the ossuary's current owner...might have purchased it only recently and added the last two words ('brother of Jesus') to the inscription. Golan was sitting in the audience and Meyers looked straight at him" (2003b: 55–56).

22.   As phrased by Stephen H. Sanchez, a doctoral candidate at Dallas Theologi-cal Seminary: "The box is an archaeological find that is interesting because it may confirm some of the historical realities Christians already believe" (2002). [Ed. Note: the URL for this article has changed since this chapter was first published; the current URL appears in the reference section.]

23.   Ed. Note: it's rather funny—and nicely makes the point—that now, ten years after this paper was first published, its reference to compact disks is itself dated, since so many people today do not even use CDs but, instead, rely either on MP3s or the internet for their music.

24.   Ed. Note: on December 29, 2004, the ossuary's owner, Oded Golan, was charged in Israel, along with several others, with being part of an archeological forgery network. Conflicting opinions among the defense's and prosecution's various expert witnesses led to no definitive judgement on the various arti-facts' authenticity, including the ossuary of James, despite the Israeli Antiqui-ties Authority having already concluded that the inscription on the ossuary was a modern fake—the continued claims of Shanks concerning its authenticity notwithstanding. Golan was eventually found not guilty of the forgery charges in the Spring of 2012. And in March of 2012 the Royal Ontario Museum announced that there would not be an exhibit of the ossuary to celebrate the tenth anniversary of its first showing at the museum.

Chapter 9

Introduction

Craig Prentiss, who took over the *Bulletin of the Council of Societies for the Study of Religion* after I left as editor in 2001, kindly sent what was then my new book, *The Discipline of Religion* (2003a) to several scholars for their comments, inviting me to reply when he published this set of review essays. The following chapter is that response.

The Discipline of Religion was my second collection of essays; for a variety of reasons I have found myself to be an essayist. I have heard Jonathan Z. Smith liken the essay genre, that he himself uses exclusively, to the place where scholars in the human sciences conduct their experiments; for example, in an interview from 2008 he comments as follows:

> if the human sciences are sciences at all, they have to have something analogous to experiment. So talk is one of those. Comparing is another one. Experiment interferes with whatever it's looking at. It's not watching a natural process just going along naturally. It sticks a pin in or drops some irritant on it or does something to it or smashes it in a multibillion dollar hole. But comparing is doing something—bringing two things that have no reason in creation to be in the same pond together—throw them in and see what happens. It's the same thing you do when you interfere with largely, fortunately, an inorganic substance, but certainly we do try to cure diseases. We interfere with bodies, we interfere with bodily fluids, and we drop something in and see. And that's all I do. I look at the Book of Mormon in relationship to the Koran. I'm dropping one in the other's pond to see what happens. So to me, if we're a science, we have to have something analogous to an experiment.[1]

As much as I agree with this, for me, the essay was a logical—perhaps inevitable—choice of format for far less principled reasons; it was the genre that accommodated a heavy teaching load as an Instructor, the demands of a highly competitive job market, the various other projects that I was also involved with early in my career (e.g., co-editing *MTSR* from 1990–2001, editing the *CSSR Bulletin* from 1996–2001, editing an anthology book series, etc.), along with a profound frustration for how an entire academic field was structured. After writing a dissertation and revising it for publication, it makes sense that another monograph failed to met the needs of those factors.

While I don't think that I had delusions of changing the entire field—and if I did, I soon was cured of them—I do know that I had little patience for some of the things that I read that were regularly published in a variety of books and academic journals. I tried to pick my targets carefully, of course, so that each piece that I wrote tackled a specific issue as exemplified in the work of a particular scholar—always hoping that a reader could make the move to generalizing the critical point I attempted to make—all of which made the essay format a pretty natural choice. Although the contract I signed with State University of New York Press for what became my first collection, *Critics Not Caretakers* (2001a) required that I sell a thousand copies in softcover or hardcover before any royalties were paid—by far, the most ungenerous contract with a publisher that I have yet signed, for one thousand copies is, by some academic standards, a rather large number—I was thrilled that anyone thought that my already published essays were worth publishing as a set.

Although I dislike the pretention of referring to pieces of writings as "interventions," looking back, I guess that each of the essays that I have published were just that. In fact, thinking back on Smith's notion of the essay as our experimental medium, I now think of my essays as interferences in the status quo, disturbing some taken-for-granted situation within the word limit of its Petri dish—for example, poking so as to discover the tolerable limits within the model of liberal, universal tolerance that so informs our field. So I stuck in some pins and dropped some irritant to see what would happen. Sensibly, I often got poked back. As with the following reply, sometimes I was lucky enough to get the final poke in the experimental setting.[2]

Sometimes, when I was given the opportunity to reply, I recalled reading Eliade's published journals, which I had read and reviewed earlier in my career (McCutcheon 1993), in which he commented about not replying to his own critics. As phrased by one of his more sympathetic commentators:

> Although he frequently attacked reductionistic approaches to myth and religion, Eliade felt little need to respond to reductionists and other critics of his history of religions… It would seem that he felt that almost all of his reductionist critics did not deserve the bother of a reply. (Allen 2002: 61, n. 29).

Or, as Eliade himself phrased it in the last year of his life, as recorded in the last of his four published volumes of journals,

15 September [1985]

From the articles which Ioan Culianu has dedicated to me, I understand that in recent years the "methodological" criticisms brought
against my conceptions of the history of religions have increased.
The fault is, in part, mine; I've never replied to such criticisms,
although I ought to have done so. I told myself that someday,
"when I'm free from works in progress," I'll write a short theoretical monograph and explain "confusions and errors" for which
I am reproached.

I'm afraid I'll never have time to write it. (Eliade 1990: 143)

This attitude[3] never struck me as the view of someone who understood
scholarship to be a collaboration between competing viewpoints and interests among equal parties, all engaged in the exercise of testing each other's
claims; instead, it seems the rather anti-scientific view of someone who
sees themselves as being above the fray, free of the petty rivalries that supposedly drive critique (for example, the sort of person who might name
those with whom he disagrees "dilettantes," as Eliade routinely did in
print).[4] Whether or not they liked what I said in reply, I would hope that
those to whom I replied at least understood that I never doubted that they
"deserve[d] the bother."

But in this particular case I recall coming to the point of simply wanting
the *The Discipline of Religion* to stand for itself—yes, I've read my share
of Roland Barthes and Michel Foucault on the death of the author, but I've
also shown up for enough invited talks at which the attendees made me feel
as if the wrong McCutcheon had shown up, inasmuch as the long departed
author of *Manufacturing Religion* was expected to be standing behind the
podium. Besides, what I took to be the most important critical comments in
the symposium, those of Robert Orsi (who was then the immediately past
President of the American Academy of Religion [in 2003], under whom the
AAR split from the Society of Biblical Literature [SBL]—if only for a time)
inspired an essay of their own, on which I soon began working (McCutcheon 2006a). That I am now introducing my own pieces written from back
then, flies in the face of what I was trying to accomplish in this reply, of
course. But who can resist the temptation to regroup and restate what you
had thought you'd already said in the first place once you've read what
others found in your writing, looking back on all of it as if with the omni-
science that time seems to lend? Not I, apparently.

A Few Words on the Temptation to Defend the Honor of a Text (2004)

Den Himmel überlassen wir
Den Engeln und den Spatzen

("We leave heaven to the angels and the sparrows")

- Heinrich Hein, "Deutschland" (1844), quoted by Sigmund Freud
in *The Future of an Illusion* (2012: 109)

First off, I wish to express my sincere thanks to Craig Prentiss for commissioning and publishing the four preceding review essays and for inviting my response to them. It is always humbling to find that one's labors have been taken seriously enough by one's peers to have been incorporated into their own work. I would therefore like to express my gratitude to the four participants—Henry Goldschmidt (2004), Bob Orsi (2004a), Carol Wayne White (2004; see also 2005), and Joanne Punzo Waghorne (2004)—for doing me the kindness of taking *The Discipline of Religion* (2003a) seriously enough to offer their criticisms and compliments. Of such things are discourses made.

Because I have had the good fortune to have had my own work, along with the work of all of my colleagues at the University of Alabama, appear in a recent issue of the *Bulletin*,[5] I believe that this reply ought to be kept as brief as possible, for fear of overstaying my welcome in the pages of this periodical. Of course I'd rather that brevity not prevent me from letting what I consider to be mischaracterizations of my position go unchallenged (for I saw a number of these that, lamentably, I have seen and addressed in print before). Neither do I wish to let readers put this collection of papers down if they have been convinced that I, or the position that I advocate—I admit that I am often not certain which are the focus of some of my critics—am condescending, contemptuous, willfully or naively ignorant of this or that, let alone puritanical (perhaps I have misread Goldschmidt, and failed to find in this a compliment[6]). It is therefore tempting to jump right into this reply for, as we saw in this year's US presidential campaign, without challenging them some claims need only be repeated a few times in order for them to become accepted as truisms.

Although brevity prevents me from offering such an itemized list of rebuttals, there is a reason other than brevity for practicing restraint. Having written and rewritten the essays that comprise the chapters in *The Discipline of Religion* while attempting to keep in mind that participant self-reports (such as, let's just say for argument's sake, the protestations of an author who feels misunderstood) carry no self-evident privilege when it comes to their public examination (as in what these four reviewers have done to the content of my text), and that wider structural contexts determine what gets to count as meaningful and thus significant content (two points to which White has drawn attention), I now find myself in the odd position of being tempted by the invitation to defend the meaning, intention, and implications of a text that, I admit, I certainly wish to call *my* text. But despite this presumed semantic propriety, this text is an unapologetically promiscuous thing, for it resides in a warehouse somewhere, ready to travel at a moment's notice, through the dark of night, into the hands of some stranger, all because of the merest click of a button at amazon.com.

I am therefore presented with a dilemma: defend the hopes and dreams of McCutcheon *qua* author, thereby undermining the book's theoretical position, or, since it long ago left the nest, let the text flap its own wings, and thereby risk leaving unchallenged some of the reviewers' comments.

Given the particular approach to the study of meaning systems that I use in my work (whether those systems be texts, self-disclosures, behaviors, or institutions), I have decided to cut the text loose and decline the kind invitation to offer a substantive reply, for I am not inclined to do battle over how one *ought* to have read it. I think here of how it seemed that Gary Ross, the director of the hit movie "*Seabiscuit*" (2003), virtually hit viewers over the head so that they would "get" the uncanny parallels between the spunky, come-from-behind horse and the spunky damaged-goods rider—I can only imagine the script: "Close-up: Seabiscuit's injured leg; close-up on Red Pollard's injured leg; return to the horse's bandaged leg; linger on the jockey limping toward the camera. Man drops crutches; man embraces horse. Cue the violins." If only reality led us, like this, by the nose to discover just what really gets to count as significant, or who, of all the human subjects that we as scholars study, gets to be asked for their permission before they come into focus in our studies. Aside: is Orsi *really* proposing this as a general methodological rule for the human sciences, or only for the study of those with whom we already agree?[7] For if the latter, then it is profoundly self-serving and if the former, then I can only imagine how he would study those who don't particularly want to sit inside the proverbial big tent and swap anecdotes. For we all know of quite a few human behaviors in which we would never entertain that the participants had a leg to stand on in advancing their self-reported perceptions in competition with the scholar's analysis. Yet why do some of my colleagues get so exercised about human subjects becoming data for the redescriptive scholar of religion? (I admit that, for some time, I have wondered which liberal humanist would get upset by my use of that particular four letter word.[8]) Why does Orsi get to characterize as "chilling" my effort to place all human behaviors on a par when it comes to studying them as socially formative actions working to reproduce conditions favorable to this or that group's interests (interests I may or may not share myself)? Is there something special about the people we study that we must tread so carefully to avoid stepping on their toes? If so, is it that the category "religion," defined in a very particular way, enables us to select out the easy cases of human behavior, like his example of a working class widower overcome by what Orsi seems to name as existential angst. Only a heartless fool, or so it is insinuated, would be bold enough to study this man in a manner different from how he perceives himself. But before waltzing in with our proclamation concerning how he feels, maybe we should linger a moment over the question: How *does* he perceive himself? Does he even have conscious self-perceptions? (Question: Are you, dear reader, now experiencing yourself as an early twenty-first century consumer of a commodity we call knowledge or, instead, are you just engrossed in the act of reading, with no care for its relation to the various other elements of your socio-historical world that, someone observing you read, might find of interest?) Or must the non-participant who, for whatever reason, finds this of all men significant, curious, anomalous, and thus worthy of focusing upon for a little while, coax his self-perceptions from him by means of questions he is not himself posing ("Sir, why are you crying?")? Given that the ethics card has been played, we might also inquire whether this hypothetical man wishes to have his apparent grief—should Orsi's description of the man's experiences be accurate, and how does one determine accuracy of such things when participants might not even be aware of the meanings of their own actions, as Frits Staal argued so long ago in his studies of Vedic ritual[9]—repackaged so offhandedly as a rhetorical trope in a piece of writing? (Note to self: scholars, all of whom live in glass houses despite their confidence in the ability to read the minds and feel the feelings of their subjects [past and present], should be careful how they throw around judgments about chilling reductionism.)

But wait; having re-read the words that I have just written, I see that I have succumbed to the temptation to pick up the glove and do battle over the honor of my text. So, having taken the required number of steps and, being ready to turn around and fire, let me stop and, instead of jousting over this or that issue of meaning (e.g., instead of me defending my reading of Foucault or replying that, because I was not intending to say that we all should model ourselves on the work of anthropologists, Willi Braun's term "anthropocentric" might have been at least one way of preventing the literal-minded reader from stumbling over "anthropologically-based"), I have decided to take away with me from this collection yet more evidence of just what might be at stake in how and why scholars of religion do what it is they have been trained to do. After all, I am merely proposing that all it is that we as scholars have to study are contestable historical (in Roland Barthes's sense of History, that is) behaviors—whether we happen to agree with them or not (i.e., whether they do or do not advance our particular group's interests). As for whether there is indeed more things in heaven and earth than we have dreamt of,[10] all I can say in reply is "Who knows?" Or better yet, "Who gets to know?" It is a serious question, of course—serious, if for no other reason, because there are so many people who proclaim to know the answer. The only trouble, of course, is that this surplus of answers must be read in light of the fact that they conflict so greatly that people are willing to kill to settle the dispute—in order to limit who gets to know. (Note to self: "our" soldiers who enlist are making no less a claim than the so-called fanatics, since all are, apparently, saying that they are willing to pay with their lives for the right to force others to live in this or that manner.) So I leave to others the celestial part of Shakespeare's equation and hope that our earthy studies will shed some light on why we invest so greatly in discourses on the heavens.

So, having had the good fortune to have been able to publicize my views on both the study of religion and "religion" by means of the text under consideration here, and having played a part in helping to provoke this exchange—thereby giving another spin to the wheel we call our discourse—the best I find myself able to do in reply is to state my hope that readers of the preceding essays will see enough difference between the characterizations of my work—whether positive or negative, for I fully realize that each contributor finds both diamonds (or at least some sparkly cubic zirconium crystals) and stones in my work—to be curious enough to read a chapter or two for themselves. Then, they might be able to apply its thesis to beliefs, behaviors, and institutions of which they are familiar, and arrive at their own conclusion concerning whether the approach proposed in its pages sheds any worthwhile light on that interesting collection of human doings we call the discipline of religion.

Notes

1. Quoted from an online interview with Smith, available at http://chicagomaroon.com/2008/06/02/full-j-z-smith-interview/; accessed February 24, 2013.
2. The first poke back of any consequence was when Paul Griffiths minimized my critique by likening me to an irritating little dog that had learned a new trick. If I had not already included my reply (1998d) to Griffiths and June

O'Connor, who both wrote responses to my article "A Default of Critical Intelligence? The Scholar of Religion as Public Intellectual" (1997a), in *Critics Not Caretakers*, I would have included it in this collection.

3.   Ed. Note: for example, from a journal entry dated January 8, 1979: "..., for many years now I haven't read what is written about me" (Eliade 1990: 3).

4.   February 10, 1981: "Ordinarily I don't read many articles about myself..., but in the ones I have read, I've never seen anyone bringing out this fact: that I am an author *without a model*. I resemble, or want to resemble, [the Romanian writer, Bogdan Petriceicu] Hasdeu [1838–1907], [the Moldavian Prince and writer, Dimitrie] Cantemir [1673–1723], and [the Johann Wolfgang von] Goethe [1749–1832]. But look very closely at our writings and ideas, our beliefs and *lives*: which of my great predecessors, indeed, has constituted for me a model? Their example gave me courage, that's all" (Eliade 1990: 41). Perhaps one would expect no less a disclosure from a scholar who repeatedly argued that his academic specialty would bring about a world-wide Renaissance of transcendental human values.

5.   Ed. Note: in issue 33/2 (2004) members of the faculty in my Department replied to Professor Martin Jaffee's inaugural Aronov Lecture, which was also printed in the same issue of the *Bulletin*. The annual lectureship, begun in 2002–2003, and named after the Department endowment in Judaic Studies, has since then brought eleven additional scholars to campus, among whom has been Jonathan Z. Smith, Arjun Appadurai, Tomoko Mazusawa, Aaron Hughes, Ann Pelligrini, and Cary Nelson. See McCutcheon (2004a) for a brief history of this Department on the occasion of its faculty publishing replies to Jaffee's inaugural lecture.

6.   Ed. Note: Goldschmidt: "[W]hile I share McCutcheon's fundamental goal of developing a richer social analysis of religion, I am entirely uninterested in his puritanical effort to set 'legitimate' forms of social analysis apart from their religious others."

7.   Ed. Note: Orsi:

> Men and women, in other words, theologians and others, who do not share McCutcheon's epistemological assumptions, his "naturalism" as he calls it, become susceptible or vulnerable to theorization, which thus takes on the qualities both of something deserved, a punishment or chastisement, and of an action performed on unwilling subjects. These subjects—and here the word means exactly that—are in need of theorization, McCutcheon says; they are to be subjected to theory. But who has determined this need? From what authoritative and normative vantage point (or political or intellectual imperatives) is this need identified? The dismissive "one more group in need of..." is chilling: nowhere—absolutely nowhere—in this volume is any reference made to the moral requirement of obtaining the consent of those upon whom this theoretical action is to be performed (even theologians). Rather, the assumption appears to be that the scholar of religion by virtue of his

or her normative epistemology, theoretical acuity, and political know-
ingness, has the authority and the right to make the lives of others the
objects of his or her scrutiny. He or she theorizes them.

8.   Ed. Note: Orsi:

> ...a devout working class man who kneels to pray at his wife's grave,
> suddenly uncertain and afraid at the end of his own life of what lies
> ahead, has attained the status of data; he has become a fit candidate
> for theorization. A suburban Pentecostal woman speaking in tongues,
> an Orthodox family preparing for high holy days, a Mexican migrant
> imploring Guadalupe for a healing, a pilgrim to the shrine of the imprint
> of Krishna's foot: these are our specimens, their words "*heuristically
> useful, everyday rhetorical fictions.*" Do the theorized have any voice
> to speak back to the italicizing theorizer? Can they challenge the asser-
> tion that they are in need of theorization or this construal of their lives?
> Can they protest being made into a theoretician's "fair game"? If they
> do, McCutcheon never says so, which is a serious omission: the data
> remain silent, as one might expect of data. A book that sets out to call
> attention to the dynamics of power/knowledge in the study of religion
> winds up proposing the most egregious exercise of power as the disci-
> plines' fundamental work. And once again, religious studies can't look
> its subject in the eyes. I used to think that John Milbank's critique of
> the discipline as the work of an elite studying "them" to be unfair and
> tendentious. Reading McCutcheon, I'm not so sure...

> We do not study data in need of theorizing but people at work on their
> worlds in the full and tragic necessity of their circumstances, in the
> present or in the past, and we do not need to posit an arrogant Western
> universalism or an aggrandizing belief in human nature to recognize
> that their lives are not alien to ours.

I admit that I found Orsi's moralizing charge curious (and I drew attention to
this in my published essay which used his review as an entry point into methodological issues in his own work [McCutcheon 2006a]), for both Jonathan
Z. Smith and Bruce Lincoln routinely use the word "data" when describing
the things that they, as scholars, work on but I do not recall either of their
writings—which are far more prominent than my own—ever receiving such
spirited criticisms from Orsi.

9.   Ed. Note: I have in mind here Staal's "The Meaninglessness of Ritual"
(1979; see McCutcheon 2001a: 209–10), in which he argued that ritual only
acquires meaning later (inasmuch as some action is said to correspond to
some doctrine or belief), when reflected upon in hindsight, and that, in the
actual doing of a ritual, the participant does not have meanings in his or her
head but, rather, is better understood as simply following rules and aiming
for propriety. Ritual, then, is better understood as a purely rule governed

behavior. Recalling (though, admittedly, with the benefit of hindsight—and therein lies the problem!) myself as a ring bearer for my oldest sister's wedding, when I was only seven years old, adds persuasive force to Staal's approach to ritual: the event had, best as I can remember, no meaning to me but was, instead, merely an occasion to worry about standing, sitting, turning, etc., at the correct time—performance and propriety, not interpretation and meaning, were the issues from a participant point of view. In fact, I still clearly remember my soon-to-be brother-in-law's own younger brother, who was a little older and thus taller than me, standing behind me, holding my shoulders, and turning me at the appropriate times.

10.   Ed. Note: this wording appeared, two years later, in one of Orsi's book titles: *Between Heaven and Earth: The Religious Worlds People Make and the Scholars Who Study Them* (2006).

Chapter 10

Introduction

The following chapter was written in response to a reply Robert Segal wrote (2005) to an article of mine that was published in *JAAR* (2004b). The essay that began this exchange, "Religion, Ire, and Dangerous Things"—which was a revised version of as a chapter that appeared in *The Discipline of Religion* (2003a: ch. 11)—was an answer to Ivan Strenski's various critiques of, as he phrased it, the "naïveté, bad faith, or ignorant mischief" (1998: 118) of those who, like myself, study the category "religion" itself. The gist of my article was to ask why the category "myth" could be so rigorously historicized, as Strenski himself had done so nicely in his own earlier book (1987), yet an equally thorough-going historicization of yet another (as he terms it) cultural *a priori* (i.e., the category "religion") would, as Strenski himself wrote, "be a disaster for the study of religion" (1998: 118). Why the double standard?

Although Strenski—whose earlier work on the politics of Eliade's theory of myth was very influential of my own thinking while a doctoral student—did not respond, his longtime co-editor at the journal *Religion*, Robert Segal—a scholar whose earlier work in favor of reductionism in the study of religion also influenced me during my doctoral studies—did respond. What I took away from Segal's reply was that, as he phrased it in his closing line, "the irrefutable demonstration of the ideological *use* of the category religion would not invalidate the category itself" (2005: 212–13).

It seemed to me at the time, and still does, that this back-and-forth, first with Strenski and then with Segal, nicely demonstrates two things: changes in my thinking over the past twenty years and the role played by the category "religion" in modern liberal democracies. I'll address each in order.

I'm lucky enough to have published a first book that, for whatever number of reasons, is still being read and used. One group that has made good use of it is the cognitivists in our field—those scholars of religion, anthropologists, sociologists, and so on, who apply findings from evolutionary biology and the broad field known now as the cognitive sciences to the study of ritual, religion, and so on, in hopes of developing a general theory of religion as an entirely natural acquisition of the human species (e.g., most recently, McCauley 2011). Although I've been critical recently of the optimism with which some of these scholars pursue their studies, inasmuch as I think they fail to recognize the historically constituted nature of the categories that they use to name seemingly stable and universal realities in all people's brains and genes (e.g., McCutcheon 2010), it is clear that my earlier work critiquing the theological/humanistic approach to the study of religion has been very useful in helping some of them to establish a rhetorical space to conduct their own work. That is, the arguments and conclusions of *Manufacturing Religion* are often cited, early on in many of their books, as being among the warrants for leaving behind one model for how to study religion, thereby helping to open the way for their naturalistic approach. Of course, this divide between a theological and a "truly" scientific approach once characterized by own work, back when scholars such as Strenski and Segal were also very influential of my thinking (especially Segal's always impassioned and well argued defenses of reductionism—that dirty word for any Eliadean—despite the fact that their own studies reduce participant self-disclosures as much as anyone's work; after all, people the world over do not seem to report the Sacred being a structure of their consciousness). But since becoming more interested in *any* use of the category to name a distinct zone of human conduct—whether used by a theologian or humanist as a source for appreciation and emulation, or a social scientist or evolutionary biologist to name a peculiar disposition in need of explanation—I find that the citations in such literature suggest that McCutcheon has not really published anything much since 1997.

That this change in my thinking—one that often makes me the think back to points on which I was pressed early in my career by Arnal and Masuzawa—seems not to discourage people from reading my earlier work in a bit of a vacuum illustrates not just the way readers conjure the authors of their pleasing into existence but also the second point mentioned above: the role played by the category "religion" in modern liberal democracies. For my later work has persuaded me that it is entirely in people's best interest *not* to take the historicity of the category religion seriously but, instead, to conceive of it as separate from (as Segal does) its various *uses*, as if there are better and worse ways of defining it, inasmuch as it seems widely known that there is some real referent in the world to which the category properly (i.e., inevitably, necessarily, etc.) applies. I say this because using the category as if it names an obvious set of items in the world, set apart in some regard from other parts of the world and all more or less sharing the same set of distinct properties (i.e., Wittgenstein's family resemblance approach to definition has won out in most cases, and which most scholars use to determine what gets to count as religion), seems to me to be linked to reproducing an interconnected set of basic elements that help people to make possible their taken-for-granted social worlds. For to call the common usage of the category into question—that is, asking "Just why do we name certain parts of the world 'religion' or 'religious'?" or "Why do we assume that 'believing in God' is somehow different from 'believing in an infinite universe,' 'believing in the free market,' or 'believing oneself to have an identity' or a 'self'?"—also means calling into question a host of other practices connected to the category, such as our commonsense distinctions (and generally prioritizing) of: beliefs over practices, individuals over groups, experiences over expressions, origins over derivations, authors over readers, meanings over interpretations, and intentions over effects. To rephrase: the category religion and how we employ it now strikes me as the tip of a particular iceberg that we call liberal democracies—a particular sort of modern social arrangement that, when coupled with so-called free market capitalism, seems at present to be the only large scale social grouping that, at least for the foreseeable future, can sustain itself (i.e., so long as yet untapped, overseas raw materials last). *Believing* that the group is merely a fiction of prior, distinct individuals' (i.e., citizens) rational consent to Rousseauian social contracts with each other, *believing* that these individuals' public actions are driven by their prior, interior states (i.e., beliefs, experiences, feelings), *believing* that a close reading of an artifact can bring to mind the intentions and meanings that motivated its long departed creator, and thus *believing* that there is an unbroken connection between the present and the immutable, authoritative past (i.e., heritage or tradition—the thing that much modern history writing sets out merely to chronicle, thereby authorizing the presumed linear causality of the past on the present) are among the conditions that, I argue, make such large scale groupings and thus identities seem persuasive to us. Although we see the discrete elements of this collective *imaginaire* all throughout social life (from how we read the most mundane of texts to how we conceptualize ourselves in relation to our family and relatives), the grouping together of these—recalling Strenski's term—various cultural *a priori* goes by the name "religion."

To historicize our propensity to believe and act as if, for example, the apolitical individual-as-free-radical is the lone experiential seat of all social life, therefore calls too much of our worlds into question and thus hits a little too close to home—making such scholarship not (as Strenksi concluded) a disaster for the study of religion but, instead, a danger for the otherwise smooth running of the liberal democratic nation-state, perhaps. Perhaps that also helps to explain why the rationalists among us—who I don't think really have a good answer to why, for example, the law of non-contradiction *ought* to apply other than that they can accomplish certain things of importance to them when it does—are quite comfortable historicizing other people's old tales that we know as myths, as well as the very category myth as well, but balk at doing the same to the category religion, even if they say they don't believe in it. For their very ability to conceptualize themselves as freely believing, rationally-choosing agents may itself be at risk should they go down that road.

Theorizing the Politics of "Religion": Rejoinder to Robert A. Segal (2005)

I appreciate both Robert Segal's interest in further clarifying some of the issues involved with critiques of such classifications as "religion" and "myth" as well as the interest of *JAAR*'s editors in facilitating this brand of scholarship by publishing our brief exchange.

I find Segal's three bases upon which one can critique categories to be useful,[1] though I am unsure why critics must defend themselves while scholars who use a term such as "world religions" are not required to justify their continued use of this antiquated concept (e.g., see Masuzawa 2005a and 2005b; McCutcheon 2005b). I'm sure Segal would agree that just because the people we study use a term in their acts of self-definition and self-description does not mean that it ought to enter the halls of academia as an analytic taxon that is presumed to have some deep resonance with all people's motivations and experiences. As demonstrated so nicely by Robert Darnton (2003: 166), dangers lurk when scholars parrot participant self-descriptions. So, apart from the fact that certain human populations have variously used "religion" to name aspects of their lives, why do we continue to employ it in our studies of them and others?

With this question in mind, I should say that I appreciate the fact that Segal correctly understands my work to avoid criticizing "religion" simply because many of the people we study do not possess the word/concept (as an aside, divorcing word from concept is a common strategy among theological critics intent on jettisoning "religion" to make room for the supposedly more real, inner thing, faith). Just because people the world over do not talk about "cultures," "economies," "genders," or "deoxyribonucleic acid" scholars are by no means prevented from using these analytic concepts to carry out their work. But, recognizing that "religion" is peculiar to a relatively small group of language users will hopefully prompt scholars to be a little more timid in claiming that their words/concepts enable them to peer into the deep recesses of the human heart. As Daniel Dubuisson (2003: 101) notes, we would not look kindly on scholars telling us that, whether we happen to know it or not, we all have dharmic experiences. So it strikes me as reasonable to inquire as to what it is about our Latin-derived "religion" that makes us—people who inhabit a no less historically entrenched world than Dubuisson's hypothetical Indian scholars—think that our words and ideas carry ontological privilege. Why is it that, as I was recently told rather emphatically at a conference, the ancient Arabic term *dīn* not only *means* religion but has always *meant* religion? (For elaboration on this example, see McCutcheon 2006b).[2]

Segal is therefore correct to conclude that it is the function commonly played by "religion"—along with the attendant split between faith and practice, private and public, experience and expression—that prompts me to see the term as being suspect when used by scholars trying to explain events in the world. That some of the people we study use this term in their efforts to describe and account for their own worlds is obvious. That our accurate descriptions (i.e., accurate insomuch as they work to avoid what Wayne Proudfoot [1985] once termed descriptive reductionism) will have to rely on a whole series of indigenous taxonomies is equally obvious. As I have suggested elsewhere, if the members of Heaven's Gate say that they have a seed that outlives their physical body, then we had better talk about their seeds when describing the group, and not their soul, jiva, or atman.[3] But, as Proudfoot also noted (and I am certain that Segal agrees with this as well), explanatory reduction is inevitable since (and here I am once again borrowing from Jonathan Z. Smith), scholarship ought to be something other than ventriloquism; it therefore requires the translation of one set of claims about the world into another language—in our case, the meta-language of the academy.

But it is a particular sort of academy in which many of us toil—one funded by a diverse citizenry and one in which it is presumed that the human data we study is, without remainder, but one element of the happenstance world of conditioned, historical events. Accordingly, the technical language into which we translate the self-descriptions of the people we study is a language that is recognized by its users to be tactical, problem-oriented, theory-based, and never in sync with some posited Reality or so-called Big Picture. In a word, it is thoroughly historical (i.e., contingent). I say "many of us" because, as with most journals in the study of religion, *JAAR* attempts to represent the interests of groups who, in my experience, not only occupy different discursive/institutional settings but, as a result, ask entirely different, sometimes contradictory, questions. Case in point, I hazard a guess that few of my readers would agree that, as scholars, all we have are tools devised in the historical world by means of which we study events in the historical world in order to satisfy curiosities specific to just our historical world. Instead, many would fight to retain some sort of enduring meaningfulness and significance to these games we play, calling it either the search for meaning, intention, truth, human nature, objectivity, what have you.

It is precisely this institutional requirement—that our discourse on the contingent be equally contingent (to paraphrase Theses 2 and 3 of Bruce Lincoln's "Theses on Method" [1996])—that the category religion, when elevated beyond mere description of how some people classify aspects of their lives, allows many of our colleagues to evade. So, despite accurately identifying my interest in the political (i.e., how power and privilege are allocated and negotiated), Segal is not entirely correct to suggest that my interests are not primarily theoretical. For my critique of "religion" is based on the position that theory is a human activity that is accomplished by means of rules that *we* have established (e.g., the three criteria proposed by Segal). "Religion" is ingeniously used by people from all across the political divide to create a zone that is somehow thought to be free of this history and thereby bears none of our traces (i.e., free of interests, power, conflict, etc.)—in my assessment, this is simply poor theory.

Case in point, consider the now well-known phrase, "the politicization of Islam." Behind this phrase is the presumption that certain mass movements (the ones we call religions) are normally, naturally, originally, ideally—whichever—something *other than* political and that their metamorphosis into a practical social force is therefore some sort of secondary step to be lamented, celebrated, chronicled, corrected, explained—whichever. But if a founding theoretical tenet of the human sciences is that both its methods and objects of study are historical products, from where does this pre-political or apolitical zone arise, the one occupied by what I presume we should call non- or pre-politicized Islam?[4] If, instead, we presume that both our tools and our data are part of the irreducibly historical world, then "politicized religion" is redundant, for there no longer remains any sense to the notion of an apolitical (a.k.a. spiritual) sphere comprised merely of disembodied faith. But if we yet harbor the hope that something escapes history— call it soul, meaning, value, human nature, whatever—then encouraging, lamenting, or simply trying to explain the active involvement of the things we call religions in the political sphere will make a lot of sense. However, for those committed to the theoretical position that all we have is history, all the way down (once again to borrow a phrase from Smith), this will make no sense whatsoever; moreover, scholars of this latter group may well attempt to call into question the means whereby the seemingly pre-political or apolitical zone is fabricated in the first place and the ways in which it is used (for elaboration on this, see McCutcheon 2005c).

Which brings me to an early July 2004 newscast of the local NBC television affiliate in Iowa City, KWWL, in which it was reported that a Des Moines-based chain of movie theaters, Fridley Theaters, refused to show Michael Moore's film, "Fahrenheit 9-11." According to the owner of the theaters, R. L. Fridley, Moore's movie emboldens terrorists and divides the country. In the words of the news anchor, the issue revolves around whether the film constitutes "political propaganda" or "free speech." Much like "the politicization of Islam," this handy distinction presupposes that human beings can sometimes float outside their choices, contests, costs, and conflicts. The distinction is a bold power move, one that nicely accomplishes the marginalization of dissent that, in someone's opinion, goes just a little too far (either to the left or right—you pick).

When not redescribed in a thoroughly historical language, claims concerning things commonly called religion, religions, religious experiences, religious motivations, religious traditions, religious rituals, and so on, are part of the same power move insomuch as they posit a site removed from history and public contest, one that periodically, or under certain circumstances, interacts in varying ways with history. This ought to make such categories, along with the presumptions and interests that drive their use, theoretically suspect for those who call themselves scholars in the human sciences.

Notes

1.   Ed. Note: according to Segal, the three bases upon which categories are commonly critiqued are: 1. "the invocation of the practitioner" (i.e., if the category is an indigenous one—say "mana"—then it is argued to be unsuited for scholarship); 2. "the invocation of its origin" (i.e., identifying the historical specificity of a concept—say the ancient Latin "paganus," a perjorative term for rural villagers, from which we derive "pagan"—thereby disallowing it from being universalized); and 3. "the invocation of its function" (i.e., demonstrating the flawed nature of categories by identifying the function they serve—such as arguing that because "terrorist" normalized only one sense of legitimate authority it is therefore ill-suited for analytic useage). This last is my "favorite," he concludes (see Segal 2005: 211).

2.   Ed. Note: see McCutcheon 2005c: 38–40 for elaboration on the Arabic term *dīn*.

3.   Ed. Note: see McCutcheon 2003a: 104ff. for a discussion of scholarship on this group.

4.   My choice of Islam as an example is based on the spate of authors currently falling over themselves to console the reading public by explaining how good piety goes bad; that I could make the same case for commentaries on each of the so-called world religions is, hopefully, obvious.

Chapter 11

Introduction

The chapter that follows was a response to a panel that took place at the American Academy of Religion in the Fall of 2003 (held in Atlanta, Georgia), which, along with the papers from the session (as well as a few additional essays that were commissioned after the conference), were all published in *Religious Studies Review* 31/1 and 31/2 (2005).[1] At the panel itself I simply acted as the chair—a largely ceremonial role, really—but was invited to write a reply to be published with the panel's papers. The conflict that I saw, during the panel itself, between those who wanted to problematize the world religions category, on the one hand, and those who just wanted to keep expanding it to include more and more (as has happened ever since it was first devised in the late-nineteenth century, back when, at least for one of the founders of our field, the Dutch scholar Cornelis Tiele [1830–1902], only Christianity and Buddhism counted as *Weltreligionen*, or "universal religions" [see Mazusawa 2005a: 109ff.]), on the other, prompted me to accept the invitation to write this reply.

Although my earliest experience as a Teaching Assistant (TA) was working with William Arnal as TAs for Michel Desjardins's introduction to the New Testament, a night course at the University of Toronto, the course that I TAed for the most was in the following years: the introduction to world religions that was team taught by Will Oxtoby (d. 2003) and Joe O'Connell (d. 2012). Several TAs ran tutorial sections (i.e., discussion sections) either before or after the lecture, during which we generally repeated the lecture or debriefed students on it, since it was a very large lecture course and, as is the case in such large enrollment sections, especially before the technological aides that we take for granted today, many students tended to get a little lost in the material. I presume that this course was the bread and butter course for the Department, as the saying goes, and I recall seeking a position as a TA in it because of advice given to me by my friend, who began at the Centre for Religious Studies at the same time, Bruce MacKay (Bruce began his PhD when I began my one-year MA, so that landed us in the same method and theory class which served as a common basis for students in that cross-disciplinary program, who ended up taking all of their other courses all across the university).[2] Whatever your specialty, as I recall him saying to me one day on the fourteenth floor of Robarts Library, where the Centre was then located, they'll always need people to teach a world religions class—so make sure you know how to do it. Bruce, who obtained a contract position at the University of Lethbridge as soon as he had written his comprehensive exams (and where he has stayed for his career), seemed to know what he was talking about; given that, at the time, I was increasingly being drawn to studying scholars of religion rather than religion itself, his advice made even more sense to me, for while I reasoned that no one would probably employ me to teach what I ended up writing on they might employ me to teach something like a world religions class. As it turned out, this was probably one of the best pieces of advice I ever received—nicely demonstrating that professionalization happens in all sorts of unexpected and informal ways, often peer-to-peer.

My first job, a one year (i.e., Fall and Spring semester) position, in 1993–94, as an Instructor at the University of Tennessee at Knoxville—requiring me to obtain a J1 work visa in the US because I am a Canadian citizen—found me teaching multiple sections of a world religions course each semester and throughout the summers as well (to help make ends meet, given the low salary of an Instructor), where I relied heavily on my notes from my days TAing the Oxtoby/O'Connell class. I used those same notes as well as various handouts that I later created when teaching a world religions course at Southwest Missouri State University three years later, when my first tenure track job started, and where I (along with Jack Llewellyn) also taught the world religions course. During that time I experimented with a variety of textbooks; for example, in the Fall semester of 1995 (and yes, I still have all those files on my computer), teaching RELST 101 in Knoxville, I used the sixth edition of the late Lewis Hopfe's *Religions of the World* (1994—in its twelfth edition as of 2011), the second edition of Roger Eastman's collection of primary source readings, *The Ways of Religion: An Introduction to the Major Traditions* (1993), along with John R. Hinnells's *The Penguin Dictionary of Religions* (1984). As I remember it, after looking at many of the textbooks then available I opted for Hopfe's inasmuch as it had an opening discussion on the definition and theories of religion, which struck me as a necessary element to any course, and I included readings from Eastman's anthology so that students read more than just scholars commenting on things; although, looking back, I'm not sure what emphasis I placed on the supposed immediacy of so-called primary sources, it certainly did strike me as important that, at least in translation, students get some sense of the things the textbook was discussing. And I can't count the number of times that I used Hinnells's dictionary as a recommended text (in fact, for a few years I just used Jonathan Z. Smith's dictionary [1995a] as the only textbook in the course, given its mix of substantive articles and short entries), under the assumption that students needed a handy guide to the technical terms that a course such as this kept heaping onto them.

But during my three years as an Instructor I also taught sections of the Department's alternative, thematic introductory course (RELST 102), along with an upper-level undergraduate course on myth and ritual—the latter class, given my interests and lack of background in the straightforward study of myths and rituals, soon turned into a course on *theories* of myth and ritual. My frustrations with the manner in which the world religions textbooks presented the globe as if it were nicely divisible into a variety of discrete –isms, all based on various things that people did or did not *believe*, was likely influenced not just by simultaneously teaching the course on theories of myth and ritual (a course that asked students to think about the intellectual preconditions to being able to talk about myths and rituals, to being able to distinguish, say, a habit from a ritual) but also by my experience of repackaging the data of religion in an entirely different way for an alternative introductory course, so that the material could serve different pedagogical goals. For instance, in RELST 102, which I also taught in the Fall 1995 semester, I used the following books: Plato's *The Last Days of Socrates* (1993), so that we could read the "Euthyphro" and thereby focus on the complexity of definition; William Paden's, *Religious Worlds* (1992), to structure the course by means of his thematic chapters (e.g., myth, ritual, gods, etc.); John Lyden's anthology, *Enduring Issues in Religion* (1995), for nicely juxtaposed readings from a variety of scholars and theologians; and, as a case study in different ways to approach the study of religion, students were asked to compare Sigmund Freud's *The Future of an Illusion* (1989) and Carl Jung's *Psychology and Religion* (1966) in a final essay. While I now think that the final paired readings were likely overly ambitious for this course—aside: I find that the longer I teach the more skill I gain at starting with increasingly simple (but never simplistic!), seemingly commonsense items (such as the brief but wonderfully useful Nix. v. Hedden US Supreme Court decision [149 US 304 (1893)] on whether tomatoes are fruits or vegetables—and yes, taxation on imported vegetables was the issue!) and then working to the more complex; looking at the introductory course that I now teach (in one form or another, I have taught some version of this course consistently for twenty tears), I see how these two earlier 100-level classes were eventually joined together and, over time, the world religions component was completely subsumed, inasmuch as my course now is completely devoted to the problem of defining an object of study, using an example here and there to illustrate the various problems of definition—though naming Mount Everest is as likely to be an example as Hinduism (see McCutcheon

2007, for example, for the manner in which I think an introductory course ought to be organized).

So, despite that Southwest Missouri Department's desire for me to continue to teach its world religion's class, sometime after 1996 my syllabi began changing, increasingly using the so-called data as but examples of issues we discussed that were of interest to us, making the so-called facts serve our curiosities (i.e., with our interests determining what would get to count as something worth talking about), as I might now phrase it, rather than seeing the data as self-evidently interesting and thus requiring description. And thus the increasing influence on me of Jonathan Z. Smith's various writings became more and more apparent over this time. That the Department I was hired to Chair in 2001, at the University of Alabama, has only now, in 2013, had a world religions course developed is just as much evidence of my utter suspicion of the genre as it is my confidence in my colleague, Steven Ramey, and the manner in which he simultaneously introduces and problematizes that traditional material, all in one lower-level undergraduate course that aims to do far more than just teach the names of rivers and holidays.

The Perils of Having One's Cake and Eating it Too: Some Thoughts in Response (2005)

> The impossibility of penetrating the divine scheme of the universe cannot, however, dissuade us from planning human schemes, even though it is clear that they are provisional. (Borges 1999: 231)

At the close of last Fall's [Ed. Note: 2003] "Religion/s Between Covers: Dilemmas of the World Religions Textbook" panel, the participants were a little conflicted, for they were evenly divided between those who thought that world religions textbooks were, on the whole, sadly truncated insomuch as women, Africans, and South East Asians were under-represented and those who recommended that we jettison the category altogether—or at least scrap some of its constitutive parts, such as "Shinto," the catchalls "Archaic" and "Primal Religions," and possibly even "religion" itself. Somewhat ironically, then, the dilemma of the panel's title had to do with the world religions genre and genus being judged to be both too restrict*ed* and too restrict*ing*. Apparently we need both more *and* less in our textbooks; either they will need to grow fatter or their readers will need to quit making trips to the world religions buffet.

While not wishing to diminish the importance of noting both the gaps in our teaching resources and the possible reasons for these gaps, I wish merely to point out that, no matter how comprehensive our schemes, gaps will inevitably remain, for—and here, I am merely paraphrasing Jonathan Z. Smith—not everything gets to count as significant and tough choices must be made. I draw attention to this because, from where I sat during the panel, those recommending including more material did not seem to be entertaining the criteria and therefore the limits of inclusion, that is, the price they were willing to pay for this inclusion. Certainly, that the principle of selection which once determined the use of the world religions category had much to do with issues of colonial politics and perceived Christian superiority is evident; with the work of Smith in mind (e.g., 1996: 394–401; 1998), and we can now add to this Daniel Dubuisson (2003), as well as the work of Tomoko Masuzawa (2005a; 2005b), it is not difficult to map the expansion of such early nineteenth-century categories "religions" and "world religions" alongside the geographic movement of European nations across the globe, fueled by second sons in search of fame and glory. For, as Smith aptly put it, "[t]he question of the 'religions' arose in response to an explosion of data" (1998: 275)—explosions that had everything to do not only with armies but also those reconnaissance workers we euphemistically call missionaries and explorers. It should therefore not surprise us that, for instance, soon after the British annexation of Bengal (the year after its victory at the battle of Buxar in 1764) we see not only the British winning the right to collect taxes in the region but also increased intellectual labors expended on understanding those who worshiped "the Boudha," as he was called by early writers. It was only a matter of time before imperial systems seeking to rule new groups of people, systems whose administrators were on the hunt for locals with whom they could work and who might share some of their interests, led to new religions being added to the ever-growing list. And the rest is history.

But if we are no longer willing to accept the price entailed by the principle of selection implicitly used by our predecessors, we must still come up with an alternative; since there is no "cost-less method, the cost-less theory" (as Jonathan Z. Smith has observed [2007: 77]), I'm not convinced that, when it comes to the world religions banquet, the no doubt well-meant "come one come all" invitation does the trick. For, just as similarity presupposes difference, so too inclusion entails exclusion, such that not everyone will fit into the big tent. So, despite the hopes of those who advocate a more expansive use of the category, the criteria whereby we choose are just *our* criteria and, as ours, they inevitably reproduce *our* interests (as do all taxonomies). Since our interests are more than likely not universal, then if pressed we might have to admit that we probably don't want everyone in our tent, playing with our toys. For example, those aspects of global culture that are currently judged to threaten the particular sort of social world that we liberal democrats take for granted will, more then likely, *not* be admitted to the menu of "the faithful" that are surveyed either in a descriptively objective or sympathetic manner in our textbooks. Despite many of us lamenting the way "civilization" was once used to do some of the dirty work of colonialist social formation, we now seem to have little difficulty using "civility" to distinguish between peaceful and tolerant religious people (who, because they pursue the life of the spirit, make their way into our textbooks) and those who have the poor manners to act out their supposedly deep beliefs (whom we relegate to the spheres known as "cult," "fanatic," "militant," and "fundamentalist"—qualifying members of such groups for an entirely different genre of book [e.g., Jurgensmeyer 2000; Kimball 2002; Krakauer 2003; and Stern 2003]).

But what of the tolerant faithful who get their fifteen minutes of fame in our textbooks? Taking seriously that we have no choice but to make choices, it makes sense that regardless how inclusive we aim to be there will always remain a remnant of the miscellany that was once grouped together under "Idolaters," "Pagans," "Heathens, or "National Religions." Much like ending your acceptance speech by acknowledging a debt not only to "the members of the academy" but deflecting credit onto the universe as a whole (i.e., thanking its creator) and thereby tipping your hat symbolically to those you forgot to mention by name because they fell beneath your radar screen, categories such as "Archaic" and "Primal" are a way of including those left out in the cold by dropping them into the expansive "other" category. But this honorific inclusion entails a pretty effective exclusion, as nicely demonstrated in a 1992 episode of "The Simpsons" in which Reverend Lovejoy, speaking to Homer, described his inclusivist vision of God as "working in the hearts of your friends and neighbors when they came to your aid, be they Christian, Jew, or...miscellaneous." To which Apu, the owner of Springfield's Quickie Mart, and resident "Other," replies, "Hindu! There are 700 million of us."

So, despite our best-intended inclusivist tendencies, every well functioning taxonomy will have to have a marginal place for the *et cetera*—if for no other reason than the fact that no classification system is sufficient, no matter how many compounded hyphens one uses to give a name to, say, one's ethnic identity on the federal census.[3] To borrow some words from Jorge Luis Borges's, we could say that, despite our complaints, the "ambiguities, redundancies, and deficiencies" in the world religions' textbook are therefore par for the course, for "obviously there is no classification of the universe that is not arbitrary and speculative. The reason for this is quite simple: we do not know what the universe is" (1999: 231). So he wrote near the close of his 1942 essay, "John Wilkins' Analytical Language." The ambiguities, redundancies, and deficiencies of the textbooks in question—a genre that generally promises far more than any classification can reasonably deliver since it claims to represent humanity at its most human(e) and thus authentic—are reminiscent of the perplexing structure of *The Celestial Emporium of Benevolent Knowledge*, that "certain Chinese encyclopedia" that Borges cites in his essay. This is none other than the fanciful book whose taxonomy of animals, as we read in the opening lines to his *The Archeology of Knowledge*,[4] prompted Michel Foucault to recall how it had "shattered all the familiar landmarks of my thought." The list—much like Oscar winners who try to name everyone from their piano teacher to their agent and God—stands out as memorable because of the sheer audacity of its ambition to be all encompassing, total, and thus final. Since everything is supposedly included, there has been no cost paid for the choices entailed by scheme. In this case, the map *is* the territory, which does nothing other than make either the map or the territory redundant.[5]

The problem here is that common problem of trying to have one's cake and eating it too: of making a selection without paying the price of exclusion (as in the "pluralistic etiquette," to borrow a phrase from Smith [1998: 280], that prompts scholars to provide an honorary yet marginal place for "other" in their systems). I suspect that something like this is operating when once dominant classification systems are judged by modern scholars as inadequate—a criticism that is generally premised on the antiquated nature of previous classification systems—only so that their own system can be sold as definitive and thus final, rather than provisional and the product of their own historically situated preferences, interests, and conjectures. It is the problem of recognizing and ignoring history *at the same time*, something the world religions genre is notorious for doing. After all, whether chronicling development within one tradition (e.g., the history of Judaism) or juxtaposing contemporaneous, cross-cultural instances of behavior (e.g., ritual in comparative perspective), the contingency of time and place is tamed by means of the presumed presence, that is, the things we group together as Judaism are presumed to comprise a timeless "tradition" that, despite changes in form or expression, endures nonetheless; and, despite not only the difference in performative setting but also participant self-understandings while engaged in the behavior, activities categorized by scholars as rituals are all believed to comprise instances of the same timeless thing. As with "other," it is the way that we tip our hat to difference, contingency, and the unpredictability of the worlds in which we find ourselves, while working diligently to ignore them. That members of the groups we study continually jockey for dominance, portraying their part as if it were the Whole, goes without saying, of course. However, that scholars do this too is a problem that needs our attention.

To put a little meat on the bones of these theoretical observations, consider the Introduction of a recent, co-written textbook that is sure to be a wide seller, *World Religions Today* (Esposito, Fasching, and Lewis 2002).[6] In a section entitled, "Understanding Religious Experience and its Expressions," the authors draw attention to the history (i.e., etymology) of "religion," by asking readers to picture themselves in ancient Rome, asking someone on the street: "What religion are you?" Not letting their admission that people in antiquity did not talk like this, much less speak English, deter them, they press on with their example: "Frustrated, you try rephrasing your question and ask: 'Are you religious?' Suddenly their faces light up and they smile and say, 'Of course, isn't everyone?'" (5).

Despite this example striking me as having something remarkably in common with stereotypical paternalism of some English speakers who think that if they just spoke loudly and slowly enough everyone would understand them (i.e., "I said, are you R-E-L-I-G-I-O-U-S?"), there is something more

that we can take away from this speculative tale. For in the process of recognizing the historicity of our terms (i.e., demonstrating that the modern word
"religion" derives from ancient Latin words, though the precise etymology
is unclear), these authors nonetheless presuppose that the adjectival form of
the modern word—which names not "something you join" but, instead, "a
way of seeing, acting, and experiencing things" (5)—is a universal signifier.
In concluding that "people [in antiquity or outside the orbit of Latin-influ-
enced modern languages and cultures] did not think of what they did as 'a
religion'—a separate reality one had to choose over against another" (5), the
authors yet presume that our word "religious" names some predicate of all
human beings (i.e., a way of seeing, acting, and experiencing). In fact, it is
not just any old predicate—like height or weight or color—but, quite possibly, the most truly authentically human quality of all. For, as they conclude:

> Religion as a form of human experience and behavior, therefore, is
> not just about purely "spiritual" things. Religion is not just about
> gods or God. People's religiousness is as diverse as the forms of
> power they believe govern their destiny, whether it be the gods
> as forces of nature, or wealth, or political power, or the forces of
> history. Religious attitudes in the modern world can be discerned
> in what many people would consider purely secular and very
> "unspiritual" attitudes and behaviors in relation to power. Hence,
> whatever powers we believe govern our destiny will elicit a reli-
> gious response from us and inspire us to wish "to tie or bind"
> ourselves to these powers... (7)[7]

Despite the fact that many people seem to think that the model of religious
studies represented by the work of Mircea Eliade has shuffled off this mortal
coil—and that scholarly criticisms of this model are pathetically tilting at
antique windmills—he told us pretty much the same several decades ago:
everyone is religious, whether they know it or not. No doubt we can hear
faint echoes of Juliet proclaiming that "by any other name a rose would
smell as sweet." Or, updating Shakespeare, we could quote David Denby,
film reviewer for *The New Yorker*, commenting on the films of Quentin Tarantino's: "a filmed image has a stubborn hold on reality. An image of a rose
may be filtered, digitally repainted, or pixilated, yet it will still carry the real-
world associations—the touch, the smell, the romance—that we have with
roses" (113).

But, Denby adds: "Tarantino wants us to give up such associations." Scholars who are suspicious of the essence/manifestation linkage that yet haunts
our textbooks—and my guess is that many of them are fans of such films as
"Reservoir Dogs," "Pulp Fiction," and, now, "Kill Bill, Part 1"—likewise

suggest we give up "world religions" or at least give up presuming that "religion" is anything but an historical accident to which we have become accustomed, a taxonomic marker some of us use in doing cross-cultural work from a very particular theoretical and historical location.

But going down this path means that scholars must relinquish not only some cherished metaphysical assumptions but also some political assumptions concerning the ability of well-meaning liberalism to set a table at which everyone can feast. Sadly, much as J. Z. Smith once noted that issues of definition raised at the outset of a textbook "never recur or are alluded to again in the body of the work which continues, unperturbed, to say what it would have said anyway" (1995b: 411 n. 6), such writers reverentially quote from the opening of *Imagining Religion* and engage in the sacrament of chronicling the etymology of "religion," all the while continuing to assume that behind their acts of historical imagination there lurks an enduring, universal presence that transcends time and place—like some definitive taxonomy that will finally let everyone snuggle under the textbook's cozy covers (if only we're allowed some version of *et cetera* in our table of contents). But the history that these writers offer in their etymologies doesn't go very far and their readers are left confident that behind the transitory world of appearances they have skimmed in a whirlwind semester that began in the rivers of India and ended in the sands of Arabia there is an enduring permanence and it is lodged deep within the immutable confines of this thing we call experience or human nature (hence the popularity not only of kaleidoscopic graphics on the covers of these books but also of such books as Mary Pat Fisher's *Living Religions* [2003], with its focus on "the personal consciousness of believers and their own account of themselves"[8]).

These writers therefore give the lie to the historian of antiquity, Peter Brown's thoughtful words: "A little history puts one firmly back in ones place." In the case of textbook writers, their place is apparently everywhere since—and *this* is the problem—the genre predetermines that *only a little history* be done. As Brown goes on to remark in his American Council of Learned Societies (ACLS) Haskins Lecture, taking history seriously

> counters the amiable tendency of learned persons to think of themselves as if they were hang-gliders, hovering silently and with Olympian ease above their field, as it has come to spread out beneath them over the years. But real life, one knows, has not been like this. We are not hang-gliders. We are in no way different from the historical figures whom we study in the distant past: we are embodied human beings caught in the unrelenting particularity of space and time. (2003: 3)

That the terrain mapped by these high-flying textbooks ends up looking an awful lot like what their authors assumed it would look like before donning their flight suits (i.e., women find women sadly lacking, Africanists go looking for Africa; South East Asianists search out South East Asia, etc.) is therefore not a coincidence. Furthermore, that one shares their lament over these unfortunate gaps tells us nothing about the way "world religions" ought to be used; instead, it tells us everything about our affinity for the work of these colleagues and the social world we wish to share with them.

Failing to recognize that one can never get outside language (both its vocabulary *and* its meanings), these books' authors overlook that—despite "Hindooism" becoming "Hinduism" and "Mohammadism" now being known as "Islam"—they are in precisely the same position as were their nineteenth-century predecessors; for they are all confident not only that a stable presence exists but that we can somehow find all the places where it lurks (of course we must recognize that it now lurks in hearts and minds rather than in souls, as was once thought). Wishful thinking notwithstanding, no one has yet penetrated the divine scheme of things (if one exists). Instead, taxonomies presupposing that behind all *religions* there exists some disembodied *religion*, are simply the way we authorize and thus reproduce the world as we happen to find it, a world apparently filled with colorful, faithful, and non-threatening people whose lives comprise the introductory course's menu. If we could just figure out how to let our students know that—as Smith has been suggesting we do for some time, now—the menu is provisional and problem-oriented, as are the utensils and recipes that we use, then maybe we'd be doing more than just adding a little historical spice to our world religions textbooks.

But I suspect that the genre itself precludes anything but high-flying aerobatics, making debates over what to add to these books comparable to debating what cargo ought to go into the Titanic. Certainly we should have more women. And more Africans. And more South Asians. Apparently we need a lot things—as the panel organizers apparently realized in transforming last Fall's AAR panel into the preceding set of published papers, for several of the essays were commissioned for their appearance here, presumably to fill yet more gaps. But what principle of selection was utilized and which gaps are worth filling? Do our textbooks need more children? What about adolescents? Is sexual orientation an issue? Ought it to be? Of course, answering such questions means we must acknowledge that we have principles of inclusion/exclusion, yet such an acknowledgment flies in the face of our "come one come all" efforts to squeeze everyone around the same table. But, as with the completely unregulated market of the "religion and..." genre—as evidenced by the endless variety of program units offered by the AAR[9]—you can imagine that we will never come up with the definitive scheme; failing to acknowledge this, we end up like Grady Tripp and the immense manuscript he can't finish in Michael Chabon's novelistic ode to dysfunctional academics, *Wonder Boys*: both the program for the Academy's annual meeting as well as the table of contents for our textbooks end up looking an awful lot like an "immense careering zeppelin" (Chabon 1995: 15).

But none of this seems to deter the world religions industry. For, as with the Titanic, the band plays on despite the ship taking on water; although three panelists leveled some pretty serious critiques, last November's panel ended not with a resounding call for an end to this antiquated conceptual holdover from the nineteenth century but, instead, with news that was eagerly greeted by members of the audience: world religions textbooks have gone digital, with moving pictures and music.

Something to watch while having our cake and eating it too.[10]

Notes

1.   The original panelists were: Carol S. Anderson, "The Disappearance of Women in World Religions Textbooks"; Mark Wheeler MacWilliams, "Shinto in World Religions Textbooks"; Ross Miller and Melanie White, "Creating a World Religions Text for the Twenty-First Century"; Selva Raj, "The Quest for a Balanced Representation of South Asian Religions in World Religions Textbooks"; Kay A. Read, "World Religions and the Miscellaneous Category"; Joanne Punzo Waghorne, "Revisiting the Question of 'Religion' in the World Religions Textbook"; and Robert M. Baum, "The Forgotten South: African Religions in World Religions Textbooks."

2.   As I recall, Will Oxtoby, Don Wiebe, and Lorne Dawson (who came in from another university nearby), team taught the course when I took it in the 1987–88 academic year, each coming to the class only for their own units. I gather that the shape and content of this course—as is often the case—were among the sites for the ongoing conflicts in the Centre for the Study of Religion concerning what (and who) best constituted the academic study of religion. See Wiebe (1999: ch. 13; originally published in *MTSR* [1995] 7/2: 351–81), for a history and analysis of the University of Toronto's program in the study of religion.

3.   Ed. Note: I think here of the recently invented category of "None" on US polls (i.e., no religious affiliation) that, over the Fall of 2012, turned into a designator for an entire group, presumed to share affinities and socio-political interests. See Steven Ramey's insightful critique of how this designator has been used by scholars, mistaking a discursive construct for an actually existing social group, in *The Huffington Post* (http://www.huffingtonpost.com/steven-ramey/what-happens-when-we-name-the-nones_b_2725169.html) [accessed April 6, 2013].

4.   Ed. Note: in the original version of this essay, preserved here, I mistakenly cited *The Archeology of Knowledge* rather than the correct book, the Preface to *The Order of Things* (Foucault 1973: xv).

5.   I think here of an earlier passage in my work (2001a: 30), citing the late Gary Lease:

> Related to Smith's comments on the incongruity of lived experience and the need to rationalize the disruptions and accidents that invade our systems of signification, is Gary Lease's attempt to delineate just such a natural history. (The work of Bruce Lincoln and Burton Mack of course come to mind at this point as well.) For Lease, religions, much like nationalisms, attempt "to be totally inclusive of all paradoxes by establishing exclusive meanings." Because historical life is rather more complex than the interpretive models of any totalized system, Lease predicts that, despite our best attempts to rationalize their appearance, the dissonances and conflicts that inevitably arise will eventually cause "the societal system to breakdown and the 'structures' which allowed such a paradoxical mutuality to dissolve" (Lease 1994: 475). Embarking on a natural history of social formations will therefore examine a religious system not as an ahistoric given but as a historical product that has a specific history, a limited future, and a wealth of possibilities.

6.   Ed. Note: I drew on this same example in 2005c (40ff.), where I used the following paragraphs as well.

7.   As of 2011, this textbook, which at that time was nine years old, was already in its fourth edition.

8.   Ed. Note: the eighth edition of this book was released in 2010 and the ninth comes out in 2014.

9.   Ed. Note: see McCutcheon (2001a: ch. 11 and 2003a: ch. 4) for elaborations on this point.

10.   My thanks to Jim Apple, Steve Berkwitz, Greg Grieve, and Kurtis Schaeffer for their helpful comments on an earlier draft of this essay.

Chapter 12

Introduction

While I was in my first full-time, tenure-track position, at what was then called Southwest Missouri State University in Springfield, Missouri (but which has since been rebranded as Missouri State University, over the objections of the University of Missouri System, given that this was once the name for their own flagship campus at Columbia, MO—a nice example of how tales of origins are sites of arm wrestling matches over identity and turf in the present), I was contacted by Charlie Reynolds, the longtime (though now retired) Chair of the University of Tennessee's Department of Religious Studies. Reynolds had been my own Chair while I was employed on an annual contract, that lasted for a total of three years, as an Instructor (1993–96). He had also been involved in the Council of Societies for the Study of Religion (CSSR—once known simply as the Council on the Study of Religion [CSR]), a North American umbrella organization, founded in 1969, to which various scholarly societies belonged so as to pool their resources and provide such things as membership services to themselves. (On the history of the CSSR, see Harold Remus's important essay in Scott Elliott's edited collection of *Bulletin* essays [Elliott 2013].) One of those services was publishing the quarterly *CSSR Bulletin*, a publication that served as part journal/part newsletter for the Council's various member societies (*Religious Studies News* largely reproduced the function of the *Bulletin* when *RSN* was established by the American Academy of Religion [AAR] and the Society of Biblical Literature [SBL] after they left the CSSR and formed Scholars Press.) With the previous editor stepping down, Charlie told me, they were looking for someone with energy and a bit of a vision for what the *Bulletin* could become. Although I was still a co-editor with *MTSR*, working on a scholarly periodical with a field-wide audience seemed like an opportunity, so I accepted the offer.

From 1996 to 2001—when I moved from Springfield, Missouri, to Chair the Department of Religious Studies at the University of Alabama—I was the *Bulletin*'s editor; briefly, at the start, I invited the late Tim Murphy (1956–2013) to join me as co-editor (which lasted only for a semester or two, at which time he thought his time and energy were best spent elsewhere), and then, near the end, when my new administrative duties were upcoming in Tuscaloosa, Craig Prentiss joined me as co-editor and, soon after, inherited the journal when I left.[1] Not being peer reviewed, I had tremendous freedom with the *Bulletin*'s contents; but not being peer reviewed, few people saw it as important enough to submit their work for inclusion in an issue of the *Bulletin*—that is, its strength was also its weakness. Given that the publication that I inherited printed few articles and was mostly filled with announcements, and that the CSSR seemed keen on just having it appear regularly with engaging content, it seemed ripe for reinvention. Needless to say, I did a lot of commissioning and solicitation for the articles that it published during my time as editor.

Looking back over the early editorials and the few pieces that I myself wrote for the *Bulletin*, the shape of the academic job market was certainly on my mind in those days—as it still is, though as a tenured Full Professor and Department Chair, I fully recognize that I'm in a rather different position than I was in the mid- to late-1990s. For example, consider my very first editorial (published in issue 26/1 [1997]) which in part read:

> This issue is comprised of papers that address the relations between the future of the field and the current pressures of the job market. Three of the papers were originally part of a panel at the 1996 meeting of the Society for the Scientific Study of Religion held in November in Nashville, Tennessee and three additional papers from this panel will appear in a future issue of the *Bulletin*... Because widespread economic constraints, cutbacks, and the pressures of the job market know no boundary, we believe that the contents of this issue should be of interest to all of our readers. Taken together, the editors believe that the papers published in this issue of the Bulletin will be of particular use to those currently on the job market, those soon entering it, and those who need to be reacquainted with it. In particular, those of our readers working with graduate students, or who are themselves graduate students, might use this issue as way to begin frank discussions in their departments concerning what it means to enter a profession of teaching and scholarship in the late-1990s. Far too many graduate programs do a disservice to their students by failing to raise the issue and far too many graduate students enter the job market unprepared and with unrealistic expectations. With specific regard to the job search, in this issue the editors also offer an open letter to department search committees in hopes of generating a constructive debate on the procedures and ethics of advertising for candidates.

The open letter, co-written with my late colleague, Murphy, and which I later reproduced, with his permission, as an appendix to a chapter (on early career pressures) that was published in *The Discipline of Religion* (2003a:

ch. 8), challenged Departments to, among other things, do their homework in advance of a search, so that their ads and criteria were explicit, rather than being shrouded in references to empty but seemingly weighty designators like "excellence."

The following set of theses, although written some years later, is in the tradition of the various pieces on the practicalities of our work that I've written over the years. Apart from the Open Letter mentioned above, most times when I've written on the job market—a market that, with the worldwide economic collapse in 2008, has just gotten worse since this piece was first written—my intended audience has usually been those who are in the situation themselves rather than those who, inasmuch as they are employed and appointed to search committees, control some of the conditions that determine the job market (though, admittedly, professors and even university administrators, control very few of the economic and political factors that impact the academic job market). My goal has often been to persuade people who obviously know that they do not control the levers of their situation that they do in fact control some of them. Although I don't think it wise to propose to people who find themselves in outrageous work conditions that, say, a positive "can do" attitude will help them to overcome their situation, I also think they will not know if the things that they *do* control will have any effect until they exercise the agency that they might not realize that they have.

Such a proposal is based on my own experience, of course. For example, as I was finishing revising my dissertation into the manuscript for what became my first book I was also beginning to write a new essay—on the then widely discussed topic of religion scholars as public intellectuals—that could very well have been included as an additional chapter to the book that I was then completing. Over the years I learned that it is important to know when a project is done and that what you are currently working on is part of the next project; whether I knew this at the time or not, I decided to submit the new essay separately to a journal. At the same time, I was also discussing with the book review editor of the same journal whether he would be interested in a review essay on resources available for courses in the study of myth and ritual. Because I was then an Instructor at the University of Tennessee, teaching a course entitled "Myth, Symbol, Ritual"—a course that I had no idea how to teach as I enthusiastically said yes when Reynolds asked me over the phone, after my hire but prior to my arrival in Knoxville, if this was a course I could teach—I had had a crash course on teaching this sort of course; so, I recall reasoning at the time that I should try to take full advantage of the work that went into preparing for teaching by writing a review essay on the various books that I had found useful in developing and teaching this course. While I do not wish to minimize the (no doubt significant) role played by dumb luck or sheer happenstance in my or anyone else's career (such as the original query sent from Knoxville to the University of Toronto for a two semester Instructor that led to my name being suggested), I often think back on that example, for, as it turned out, the editor and the review editor had two separate review processes and, I gathered later, both, without knowing it, separately agreed to publish my work. So, as it turned out, within the span of a year, my first book was published as well as a long peer-reviewed essay (that itself prompted a spirited, published exchange with two scholars, a few issues later) and a detailed review essay, both in the *Journal of the American Academy of Religion*. I think this is what I mean by advising younger scholars to be entrepreneurial.

My point? Social theorists must take their own theory seriously when examining the conditions in which they do their own work. Given that my own interest has often revolved around what I understand as the necessarily dialectical relationship between agency and structure (a point I first learned reading the British social theorist, Anthony Giddens [see, for example, McCutcheon 2001a: 28])—in an attempt to correct what I find to be the unwarranted reliance on agency and first person representation/interpretive authority that we often find in the work of scholars of religion—when it came to thinking about the institutions in which we do our own work it just made sense to examine them in precisely the same way. While it does not guarantee the result that any one social actor might wish to see realized, seeing oneself as an agent working within prior structural conditions not of your making—but which, as contingent conditions determined by history, are apt to being changed—does prompt one to try to take a risk or two, to influence those factors that might be within one's own control.

These thesis statements concerning the (yes, lamentable, but changing that is beyond my agency) nature of pre-professionals needing to excel at the measures of a profession to which they have yet to be admitted as full partners, were aimed to persuade people of just that.

This was also the theme that I tried to impress upon students in our own Department in the Fall of 2012 when I posted a blog the day after our Department's inaugural lecture in 2012–13's lecture series on the place of the Humanities and Social Sciences in the contemporary university. I posted it because I was troubled by the student feedback that I had heard immediately after the talk; it came from some of our undergraduate majors, who attended, as well as from an assortment of students enrolled in my 100-level introductory course who also attended. ("Write me a one page description and you can earn some extra credit in the course"—the professor's old trick to get students new to the university to think a few new thoughts, and, as we used to say, expand their horizons.) Whether or not it was the intended message of the speaker—Professor Gregg Lambert from Syracuse University—the students seem to have heard a message of lamentation for the future of the Humanities, and not a description of how we got here or a renewed defense of our relevance; instead, a (to their ears, at least) dire message from a senior professor concerning the fact that they may be deluded to think that grad school might be for them (since they'll possibly be mired in student debt that will take them decades to repay—making grad school sound like a bit of a scam). Because they're all just human capital, spewed into the global market from a never-ending pipeline, why continue in their studies (as they seem to have heard it)? As one first year student who attended the lecture said to me the following day, who sounded both intimidated and incredulous: "Declaring a major may be the most important decision of my life?!"

Now, this is not necessarily the lecture that I heard (e.g., the pipeline imagery was directly contested by our speaker, but the image of graduates with few practical skills being spewed into the job market stuck with many students nonetheless), but I can understand why certain parts stood out for them—the shocking often proves the most memorable (is this not Harvey Whitehouse's thesis when it comes to cognitive studies of ritual?). And maybe that was our lecturer's intention—a little cold water to wake us from our dogmatic slumbers. Perhaps these sobering words caught some of our students off-guard because we, as their professors, have not hammered home often and loudly enough that education is now (whether it always was, and we just had the luxury to pretend that it wasn't, is a discussion that we ought to have) a part of the cost/benefit economic system as much as anything else. Given the uphill argument that we, in the academic study of religion, feel that we have in helping students (and, more importantly, perhaps, their families) understand that this undergraduate major is as relevant as any other (did you ever wonder why "If you're not going to become a History teacher, then why major in History" is *not* a question for people in that field?), you would think that our students, perhaps more than anyone else's, had already done some of the hard-nosed decision-making long before declaring their Religious Studies major. And given the complex careers that some of us have had (as evident in previous chapter introductions, it should be evident that I know what it is like to be an Instructor on a nine-month contract and to have seriously considered the hard truth that, having earned a PhD, I had not also earned the right to feed and clothe myself by means of those skills), we are particularly cognizant of these issues and try to make sure students know too. But perhaps they need to be told again: structural factors well beyond your control kicked the sand out from under so much of the national and global economy in the late-2000s that it may take decades to recover (if recovery is even the right word).

But tied to that structural level analysis there needs also to be one that focuses attention on individual agency—and I wonder if this is what the students also needed to hear. Now, I'd likely never be accused of erring on the side of the rugged, can-do, lone individual, boldly making meaning in the world, like Prometheus pushing that rock—so fear not: I am not descending into some argument for the self-evident, intangible value of the Humanities for the existential good of the noble self. No, not at all. Instead, I'm taking a basic insight from structuralism seriously and noting that, while we may emphasize one or the other for analytic purposes, no analysis of a binary pair is sufficient if it neglects the other side of the coin. After all, the way that the Other-in-our-midst is silenced or at least ignored (whether it's worth recovering is, of course, another conversation) is a basic building block of the critical theories that have shaped so much of our work in the academy over the last generation or two—from the work of Social Historians to Postcolonial theorists. So, taking a page from our own critical thinking playbook I think that, while focusing on structure, we also need to draw attention to the agents within that structure; for the so-called system did not invent itself (and it isn't homogenous either) and neither did the agents invent themselves from whole cloth—none of us would be here without the dating and mating rituals that were not of our parents' (or grandparents'!) own making, though they tweaked the rules and each other, to be sure…. And around and around it goes: structure made by agents made by structure made by… It's turtles all the way down, as the old saying goes. At least that's how the critical thinker in me sees it.

And this is the part of the message that our students did not hear at that lecture—that they are agents within that structure, determined by many factors well beyond their influence, yes, but that they are nonetheless agents who, by their very activity, necessarily affect the structure (is not this the moral of the Quantum physics?); they collaborate and thereby continually re-make it—and in the process remake themselves.

Now, I'm no Pollyanna, of course, and I'm certainly no Dr Pangloss—no one is going to pull themselves up by their own bootstraps, despite how popular the "I made it myself" sentiment was in the 2012 US Presidential election, in response to the Democratic party's attempt to highlight the collective nature of society. But I would also not like to erase the presence of the actors within these structures, those who made the rules, benefit from them, labor under them, and who can and will change them—how, we have yet to see, of course.

So the following theses are not inspired by some dreamy-eyed message of hope—I will leave spinning that tale to the political campaigns. But it is a message to early career readers to pay attention to the wider, structural circumstances in which they do their work—the structures that work on them: all those turtles above you and below—but also to know that those social worlds did not spring from the ground like a mushroom overnight; instead, people—huge numbers of people, to be sure, people who didn't know each other, people collaborating, competing, and contradicting each other—made them. And since you're people then maybe you can re-make it.

So, of course, be modest but be strategic. Know that your good looks will only get you so far. Know that, at times, you're an almost powerless item exchanged in a faceless network of international capital. But also know that you have agency—within structure within agency within structure, et cetera, et cetera, all the way down. And knowing one's place within this never-ending system of reciprocal actors in situations-not-of-their-making means that one has what the ancient Greek called mêtis (μῆτις)—cunning intelligence. Undoubtedly, you will pay prices, sometimes steep prices—we all have; the grass only *seems* greener in other people's careers—but you hopefully will be empowered to decide which wagers are worth making and which prices are reasonable to pay for which desired outcomes. And in the current academic job market in the Humanities and Social Sciences, which has been atrocious since the late 1960s but which has become even worse, in many places, since 2008's global financial crisis first struck, this is just the sort of intelligence one needs.[2]

Theses on Professionalization (2007)[3]

1. Academia is unlike other professions in that the pre-professional period of training—which includes coursework, dissertation research and writing, and teaching assistantships—is not akin to an apprenticeship. Accordingly, there is no direct linkage between the accumulation of credentials and admission to the profession, no necessary relationship between feeling oneself to be qualified and the ability to obtain full time employment as a university professor.

2. A PhD is awarded not only as a mark of intellectual competence and disciplined method but also as a professional credential that signals one's eligibility for employment as a researcher and teacher within academia. Although these two aspects of the degree can complement one another, they can just as easily conflict, as in when one's research expertise fails to overlap with ever changing employment needs.

3. Pursuing a PhD purely for the "love of learning" is one among many legitimate reasons for graduate studies. Pursuing such studies for both intellectual stimulation and eventual employment requires candidates to be as intentional as possible about opportunities to increase their competitiveness on the job market.

4. Applying for full-time employment prior to being awarded the PhD degree (i.e., when, after successfully completing comprehensive or general exams, one holds the status known as ABD [All But Dissertation]) is not uncommon; however, failure to gain employment at this stage must not undermine one's confidence. Apart from extraordinary circumstances (e.g., the so-called "fit" between your expertise and a Department's needs), the doctoral degree remains a necessary condition for entrance into the profession.

5. Whether as an ABD or after having been awarded the PhD, some candidates accept year-to-year work as a full-time Instructor or Lecturer (sometimes also called a Sessional position or a Part-time Temporary Instructor). Such positions often entail teaching loads that are heavier than tenure-track or tenured faculty members and, depending on the salary offered, may necessitate supplemental teaching (e.g., evening or summer courses) for one to earn sufficient income. Although the benefits of teaching experience and an academic home can be invaluable to an early career person, the costs such temporary employment entails for one's ability to carry out research and writing can be high. Navigating these costs/benefits is no easy task; for instance, one might learn that, sometimes, time is more valuable than money.

6. Although it is necessary, the doctoral degree alone is hardly a sufficient credential for being admitted to academia as a full-time employee

because most of the other applicants also possess this credential (i.e., it is the level playing field onto which ABDs have yet to be admitted). There was a time, prior to the early 1970s, when the job market was such that merely possessing a PhD would lead to multiple tenure-track job offers; in the Humanities that time has long past.

7. For some of those who will be judging candidates' credentials to determine their admission to the profession, the reputation of the school from which they have earned their PhD plays a significant role in assessment of applicants' skills and future promise as colleagues. Although one's alma mater does communicate with whom one has trained and what traditions of scholarship one may pursue, for yet others the reputation of candidates' schools is secondary to the quality of their current research, the places where they have published their work, and the experience they have had in the classroom.

8. Like all institutions, academia provides a case study in the complex relationship between structure and agency; for, although there are a variety of things that one can do to increase one's competitiveness, job candidates must recognize that there are also a host of factors of which they are unaware and which are therefore beyond their control (e.g., the unstated needs, interests, goals, and even insecurities of the hiring Department; the number of other candidates qualified at any given time in your area of expertise; the impact of world events on the perceived need for scholars in your subject area, etc.). Success likely requires one to learn to live with the latter while taking control of the former.

9. A structural element that must be taken into account is that Departmental search committees often fail to entertain the difficult questions in advance and, instead, go on "fishing expeditions" by defining their open positions far too broadly and vaguely, such as looking for "the best qualified" applicant. Making explicit their implicit and often competing preferences may strike members of a Department as being too costly an exercise. It is into this mix of unstated disagreements and longstanding rivalries that job applicants can be thrust, affecting such things as how their letters of application are read, their credentials judged, and their performance during campus interviews measured. While one cannot control such factors, when representing oneself one at least ought to be aware of their potential presence and impact.

10. Whether working at a publicly or privately funded institution, professors are comparable to self-employed entrepreneurs inasmuch as they can increase their social capital (i.e., reputation) by seeking out new books to read and review, unique topics on which to research and write, novel and timely courses to develop and teach, and different professional service

opportunities to provide them with additional experience as well as new national and international contacts. Graduate students are in much the same position and the additional qualifications that result from their entrepreneurial pre-professional activities can serve to distinguish one job applicant from another. Documentation from such activities, as recorded on one's CV, communicate to the hiring committee that one is already skilled at participating in the many aspects of the profession that will surely be required of a tenure-track Assistant Professor.

11. While higher education is organized so as to train ever increasing specialists—a process that begins with surveys and broad course work, examines candidates on their knowledge in general areas, and then culminates in writing a dissertation on a highly technical topic—eventual full-time employment can just as easily depend upon one's ability to contribute lower-level, so-called Core or General Education introductory courses to a Department's curriculum. Because many Departments of Religious Studies justify their existence not simply by appealing to the number of their majors or graduates, but also the number of Core or General Education courses that they offer to students pursuing degrees in other areas of the University, gaining early experience in such courses as a Teaching Assistant is an important step toward being able to persuade future employers of one's ability to be a colleague who helps to teach their Department's "bread and butter" courses.

12. Many doctoral students do not realize that finding authors willing to write book notes, book reviews, and so on, is sometimes difficult for journal editors. As a first step in professionalizing themselves, graduate students should become aware of the journals in their field and write to their book review editors, suggesting that the journal allow them to write and submit a review (especially for books that they are already reading for their courses or research, thereby minimizing on work additional to their class and dissertation research). Besides providing experience in writing and a much needed line on one's CV, one never knows who will read the review or what other opportunities might follow upon it.

13. Because there is no direct relationship between seniority and the quality of one's writing, one's familiarity with the literature, or the novelty of one's ideas, graduate students ought never to refrain from submitting their work to a scholarly journal for possible peer review publication simply because they understand themselves to be novices. Even if rejected, the comments that result from the blind review process will be of benefit to students who have so far only received feedback from professors already familiar with their work.

14. Depending on the type of institution into which one is hired (i.e., its teaching load, service obligations, emphasis on research, sabbatical

opportunities, etc.), the dissertation may constitute one of the few, or quite possibly even the last, opportunity a candidate has to devote an extended period of time to one, focused project, free from the many obligations routinely expected of an Assistant Professor. Given the pressure to publish that, for some time, has attended academic careers, graduate students would be wise to write their dissertations while keeping in mind their eventual submission for possible publication—whether as a monograph (which, depending on a Department's "Tenure and Promotion" requirements, may be preferable) or as separate peer review essays.

15. Having successfully defended the dissertation, the manuscript does candidates no good in their desk drawer. However, before making revisions (unless they are dissatisfied with its argument or quality), graduates should create a prospectus containing a brief cover letter, annotated table of contents, and sample chapter (e.g., the Introduction) and submit it to a select number of top tier publishers in their area of expertise. Obtaining an outside experts' assessment of the manuscript—a step often essential to a publisher's process of evaluation—provides the best place to begin one's revisions of a manuscript with which one is intimately familiar and, perhaps, too closely tied.

16. Apart from professionalizing themselves through research and publication, candidates should consider the cost of regularly attending regional and national scholarly conferences simply as the price of being a graduate student. Waiting until one is on the job market is therefore too late to consider attending and trying to participate in such conferences—especially when one learns that being placed on the program of such annual meetings often comes about gradually, over the course of several (or more) years. Whereas regional meetings are often useful places to try out one's research, become accustomed to speaking in public, and learn the rituals of the question/answer sessions that follow the presentation of papers (knowledge especially important during on-campus interviews), national meetings play a crucial role in efforts to integrate oneself into networks of colleagues at other institutions who share one's interests.

17. National scholarly conferences and professional associations often host on-site job placement services and publish employment periodicals. Becoming thoroughly aware of such services and resources, long before actually being on the job market, may not only assist one's decision-making when it comes time to select an area of expertise (i.e., judging national employment trends over time may shed light on areas likely to require staffing in the coming years) but also prepare one for the eventual time when one is on the market and seeking campus interviews.

18. Despite being the primary, and sometimes even the exclusive, focus of candidates' attention during the last years of their PhD, once hired into a

tenure-track position a variety of other just as time consuming tasks compete for their attention. Learning to juggle many balls simultaneously—knowing which will bounce if dropped and which will break—is therefore an essential skill for early career professors who wish to continue carrying out original research while also teaching a full course load and serving the needs of their Departments and the profession at large.

19. Although it can be intellectually stimulating, developing new courses is time consuming. Depending on the needs of their Department, teaching multiple sections of the same course provides early career professors with fewer course preparations, helps them to quickly establish their area of expertise in the curriculum and among students, and allows them to gain teaching competencies far quicker, thereby enabling them to devote more time to their research and writing.

20. Despite what some maintain, teaching and research are complementary activities, inasmuch as teaching, somewhat like publication, constitutes the dissemination of information gained by means of prior research. Based on one's strengths, candidates can understandably emphasize one over the over, but declining always to carry out both, integrating them together when possible, is to shirk one's responsibilities as a scholar.

21. As with the effort to enter any profession, a price must inevitably be paid—economic as well as social—in terms of the other activities and goals one might instead have worked toward and possibly attained. Candidates must therefore not only be as deliberate as possible in determining which costs they are willing to pay and which they are not, but they must also learn to trust their own judgments when, regardless how their job search turns out, they someday look back on the decisions they once made.[4]

Notes

1. Scott Elliott and Matt Waggoner, both former MA students when I taught at Southwest Missouri State University, and then working on their PhD degrees, eventually inherited the *Bulletin* from Prentiss and, when they departed, Craig Martin took over. Martin, who departed from the *Bulletin* only recently, after reinventing is as *The Bulletin for the Study of Religion* and founding its associated blog, left it to the then co-editors Kelly Baker and Philip Tite.

2. The closing pages of this introduction—making reference to my response to a public lecture held in our Department—derive from a blog post that I wrote on September 25, 2012, for our Department's blog concerning our ongoing lectures series. See the original post at: http://www.as.ua.edu/rel/blog/2012/09/turtles-all-the-way-down [accessed April 4, 2013].

3. Too many graduate students seem unprepared for what awaits them once they complete their dissertations. Sadly, in many cases their professors seem not to have considered it to be their responsibility to provide them with some of the tools necessary for navigating the job market. It is into this gap that the following theses—which have benefited from the comments of a variety of people at different career stages—are offered. I do so with a deferential nod not only to Martin Luther's ninety-five and Karl Marx's twenty-one, but also the thirteen offered more recently by Bruce Lincoln (1996).

4. Ed. Note: these theses were also posted, with permission of the original publisher, at The Religious Studies Project (http://www.religiousstudiesproject.com/2012/02/29/russell-mccutcheon-theses-on-professionalization/ [accessed March 14, 2013]).

Chapter 13

Introduction

In October of 2008 I participated as a respondent to Robert Campany's paper at the inaugural conference of what promised to be—and has turned out to be—a multi-year "consortium" involving scholars at a variety of universities throughout Germany, Europe, and the world. Taking place at Ruhr University in Bochum, Germany, the conference was entitled "Dynamics in the History of Religions Between Asia and Europe." Funded generously by the German Federal Ministry of Education and Research (i.e., *Bundesministerium für Bildung und Forschung*), the results of the consortium's members' individual research and collective conferences (to which they have regularly invited international participants) are being published in a series with Brill; the first conference's volume, including a revised version of the paper Campany read at the conference (which was somewhat different from the paper that I was sent ahead of the conference), along with the reply that I wrote to his pre-conference paper, appeared in 2012 (see Campany 2012).[1]

The consortium's book series' description, which closely parallels what I understood the inaugural conference to be about, opens as follows:

> The so-called world religions and other religious traditions are not, and have never been, homogenous, nor have they formed or evolve[d] in isolation. Trying to overcome cultural stereotypes and their ideological misuse, the series *"Dynamics in the History of Religions"* focuses on the crucial role of mutual encounters in the origins, development, and internal differentiation of the major religious traditions. The primary thesis of the series consists in the assumption that interconnections of self-perception and perception by the other, of adaptation and demarcation are crucial factors for historical dynamics within the religious field.[2]

Such terms as syncretism, diaspora, hybridization, and creolization, not to mention dialogue, encounter, and transgression have, for sometime, been categories of choice for those who wished to present social life as far more dynamic than we might have previously thought. While attending this event it struck me that, although scholars of religion are often a little late to the party,[3] its participants were very much interested in applying such work to the study of religion so as to obtain a more nuanced understanding of religious interaction and change over time.

But I admit that, when it comes to carrying out research that requires such significant external funding from such bodies as, say, the nation-state or even such granting bodies as The Templeton Foundation or the Lilly Endowment, especially multi-million euro/dollar grants that are above and beyond what the universities already cost to run,[4] I become, if not a suspicious hermeneut then at least a curious one. I therefore find it helpful to think about some of the "destabilizing and irreverent questions" posted in one of Bruce Lincoln's "Theses on Method" (1996), specifically number 4: "Who speaks here?... To what audience?... In what immediate or broader context?... With what interests?" For example, what in the life of the EU in general, or a country like Germany in particular (or, say the Netherlands, whose Organization for Scientific Research [Nederlandse organisatie voor wetenschappelijk onderzoek], "generously funded" [de Vries 2008: xiv] "The Future of the Religious Past: Elements and Forms for the Twenty-First Century" research initiative[5]), would prompt those who control the (always limited) resources of its various granting agencies to fund so heavily, in the early twenty-first century, such a multi-university, scholarly consortium, devoted to, of all things, understanding religions as internally diverse and thus heterogeneously in motion and invariably in contact with one another? Or, why would a Ministry of Education, charged with setting the minimal educational conditions for a nation's youngest citizens, be interested in this topic? Breathing new life into the German humanities programs, and raising their reputation in the world, as well as to promote interdisciplinary cooperation are certainly among the stated reasons (e.g., Steinicke 2012: 1). But I suspect that there may be more to this than might at first meet the eye, since they could have funded any number of other things to achieve that goal.

In and around the time that I was at the first of these conference, back in 2008, the issue of immigration across Europe was (and still is, of course) very much in the news, especially the, to some, questionable role played throughout the EU of this thing called Islam. From the much publicized and debated laws concerning women's headscarves in France to the Danish cartoon controversy (of September 2005) and ongoing debates over the role of publicly-funded Muslim religious education in Germany (since religious education is Constitutionally-mandated, and thus state supported, in many of Germany's sixteen federal states, in which religious bodies provide the content and the training for the teaching, though both must be approved by the state—though students can opt out for an "ethics" course instead)—all of which comes in the wake of the post-9-11 discourse within almost all liberal democracies concerning what constitutes legitimate versus illegitimate forms of Islam (i.e., newspaper or magazine headlines, not to mention an array of scholarly books, concerning Islam being a "religion of peace" as opposed to the "radicals" and "extremists" who have "hijacked" Islam)— the place of Islam in general, and Muslim immigrants and citizens, in particular, in the future of various nation-states remains a topic very much on the minds of politicians and academics. It is also on the minds of many others throughout the public who are themselves not Muslim—as well as those who identify themselves as Muslims but nonetheless also share significant economic and political interests with most others in these liberal democracies. "How to deal with the problem of Islamic radicalism?" is the question that all of these groups seem to be asking, employing the common designator "radical" to name versions of the social formation seen to be in competition with the taken-for-granted norms of national life.

Although it was never stated explicitly (and I would, of course, need far more evidence to make this claim in any manner other than sheer speculation) I left that conference wondering if this so-called problem of Islam—or, far more widely, what is commonly called fundamentalism or extremism— was the elephant in the consortium's room. That is, the event struck me as possibly being an example of how scholarship can develop and deploy techniques that are conducive to the interests of the nation (somewhat akin to late-nineteenth-century scholars developing tools to study "superstitious primitives," perhaps—intellectual tools and scholarly findings that certainly did not hamper the worldwide spread of colonial "civilization"). For the tools that the consortium intended to develop would be very useful to divide and conquer—that is, to counter some participants' claims concerning their own alternative or perhaps non-national identity by turning their once seemingly monolithic, alternative social worlds (and the apparent legitimacy, momentum, and thus authority behind them) into a veritable kaleidoscope of potentially competing sub-interests and slipping sub-allegiances—some of which are likely aligned with the nation's dominant groups. By complicating what are currently portrayed as uniform identities in this way, by emphasizing their "interconnectedness" and "adaptation," their "differentiation" and "encounter," it may be possible that now mutually beneficial alliances between parties who had previously seen themselves as distinct and competitive, might develop; for now the only monolithic identity that remains will likely be assumed to be the nation itself (the case of how French or US national identity is usually [i.e., ideally] understood provides an excellent model for thinking this through), the foundational melting pot within which all other identities are presumed to be *ad hoc*, private, and changeable.

My point is that there are times when the complicating that comes with a partial dose of social theory may not be as progressive as it may sound.

While I could cite the many times in the consortium's first volume that some apparently uniform thing called, for instance, "Judaism" is juxtaposed to equally uniform "Islam" and "Christianity" (e.g., just what was *the* Jewish reaction to *the* Islamic conquests?), consider Volkhard Kresch, Director of the consortium, writing in his "Preliminary Considerations" to the first conference volume: "To be able to identify religious communication, i.e., to distinguish it from other forms of communication, we must examine what makes it unique…" (2012: 23). But why "must" we distinguish it, if all is interconnections and adaptations? The manner in which the imperative is taken for granted suggests to me a curious contradiction at the heart of this project: on the one hand, religions are each not as homogenous as they might appear but, instead, they invariably blend with each other, while on the other, inasmuch as they *are* all religions they are, as a class, homogenous enough to be uniquely distinct from all other cultural forms (Kresch, after all, cautions against how my own work risks "the dissolution of religion in 'culture'" [2012: 16]—though I am unsure why only the latter noun warrants the ironic quotation marks); in the midst of theorizing, and thereby relativizing, one level of the discourse, a normative and distinctly monolithic core is strategically reinforced at another. "Religion" is apparently not just a handy analytic we as scholars use to separate out but one element of the wider and endlessly intermixing cultural field, doing so for our scholarly purposes for, "[w]hat we call religion is not just a purely academic invention (as, for example Mac-Cutcheon [sic] concluded),…. Religion has its own dynamics…" [Kresch 2012: 17]. As such, it is turtles (i.e., blending, ambiguity, intermixing, etc.) *almost* all the way down.

Since the nation-state finds the category "religion" good to think with (a point argued in the last chapter of McCutcheon 2003a as well as in McCutcheon 2005c and all throughout Arnal and McCutcheon 2013), I find this to be the case in much work that is now being carried out on identity. For example, despite the apparent progress (over those who once portrayed early Christianity as utterly unique and thus special) made by considering early Christianity to be a syncretistic movement—as it was once provocatively theorized to be—the two sources from which it was thought to originate (Judaism and Hellenistic culture) were necessarily presumed to be homogenous, autonomous items that, once colliding, produced their syncretistic offspring. The more provocative approach would be to see it as syncretism—and thus turtles—all the way down, thereby making syncretism a rather unhelpful term inasmuch as *all* identity is now understood to be inevitably blended and thus derivative, ensuring that we, as scholars, can talk about sources and origins only inasmuch as we own up to the fact that we created each for our own analytic purposes—for without those purposes, each hypothetical source is but the destination for some prior dynamism. But this is not the approach taken by studies of syncretism or diaspora (inasmuch as a static and authoritative origin/orthodoxy is a necessary postulate for judging what counts as change and movement) and it is not the approach taken if, for example, religious communication is considered to be unique.[6]

It was just this sort of partial theorization that I found in the paper to which I replied while in Bochum, as argued in the following response. But whether there is more than just a hunch for concluding that such large collaboratives are deeply linked to the interests of the nation-state I leave, for the time being.

A Response to Professor Robert Campany's "Chinese Religious History and its Implications for Writing 'Religion(s)'" (2008)⁷

Because I suspect that Professor Campany and I have some theoretical differences when it comes to the role played by classification in knowledge systems, before I offer my reply let me first briefly illustrate how I understand classification systems to work.

I draw my example from the first US Presidential election debate, held on September 26, 2008; in his opening remarks, the moderator, American journalist Jim Lehrer, set the evening's parameters as follows: "Tonight's [debate] will primarily be about foreign policy and national security, which, by definition, includes the global financial crisis." Now, for anyone following the US news during the last weeks of September, it was obvious what he was talking about, for at the time of the debate a proposal to inject $700 billion tax dollars was being considered by the US Congress, transferring what the press was already calling "toxic debt" from private banks to the government. The two parties' Presidential candidates had, earlier that day, flown to Washington DC, at President Bush's invitation, to participate in meetings intended to create a consensus among the two parties concerning how to address what pretty much everyone was by then calling a crisis. The meetings failed and so, at the time of that evening's debate, the government had arrived at no plan to rescue US banks.

Although that first debate was previously scheduled to be on foreign policy and national security—focusing on topics *external* to the nation—events *internal* to the US, which already had obvious worldwide consequences, could not be ignored, suggesting that the common distinction between inside and outside was no longer as useful as the Commission on Presidential Debates had previously thought. In fact, the moderator's choice of opening words—calling what was then simply one nation's problem a "global financial crisis"—made evident that, at least when it comes to banking, the day had long past when such classifications as "domestic" and "foreign" could sensibly be used as if they applied to separable things. (A fact made evident as the American banking and insurance crisis began sweeping across the rest of the world.)

I assume it was because he recognized that his viewers' common-sense understanding of the world—what a scholar might term their folk classification system—normally distinguished between the domestic and the foreign that the moderator made the linkage explicit when prefacing the debate by saying:

> General Eisenhower said in his 1952 presidential campaign. Quote, "We must achieve both security and solvency. In fact, the foundation of military strength is economic strength," end quote.[8]

Despite a generation of scholars theorizing this process that we now know as globalization, I'd hazard a guess that most of the debate's viewers assumed that the local is easily distinguishable in some essential way from the global. That this distinction does not necessarily reflect how such things as corporations and banks actually work has become painfully evident to investors around the world.

What I find interesting about this minor episode in classification is that it makes apparent that there are times when the analytic utility of widely used folk taxonomies—that is, conceptual systems that members of social groups use to manage their environment and their place, and the place of Others, within it—can be so diminished as to make their continued use part of the problem. Although there are times when one can unreflectively distinguish between such seemingly different things as, say, military, political, and economic issues and events, or when the usually self-evident boundaries of a nation-state enable one to distinguish, say, an American issue from a French or German situation, the fact of the US waging a war which is currently estimated to cost $12 billion per month[9] while also injecting nearly a trillion dollars into a trans-national investment and insurance system[10]—money that has to be borrowed from lenders abroad—and doing all of this in the final weeks of a US Presidential election, well, this made apparent that it was in no one's interest to continue to distinguish between the domains formerly known as domestic and foreign.

I open my response to a paper on the place of the category "religion" in writing Chinese history by referencing this example to make the following point, one that I think ought to guide us in our work on the category "religion": for historically-minded scholars—that is, scholars who conceive their object of study, the world of human doings, as a contingent affair with no pristine originary moment and no Hegelian end point to which events are irresistibly moving—the tools that we use to name and thereby divide up and organize the world (such tools as the categories of "the past," "the nation," "tradition," "meaning," and "religion") are *our* tools and are thus no less a part of the world of human doings than the subjects we study by using them, making our categories not neutral descriptors of stable, self-evident realities but, instead, products of human interests that are used by social actors in specific situations. What's more, should those social actors, their situations, and their interests change, then the tools will need to be retooled, perhaps even discarded entirely—much as the once prominent categories "taboo" and "mana" have long departed from our scholarly, analytic vocabularies. The scholars that I have in mind therefore do their work presuming that there is no god's eye vantage point and thus, as Professor Campany points out near the opening of his paper's pre-distributed version, that there is no neutral language—which I read as recognizing that there is no significance to be found without also evidence of prior systems of signification—themselves historical products. To illustrate the first: despite its inventor's hopes for universality, Esperanto is but one more language among others. To illustrate the second: without prior sets of interests (such as US voters' concern for their retirement savings and their homes' values), there would have been no reason to spend half of that first Presidential debate discussing banks and home mortgages.

With all this in mind, I propose that studying classification systems—such as the longstanding practice of naming a part of the world of human doings as "religion" or "religious"—by examining, as Professor Campany proposes, which taxonomy *better fits* the facts on the ground, so to speak, is an unhelpful way to advance our studies, for the positivist facts on the ground can be argued to be a product of the classification systems themselves. To appeal to a biological example, it makes little sense to ask whether a whale *really is* a fish or a mammal (that is, which category better fits the apparent biological reality of the whale), for in and of itself—whatever that sort of ontological speculation may actually mean—a whale is neither. Instead, what we know as a whale becomes understandable *as* a fish—that is, can be seen to share a certain number of traits with those other things we call fish—only once we use a specific set of criteria to name, sort, and thereby manage our surroundings. Change our interests and needs, change our criteria, change the way in which we establish relationships of similarity and difference among items we deem significant and worth paying attention to, and the whale ends up being a mammal—a case made abundantly clear in Graham Burnett's recent book, entitled *Trying Leviathan* (2007), in which he examines an 1818 New York state court case on this very topic—a case that took place just as once dominant morphological classifications of the biological world were giving way in Europe and North America to taxonomies based on anatomical studies. Should your interests be to exchange barrels of whale oil for profit, without paying what was then a New York state tax on the sale of *fish* oils, then you might understand what drove the effort to reclassify what was then the commonsense designation of the whale as merely being a big fish.

What I hope is evident from this example is that a close examination of the facts on the ground—whether whales in the sea or people doing supposedly religious things (or, better put, leaving artifacts that we can name *as* religious) in ancient China—cannot settle such a taxonomic debate; it can only be settled by adjudicating between the competing sets of interests that drive, and the effects that result from, the application of differing systems of classification. And it is this focus on unspoken criteria, and the theories and interests that drive them, that I bring to my reading of Professor Campany's paper. I will therefore pose six questions in response, questions whose answers may shed some light on what he has described as the "conceptual and terminological pitfalls [that] arise when writing about religion in premodern China" (1 [Campany 2012: 274]).

1. Although it seems to prioritize actual historical data over merely imported theory, I do not believe that Professor Campany's inversion of his original paper title is all that helpful—such as when he opens by saying, "I will ask, in short, not so much how the modern Western notion of 'religion' shapes our writing of Chinese history as how Chinese history might impact our use of the notion of 'religion'" (1 [Campany 2012: 273]); for without the prior category religion, defined in a particular sort of way (and more on this below), I am unsure what criteria he employed to narrow down the human doings within that grouping he names as "early medieval Chinese history" to just those that, in his words, "are relevant to our topic" (1 [Campany 2012: 273]). For as I understand discourses on the past, they *must* employ some mechanism of constraint to enable one to conceptualize anything as constituting this thing we call "the past." I say this because I assume that the archive of human doings that have preceded our own is virtually limitless (even taking into account that this archive only contains those acts which left some sort of empirical trace for us to find). So if we start, as in his inverted paper title, with the so-called historical facts on the ground, to see how well they fit our category—what Professor Campany elsewhere refers to as "the realia of Chinese religious history" (4 [Campany 2012: 277]) or simply "the historical phenomena" (5 [Campany 2012: 280]) that, as I read him, seem to precede the "often-unconscious assumptions about religion(s) made by writers"—then what system of constraint has he employed to find in that massive archive of long past human doings, all of which, he agrees, predate or at least fall outside the invention of the category "religion," just those that, to quote again, "are relevant to our topic"? So my first question is: How, without starting with the

category "religion," did he select the historical acts discussed in his paper from the many things that constitute early medieval Chinese history? I ask this because all of his data strikes me as remarkably alike those particular beliefs, behaviors, and institutions that would normally be grouped together in a world religion's textbook's chapter as comprising this thing called early medieval Chinese religion. My point? I detect here a methodological problem similar to Max Weber's well-known opening claim, in his *The Sociology of Religion*, that religion could only be defined at the end of his study[11]; despite working without a definition, Weber somehow yet knew that his study ought to have chapters on gods, priests, ethics, prophets, congregations, pastoral care, preaching, and so on. So my point has to do with the fact that, at least as I see it, we have no choice but to employ imported, so-called alien categories when we, as scholars, confront the world—a point that, I believe, runs contrary to what I suspect is Professor Campany's phenomenologically-based, historiographically positivist assumption that an external world of historical phenomena precedes our use of theoretical, organizing concepts.

2. Despite how popular it has become to distinguish between the plural noun "religions" and the singular noun "religion," I think that this distinction is terribly misleading. While I understand that many today think that, for example, talking about, "Judaisms" rather than "Judaism" is evidence of a more nuanced approach to social difference—inasmuch as it *seems* to avoid the sort of essentialism and reification that comes with presuming religions to be monolithic things—such work leaves untheorized just what it is about these many Judaisms that enables us to see them, in the first place, as each constituting a distinct species and, in the second, to see them as members of the same genus. Simply put, I am unsure how one regulates this endlessly plural economy, for, according to this line of thought, would there not be as many Islams as there are Muslims? Or, as I suspect to be the case in such scholarship, are there certain unarticulated, and thus untheorized, differences that we can obviously overlook, in order to produce such workable generalizations as, for example, "Mainline Protestantism" versus "Evangelical Protestantism"? To press further, do we overlook the differences and accentuate the similarities that group members themselves overlook or focus upon in their effort to form group identities or are we, as scholars, not limited to the participants' folk taxonomies? For, according to my opening illustrations, uncritically reproducing—instead of studying!—local classification systems will lead to us, as scholars, normalizing

participant distinctions and the interests that drive them, such as when we, for example, adopt a distinction specific to a group and end up talking about Shi'ites as being obviously different from Sunnis. Sadly, in adopting these participant distinctions we fail to ask: different according to whose criteria?—a question that, once posed, would allow us to examine the mechanisms by which identities are created and contested. Therefore, to my way of approaching these topics, the seemingly progressive move to the plural simply side-steps the tough work of identifying the supposed theme upon which differences are said to play. So let me ask my second question: Of what are these things called religions composed so as to make them all members of a genus that is apparently distinguishable from, say, social and political systems? Depending how this question is answered, the discredited but resilient category of *sui generis* religion re-enters our field.

3. I am also unsure how looking for "indigenous analogues" (6 [Campany 2012: 280]) for our notion of religion helps us—whether we go looking in China's past or anywhere else, for that matter. I say this because, as everyone knows, there are more definitions of religion than we know what to do with—back in 1912 the appendix to James Leuba's *A Psychological Study of Religion* famously informed us that there are more than fifty. So, before looking for analogues of our concept religion in ancient China, I think we need to ask my third question: Analogues of what? That is, why did Professor Campany settle on the prototype that he did as the basis for his cross-cultural comparative work? For when he states that "[t]here were certainly many things going on in early medieval China that anyone familiar with the term ["religion'] would now say were 'religious' in nature" (8 [Campany 2012: 285]), I wonder with *which* use of the term "religion" we must be familiar in order to recognize these things—for will we not see different things, all depending which concept we come armed with? From the data on which he draws—things called Buddhism and Daoism which apparently involve such things as tales about founders, sacrificial ritual, temples, monks and nuns, textual traditions, ancestor veneration, and some sort of distinction between the spiritual and the mundane or this realm and some other—it is obvious that he is not employing either Sigmund Freud's definition of religion as illusory wish-fulfillment or Karl Marx's understanding of religion as a form of bourgeois ideology, let alone Ninian Smart's view of religion as but one among the host of worldviews—for using any of these old but well-known models as his prototype would not have limited his cast of historical characters to the usual suspects.

So it seems to me that, in looking for analogues to a particular folk conception of religion prominent in our own social group, his paper naturalizes one local, historically specific understanding of the term (an apparently classical, phenomenological sense of the term, though I admit I did not find his definition of religion explicitly stated anywhere in the paper—more than likely because it is simply the popular folk concept operative throughout our own social group and thus one that most readers simply assume from the outset)—something which is less than helpful if scholars wish to historicize the discourse on religion and the interests that are furthered by reproducing the notion that certain human institutions are something other than, or more than, social, political, and economic.

4. After describing the metaphorically loaded nature of discourses on religion—and I recall here my appreciative citation, earlier in this reply, of Professor Campany's thoughts on the situatedness of language—he suggests, again, in a surprisingly positivist manner, that we proceed by "set[ting] metaphors aside to ask what the purported things we call religions really, non-metaphorically speaking, are in an ontologically rather literal sense" (3 [Campany 2012: 277]). He concludes that, instead of being what many people take them to be—that is, seeing religions as entities, agents, organisms, or containers, all of which can act in the world and do things for people—they instead ought to be understood as "repertoires of cultural resources" and "imagined communities" (3-4 [Ed. note: this was not included in the published form of his essay]). Now, I admit that I have some difficulty placing his claim about literal meaning in anything but a contradictory relationship with his earlier claim that "language is metaphorical in character" (2 [Campany 2012: 274]), unless, of course, Professor Campany's scholarly language is somehow exempt from the limitations of ordinary language—a position I suspect that he is not trying to assert, given that his paper, like my own, is filled with metaphors. Now, as I understand it, meaning-making is, by definition, a metaphoric activity whereby relationships of similarity and difference are established (as opposed to being passively recognized) within systems of constraint (such as a grammar)—systems that are themselves social and historical and thus by no means in any sort of necessary correspondence to the way things *really are*. It is precisely in this way that we can say that, despite that old saying, apples and oranges are indeed comparable since they both possess sufficient traits that we have identified as belonging to our higher order concept, "fruit."[12] To press the point I could make reference to Professor Campany's

earlier claim that historical phenomena "impact" our theoretical categories (for the word "impact" suggests an attribution of agency and
massive solidity that, at least when found in descriptions of religions,
he finds problematic) but, instead, consider how moving from saying
that a religion *is like* an agent that grows (a position he finds limiting because it reifies) is any different from saying that religion *is
like* a repertoire of resources that get used. My fourth question, then,
is: By what standard can we judge which metaphoric way of talking
about the world is any closer either to the literal truth of the situation
or the so-called facts on the ground? Moreover, will not our criterion
of judgment, used to decide between these options, be metaphoric as
well? Why, in other words, should I be persuaded that the Buddhist
metaphor, as Professor Campany identifies it, of "path" is any more or
less adequate to the study of religion, than is "religion"?

5. I would also like to ask: How can our assumptions about religion
be judged to "create misunderstandings and falsify our representa-
tions of the Chinese religious situations" (4 [Campany 2012: 277])?
I would like this answered because, without the category of religion
up and running, I do not see how Professor Campany can qualify any
Chinese situation *as* religious—a qualification that, once made, he
then uses to judge some modern uses of the category "religion" as
inappropriate (I recall how this problematic circularity arises in the
second question he sets out to answer in his paper: "How does Chinese religious history invite us to rethink our models and assumptions
about religion" [1 (Campany 2012: 274)].) The use of the adjective
"religious," here and in many other places throughout his paper, is
apparently unproblematic, much as those who seem to be untroubled by the assumption that, although the noun religion is a reifying
colonial import, the actual people who are inappropriately grouped
by means of this singular noun nonetheless have active and rich religious lives. Only if one assumes a specific view of the individual, a
view more than likely limited to post-seventeenth-century Europe,
is the adjective, which apparently qualifies the individual, somehow
free of the problems of the noun—whether singular or plural.

6. And finally, I am curious what other modern field of intellectual pursuit has the problems that Professor Campany finds to plague our
own. For if, as he argues, "conceptual and terminological pitfalls
arise when authors…write about religion in early medieval China, a
culture which…lacked analogues to our generic sense of 'religion'"
(4 [Campany 2012: 277]), then what about the no less alien, Latin-
based concept "culture" that he uses in that very sentence, let alone

the presumption that the relatively recent nation-state designation, "China," can be pitched backward in time to unify a few thousand years of history, as well as the imported chronological designation "medieval"? Now, please do not misunderstand me; I am not suggesting that we cannot use local terms to talk about things removed from us in time and space; on the contrary—I think that's all we are able to do. So, my sixth and final question is: Which of our alien imports must be used with caution and which can be used without thinking. For I suspect that Professor Campany would have no trouble talking about, say, the DNA or the ideology of ancient Chinese people; if so, then why the difficulties with the concept "religion"?

I pose these six questions in hopes of pressing further with our work to historicize the means by which we as scholars name and study the world we inhabit—itself an historically specific practice that I think ought not to involve authorizing certain folk taxonomies that we may come across in our work, as if they adequately describe the very nature of things—even if they be the taxonomies of the groups that we ourselves go home to when we leave the offices and classrooms.

Notes

1.   Citations to his paper, in the chapter that follows, include the ms. pagination accompanied, in brackets, by the comparable passage in the published version (my thanks to the volume's editors for finding the matching passages).
2.   Find the full series description at http://www.brill.com/publications/dynamics-history-religions. For more information on the research consortium itself, see http://www.khk.ceres.ruhr-uni-bochum.de/en/about/ (both links accessed on February 28, 2013).
3.   For example, it would not be difficult to imagine someone describing my own *Manufacturing Religion*, written in the early- to mid-1990s and published in 1997, as a somewhat derivative application of debates that took place ten or fifteen years earlier, say, in Literary Criticism, in particular, and Departments of English, in general.
4.   The grant, from 2008–2014, was worth a total of 12 million euros.
5.   For a description of this 2002–2012 project, which aimed to ascertain the new forms that so-called traditional religions will take in the future, see: http://www.nwo.nl/en/research-and-results/programmes/the+future+of+the+religious+past (access April 15, 2013).
6.   Taking this point seriously is the goal of a research collaborative in which I participate—entitled Culture on the Edge—along with six other scholars: Craig Martin, Monica Miller, Steven Ramey, and Merinda Simmons, Leslie

Dorrough Smith, Vaia Touna. The first volume of papers by the group are scheduled to appear from Equinox Publishing Ltd in 2015.

7.   Ed. Note: portions of this paper were subsequently used as the Introduction to Arnal and McCutcheon 2013.

8.   The complete transcript of the debate used can be found at http://www. clipsandcomment.com/2008/09/26/full-transcript-first-presidential-debate-barack-obama-john-mccainoxford-ms-september-26-2008/ (accessed September 28, 2008).

9.   See http://abcnews.go.com/International/wireStory?id=4418698 (accessed September 28, 2008). See http://www.cbo.gov/ftpdocs/86xx/doc8690/10-24-CostOfWar_Testimony.pdf for the US's Congressional Budget Office document from March 24, 2007, which estimates that $604 billion had been spent on the two wars from September 2001 until the end of 2007.

10.   According to the Whitehouse's Office of Management and Budget, the 2008 budget's projected income will total $2.662 trillion (the expenditures will total $2.9 trillion, adding $239 billion to the Federal deficit), making the proposed "bail out" approximately 38% of 2008's receipts; see http://www. whitehouse.gov/omb/budget/fy2008/summarytables.html (accessed September 28, 2008)

11.   Ed. Note: as Weber famously writes on the opening page of his 1922 classic, *The Sociology of Religion*: "To define religion, to say what it *is*, is not possible at the start of a presentation such as this. Definition can be attempted, if at all, only at the conclusion of the study" (1993: 1).

12.   Ed. Note: the first time I thought of this example was as a result of William Paden using it during the Q&A that followed a panel on which we both participated at the 1995 IAHR Congress in Mexico City. The panel—the papers of which were published (see Geertz and McCutcheon 2000: 287–338)—was devoted to reviewing Benson Saler's *Conceptualizing Religion* (1993).

Chapter 14

Introduction

In early June 2006, I was a participant in the inaugural meeting of the Greek Society for the Study of Religion, held at the Museum of Byzantine Culture in Thessaloniki, Greece, in cooperation with Aristotle University. Both the conference and the society had been organized by Professor Panayotis Pachis, whom I had met some years earlier while he was a Visiting Professor at the University of Vermont, working with Luther Martin, and who, subsequently, had also arranged for the Greek editions (translated by his then student, Dimitris Xygalatas) of *Manufacturing Religion* and the *Guide to the Study of Religion*; the conference involved a variety of academics from elsewhere in Europe and North America, as well as Greek scholars and a large number of Greek undergraduate and graduate students who attended the sessions. More like Canada or Denmark than the US (in terms of lacking a constitutionally-mandated separation of church and state), I learned that the students interested in the academic study of religion were nonetheless enrolled in their public university's Faculty of Theology, taking a wide variety of courses in the history and theology of the Greek Orthodox Church while also carving out a part of their curriculum for courses with instructors who, like Pachis and Angeliki Ziaka, whom I also first met that year, went about their studies in a manner rather different from many of their theological and priestly counterparts; the colorful, framed icons that adorned the classrooms walls at the university made the difference from what I took to be the usual context of the study of religion very apparent.

Although I was not able to return to Thessaloniki the following year (to teach for a week or so, as I had hoped when I left in 2006), I was able to return in 2008, but this time accompanied by four undergraduate students from my Department. For a colleague on my campus had cancelled her otherwise annual summer study abroad trip to Greece and, knowing that I was going myself, I decided to offer my own hastily organized course for students majoring in the study of religion. Subsidized by my own Department and the College of Arts & Sciences, and accepting no salary (since the airfare, hotel, and food reimbursements struck me as deal enough), I was able to go with a very small group. (Because such courses are self-funding, large groups of students are usually needed to fund the costs of the professor's salary, airfare, hotel, and food, along with the students' own expenses, of course; the benefit of a small group, however, is in the unplanned opportunities that present themselves when you are a group of five or six, rather than twenty or twenty-five.) Having met several of Pachis's grad students in 2006, one in particular—Vaia Touna—had stayed in touch over email since then, and by the time that I had returned in May of 2008, she was, unbeknownst to me, all set to suspend her own life for ten days while guiding our small group all around Thessaloniki, as well as taking us on day trips to nearby archeological sites, where Pachis, joined by some of his other students, generously shared his knowledge on the ancient world with us (e.g., at the ancient city of Dion, in the shadow of Mount Olympus, or Vergina, home to a beautiful museum built into a reconstructed burial mound that is believed to be the tomb of the Macedonian King, Philip II, the father of Alexander the Great). However, among my best memories that year was an impromptu afternoon coffee—something not possible had we had twenty-five students in our group, all riding a bus around the countryside—in the shade of a beautiful garden at Vaia's grandmother's house, in the upper old city. Only Vaia spoke both Greek and English but somehow we all—including Vaia's mother and her late father—understood each other rather well. (The *tsipouro* didn't hurt either.)

When, in May of 2009, I returned again, but with three different students, Vaia, who also returned as our local coordinator and who was by then beginning her PhD at Aristotle University (having recently completed her MA), had organized a small, half-day conference, along with three other students: Olympia Panagiotidou ([2009] who had just completed her MA at Aarhus University, in Denmark, via the Erasmus EU exchange program for students), Thanos Koutoupas ([2010] working then on his MA at Aristotle University), and Klearhos Stamatoulakis ([2009] who was then working on his BA at Aristotle University). The four Greek students each read their papers, graciously in English—each paper based either on their coursework and past research or, if just starting their degrees, their planned research—allowing my students to hear the work being done by Greek students of religion.

To say that this was an honor for us, as visitors and guests, both to hear *and* understand their papers and to witness this collaboration on the part of these four students, would be an understatement. In fact, by the time I had returned to the US later that month, I had already begun to consider how this one-time event could be given legs, as it were, because of how impressed I was with the students' initiative—it therefore struck me as something worth acknowledging and encouraging. After confirming with the presenters and their professor that they were indeed all interested in the possible publication of their papers in the US, I decided to contact Craig Martin, then the editor of the *Bulletin for the Study of Religion*, to see if he would be interested in a submission of not just the four papers but, to make the collection of student papers even more interesting, also a critical response to each from a seasoned North American professor (nicely exemplifying what I think is important about professionalization—working across academic generations—as well as recognizing that, often, students are more along the cutting edge than those of us who think we are already working there). Generously accepting my invitation to write responses to the students (who, in some cases were completely unknown to them) were: Luther Martin (2009), commenting on Panagiotidou's paper; Bill Arnal (2010), replying to Koutoupas's; Randall Styers (2009), responding to Stamatoulakis; and I decided to write on Touna's paper (2010)—which is the response that appears as this chapter. Willi Braun (2010)—who, as with so many other conferences over the years, was my roommate for the 2006 conference in Thessaloniki, and who also joined me and my students that first time we travelled as a group to Thessaloniki in 2008, had met all of the student presenters on his earlier trips and agreed to write a brief introduction to the set of papers.

Although the *Bulletin* only accepted two of the four main papers that we submitted (i.e., those of Koutoupas and Touna, along with the responses to each—though, I should add, that Panagiotidou later had a different paper published by the *Bulletin* [2011]), it was my hope that, whether or not they were published, everyone involved benefited from reading each other's work and exchanging views across the Atlantic on such topics as applications of cognitive science to Mithraism and the use of the category "magic" to understand the ancient and the modern world. Although I have not returned with students since the year when the conference was first mounted, I have heard told that the conference apparently continues annually (though not in English, of course) and that it now is attended by a wide variety of students, both as presenters and as attendees (in 2009 the audience for the inaugural event was primarily comprised of myself and my own students)—its continuation being a wonderful tribute to those four students' self-initiative and collaboration that first year.[1]

I have returned several times to Thessaloniki since my last trip with students, all in an effort to aim higher than just a regularized study abroad course in our Department; instead, the goal is now to establish a longer term "cooperation" (as it is called there) between my own University of Alabama and Aristotle University, one that would benefit many other Departments besides my own. With the enthusiastic support of Dean Robert Olin, of the University of Alabama's College of Arts & Sciences, a semester's worth of events took place on our campus (organized by a committee, comprised of myself along with Steven Ramey and Merinda Simmons [both of Religious Studies], Tatiana Tsakirpooulou-Summers [Modern Languages and Classics (and a native of Thessaloniki, who did her BA at Aristotle University)], and Andrew Dewar [New College, and a musical collaborator with Danae Stefanou, one of our eventual Greek guests in Tuscaloosa]), all revolving around the study of Greece as carried out on our campus—ancient and modern. That semester also saw two scholars from Aristotle University invited to our campus to perform/lecture (Danae Stafanou, a musician and music professor, and Angeliki Ziaka, a professor in the study of religion).[2] What's more, with funding from our Dean, our Department also was able to bring a Greek doctoral student on a work Visa to join us for a semester as a temporary but full-time Instructor, gaining what we hoped was valuable experience in a US public University; Vaia Touna so surpassed our expectations in the Spring semester of 2010, when we inaugurated this program, that we did it again in 2012 with Spyros Piperakis. Although this program was not continued, my Dean and Luoheng Han, the Associate Dean for the Natural Sciences and Mathematics, both travelled to Thessaloniki in May of 2012, assisted closely by Touna as well as by Stefanou and Ziaka, to meet senior Aristotle University administrators in person; since then, a formal agreement between our two schools has been drafted and signed by both schools. Where this program goes—Exchanges of scholars? Exchanges of students? Collaborations among researchers?—is of course, something we will have to wait and see.[3]

While I would be either naïve or pompous to think that I single-handedly brought this all about (for where would I be had Martin not introduced Pachis and I to each other that day in Burlington, Vermont and had I not been able to attend that inaugural conference and met so many interesting people on my first trip to Thessaloniki? Or had one of my students, two years later, not been wanting to go on the cancelled study abroad that was usually offered by my colleague? Or had our Department's Office Administrator, Betty Dickey, not encouraged me to formalize my idea for taking students with me, thereby creating the study abroad program that first year? Or had my Dean not assisted by providing some of the funding for our adventures Greece? Or had Touna not volunteered all of her time each of those years, acted as our guide and translator, and taught us, for example, the dangers of seemingly innocent hand gestures that we needed to avoid making at other drivers while they zoomed by us in little cars and scooters on equally little streets!), and while I recognize from the outset that, although I wrote one of my doctoral comprehensive exams on religion and philosophy in Ancient Greece, I have no special expertise in the study of ancient or modern Greece—that is, despite a semester in Biblical Greek many years ago, I can pretty much only say hello, good morning, good afternoon, good evening, please, and "My name is Russell" or "What is your name?" in modern Greek—what all of this illustrates to me is the manner in which some entrepreneurial spirit, generosity of time, and a little hard work can (if the stars are in the correct alignment, if the gods are willing, or if luck is on your side [pick your fiction]) gain considerable traction and go who knows where, so long as a variety of actors feel that they are getting something out of it and thereby join together. Simply put, it has been a seven-year experiment in social formation—not always successful, but always rewarding. While it is foolish to think that any of us determines larger structural circumstances, of course (for, although many of us police it while grading, who among us single-handedly determines grammar?), it is equally foolish, I would argue, not to recognize that structures, rather than springing like Athena from the head of Zeus, are the results of innumerable past agents interacting with each other, all with a variety of interests that both differed and overlapped with their peers—all of whom were potentially able to influence the structure while working within it. My experiences in Greece confirm this recursive relationship between structure and agency.

And it is this oscillating relationship between structure and agency—and what is at stake in too greatly emphasizing one over the other—that, I think, best captures what the following chapter explores in response to what was then Vaia Touna's plan for her doctoral studies.[4]

"As it Was in the Beginning...":
The Modern Problem of the Ancient Self
(2010)

> In history...everything depends upon turning narrative into prob-
> lems.... Break the drowsy spell of narrative; ask yourself ques-
> tions; set yourself problems; you will become an investigator; you
> will cease to be solemn and begin to be serious.
>   - John Robert Seeley (1971; quoted in Smith 1988: 729)

Having never read Euripides's *Hippolytos*—the Greek tragedy mentioned in
Vaia Touna's very interesting paper, "The Manageable Self in the Early Hellenistic Era" (2010)—I made a point of reading it in the Summer of 2008. I
did so because I had by then begun to work more closely with Touna in her
role as the local coordinator for a study abroad program that I direct, which
takes University of Alabama undergraduates to Thessaloniki, Greece, each
May.[5] Given that her recently completed MA thesis (Touna 2008) was on this
play, and given the manner in which our many conversations on social theory
would often come around to ancient Greek and Hellenistic materials (which
comprised her "e.g.," as Jonathan Z. Smith might phrase it), reading it and
then knowing something of what I was talking about seemed the right thing
to do. Not owning a copy, and not being much (at all) of an ancient Greek
reader, I borrowed one of our university library's English translations: that
of the longtime University of Massachusetts Professor of English, Robert
Bagg (Euripedes 1992). That the book was a paperback—unlike Kovacs's
more authoritative Loeb volume (Euripedes 2000)—and thus easily packed
into luggage for a summer trip to Canada, to visit family for a week, was
appealing.[6]

The play, I learned, was performed in 428 BCE at the festival of Dionysos
in ancient Athens, not long after an earlier version (known as *Hippolytos
Kalyptomenos* [commonly translated as *Hippolytos Veiled*]), received much
public criticism. Euripides's later revision, often characterized by commentators as a correction (known as *Hippolytos Stephanophoros* [or "Hippolytus wearing a garland, or crown"]), however, was awarded first place when
it was first performed. The difference between the two plays is difficult to
determine, since the original is lost (a forty-one line fragment remains [see
Euripedes 1964: 18 ff.]), though Euripides scholars are in general agreement
that the first play's treatment of the female lead—Hippolytos's stepmother,
Phaedra—was deeply troubling to the audience at that time, inasmuch as her

lust for her stepson was likely portrayed openily on the stage—a taboo subject, especially in a society in which the woman's place was within the private, domestic space.[7]

Now, for those who, like my former self, are unacquainted with the extant plot—much less the history of the multiple versions—it is the story of a rather self-confident young man who is an ardent and thus exclusive devotee of the goddess Artemis (associated with, among other things, the hunt, the countryside, virginity, and thus youthfulness); the play's narrative engine is announced in its opening lines: the response that his single-minded dedication evokes from the beautiful Aphrodite (a goddess associated with, among other things, mature, erotic love). In a long, opening speech, her displeasure is evident and she announces her revenge: his stepmother will be compelled by a powerful sexual attraction for her stepson, which will be his undoing—"That youth who crosses me must die" she announces, adding, "His father will kill him" (Euripides 1992: 19, henceforth cited as Bagg).[8] As the play unfolds—which involves Phaedra hiding her longing to the detriment of her own physical and emotional well-being, eventually confiding her terrible secret in her maidservant (i.e., the character usually identified simply as Nurse), who in turn discloses Phaedra's lust to Hippolytos, hoping that he will help, shall we say, quench his stepmother's desire but who, instead, is revolted by the very idea, going so far as to condemn all woman[9]—it narrates the downfall of a household and not, as Aphrodite's prologue suggested, just one man.[10] For Phaedra soon commits suicide, rather than shame herself by acting on her virtually incestuous passion; what's more, she lies about her motives by leaving a note that accuses her stepson of raping her, so as to protect her own biological children's inheritance from her husband, their stepfather; Theseus (the King of Athens, her husband and Hippolytos's biological father) learns of her death and, siding with his wife's version of events, is outraged, cursing his son and calling on his own father, the god Poseidon, to kill Hippolytos for committing such a terrible deed. Thus, by the play's end, after a ferocious bull has arisen from the sea and crushed Hippolytos while driving his chariot away from his home, Artemis appears to the dying Hippolytus and explains to Theseus his terrible mistake; the King's family is by now in ruins, but the son forgives his father and the play closes with Theseus lamenting his son's death and condemning Aphrodite—whose name and whose deeds frame the play's beginning and end.

Sitting in my brother-in-law's house one morning, just outside Niagara Falls, Ontario, with a fresh cup of coffee and the sun just coming up, I recall reading the play's closing lines:

> Athens, you will have your splendor, but never again
> The splendor of this man you lose.

> Aphrodite, I have no heart for your graces.
> I remember forever only your savagery. (Bagg: 85)

My judgment about the play, however, had been made long before these concluding lines brought the goddess, the city state, and our hero into such close proximity. As phrased by Bagg in his translator's introduction—which I had dutifully read prior to beginning the play—the "brutal will" (5) of the "cruel and vindictive," even "savage" (4), Aphrodite had led to the downfall of a truly pious and thus innocent man.[11] For, much like Job from another tradition of storytelling, the audience/reader knows from the outset that he is indeed innocent (just as we know that Phaedra is innocent—merely a tool in Aphrodite's vengeful plan). Hippolytos, we find, boldly, though tragically, resisted the conventions of the city state, that is, devotion to all of the authorized gods, by pursuing instead an intimate, personal relationship with but one god (what scholars often characterize as an example of personal religion[12]), a practice well outside of the city state's usual cultus—opting to live what Bagg characterizes as "a unified spiritual life rather than a promiscuous one" (8). Confirming the way in which the Greek gods are often portrayed, the play turned out to be a lesson in what awaited the truly pious individual when confronted by the unfeeling whims and jealousies of ancient supernatural powers—mysterious and uncontrollable powers that created deep insecurity in the lives of our ancestors,[13] much as was created in Hippolytos's formerly idyllic life, not to mention that of his stepmother, by Aphrodite.

With an orientation provided by the translator's introduction, it therefore seemed reasonable to conclude that the play was an early, individualist morality tale about the tragic end that results when personal moderation (the much prized ancient Greek quality *sophrosyne*), as signified in Hippolytos's virginal restraint and dedication to Artemis alone, comes into conflict with larger societal pressures, as signified in Aphrodite's erotic excess as well as her devotional expectations. Even the behavior of his dear Artemis confirmed such a reading, given her surprisingly aloof response to the suffering of her dying devotee; for, to Hippolytos's question, "Mistress, can you see how badly I am hurt?" she impassively responds:

> I see. But a goddess may not be in tears…
> It is forbidden gods to see death come to a man.
> We must not be touched with the pollution of last agonies and gaspings.
> I believe you are close to this. (Bagg: 81, 84)

The moral of this tale, then? As phrased by Bagg, "the reflection is *inescapable* that the gods are cheerfully indifferent to the contradiction in their code which allows the supposedly cherished innocent and pious to perish through no fault of their own" (5; emphasis added). The tale is therefore a two thousand five hundred year old critique of the gods and, by extension, the city state that was supported by their forced ritual worship. If left unchallenged, the bold individual will be crushed by the uncaring weight of society; it is therefore a cautionary tale that a contemporary author such as George Orwell might well have told—which is perhaps why Bagg, an English Professor, finds it so useful to quote throughout his introduction such other modern writers as Shelley, Shakespeare, Thoreau, Robert Frost, and Henry James, all in support of his reading of the play.

Bagg, it seems, had me convinced; I was therefore content with his apparently commonsense, uncontroversial, and thus (as he phrased it himself) "inescapable" reading until, that is, I shared it with Touna via an email message that I typed out on my PalmPilot, shortly after I finished the play. Identifying with the tragic hero, and doing so without really thinking much about it, I recall writing something about how unjust his suffering was and how terribly Aphrodite had behaved, going so far as writing something, half joking, about "that poor man" and then using this reading to compliment the socially progressive judges who awarded Euripides's anti-traditionalist message.

But this was hardly her reading of the play. Because she had far more historical detail on the period than I, I paid attention to what Touna wrote back. Although I no longer have her reply, I recall her politely disagreeing with me (a politeness that, in hindsight, goes to the very heart of an alternative reading of the tragedy), saying something about just how dangerous the social values represented by the Hippolytos character would have been in the ancient world. Far from being a pious and moderate innocent (e.g., an adult virgin who modestly chose not to play a role in so-called public life), she argued that, as a grown man unwilling to accept the usual obligations of adulthood, Hippolytos was indeed dangerous to the world of Euripides's audience—a world that was, when the play was first performed, already three years into what would eventually prove to be a long and devastating series of battles that we today know as the Peloponnesian War (431–404 BCE); the tragedy of the play, therefore, was not, as Bagg had argued, the innocent protagonist's death at the hands of an uncaring world but, instead, Hippolytos's *hubris*, his uncaring attitude to his fellows, and thus his sad lack of self-awareness (despite his proclamations to the opposite). Contrary to Bagg's reading, then, Hippolytos was anything but moderate in Touna's reading; somewhat like the irony buried in the boastful claims of Plato's character Euthyphro, concerning his own unrivaled expertise on all matters pertaining to piety (*eusebia*),[14] it became evident that Hippolytos's claims of his own privileged relationship to Artemis[15] may have effectively signaled to a Hellenistic audience that the character was anything but restrained and innocent—a sign made evident in the early speech of the servant who, perhaps speaking for the audience, is aghast at his master's petulant and thus impious behavior toward Aphrodite.[16] And because such immoderation, such a preoccupation with the self, was a threat to his fellows (and what threatens such a society more than a man who refuses to reproduce and, during a time of war, to defend the city state?), it is not inconceivable that this character's death would have been understood by the members of that ancient festival's audience—or at least by what I now understood to be its socially conservative judges—as richly deserved and thus justly given.[17] The tragedy of the play, then, is not Hippolytos's ruin; instead, the true tragedy of the play is the ruin that his self-centered actions wreak on his father's household (i.e., the kinship group). It's plot is therefore indeed a warning, but not for individualists to be wary of oppressive social forces; instead, if we leave behind our own post-Enlightenment, modern notion of the individual as being the building block of society, we can re-imagine an ancient world in which *Hippolytos* could be seen as a warning for a society already under attack by the outside world also to be on the watch for those who threaten its existence from within.

Reading Touna's email reply, and based on my understanding of ancient Greek society, the social value of piety, and its link to systems of rank and social deference (in a word, *eusebia*; see the discussion in McCutcheon 2007: 25–29; 90), I suddenly realized not only why Bagg was not so much wrong as historically rather sloppy in advancing his reading of the play, but why the view of the individual that we today possess, a view that informs Bagg's reading of the play, is so useful. For even though I have written on a number of occasions on the socially constructed nature of the self, and even though I have often criticized the individualist approach to the study of religion[18]—what we might call our modern, Rousseauian understanding of isolated actors as the basis for society—this model has deep roots in the way that we today think and act. With the help of Touna's reply, what was now apparent to me was that I had read Euripides's text a little too cavalierly as I sat there drinking my coffee at sun up, unwittingly using the play to reconfirm a modern, liberal humanist model of the self as being prior to, and thus this in strict opposition to, the larger social group—a model very much at home in liberal democracies but one surely alien to the historic world of the play. Simply put, I had failed to read the text as a piece of historical data and, instead, had projected onto it a contemporary set of concerns motivated by a modern view of the individual's place outside of society; doing so, I had failed to take the past seriously *as past*, for instead of seeing it as a foreign land, I instead imagined it, as do many historians, simply as a Hegelian precursor that "inescapably" moved toward our present.[19] When it came to analyzing the play I therefore uncritically followed Bagg and described as self-evident (i.e., the apparent universality of our modern view of the individual) what instead ought to have been explained (i.e., how to understand different historical and cultural conceptions of the biological person's place within society). To appeal to my epigraph—quoted from Jonathan Z. Smith, who has already taught me so much but from whom, apparently, I still have much to learn—I made a rather basic error: I had failed to turn a narrative (in this case, not so much an ancient tragedy's plot but, instead, the story that a thoroughly modernist translator placed onto the back of the ancient play) into a problem to be studied. For Smith, making just this move, from mere description of self-evidencies to explanations for how they became self-evident in the first place, is—as he describes it in commenting on Seeley's quotation—an imperative if our work is to count as scholarship rather than merely idle repetition or paraphrase.

And this is where I return explicitly to Touna's interesting proposal for her doctoral work, "The Manageable Self in the Early Hellenistic Era"—although my hope is that readers understand my self-incriminating, opening narrative to have illustrated the problem Touna will be examining in arguing her case concerning the social, political, military, and economic conditions that made possible the invention of new sorts of Hellenistic selves. I predict that the majority of her modern, scholarly sources (following, to whatever extent, Festugière's [1960] obviously outdated but, despite this, still representative statement of how the ancient development of personal religion foreshadowed modernity, if not Christianity)[20] will be doing precisely what Bagg did in his translation and commentary: using ancient materials to make modern arguments about the place of the private person in society, doing so by naturalizing (i.e., authorizing) contemporary and thus contingent positions by concluding that, if we can find them in our society's so-called classics, then they must have always been, and will always be, present in the human heart—which amounts to a scholarly version of the Christian doxological *Gloria Patri*: "As it was in the beginning, is now and ever shall be, world without end. Amen."

For example, consider the case of the noted French scholar Paul Veyne (author of the important *Did the Greeks Believe in Their Myths?* [1988]), who, unfortunately conceives of privacy as a substantive domain naturally distinguishable from the public—rather than entertaining that social contest and force may be necessary to establish and reproduce the appearance of privacy, domesticity, and interiority in any society. Although I have critiqued him elsewhere for overlooking this social work (McCutcheon 2003a: 263), consider how his essay on Roman religion, in his edited volume, *A*

History of Private Life, is structured around the seemingly commonsense, yet curiously modern, position that religion is primarily a matter of private sentiment. For, despite providing the required acknowledgement that ancient piety "lay not in faith, works, or contemplation [to name three modern Christian approaches to which he is obviously referring] but in a whole range of practices" (1987: 211), he nonetheless drops back into a suitably idealist approach when speculating on, for example, the motivation for beliefs in life after death: "Consoling ideas about the afterlife stemmed from the *desire* to believe, not from the authority of an *established religion*" (221; emphasis added). According to Veyne, belief systems arise from individual desires (perhaps, if presupposing some sort of human nature, shared across the species?)—despite, rather than because of, social institutions.

It should be obvious that placing such causality within the isolated individual is in opposition to what a thoroughly social theory of belief would look like (an approach akin to Touna's interest in a thoroughly social theory of the ancient self). Although space does not allow a detailed elaboration here, consider how different Veyne's approach is from, for instance, that of the philosopher and social theorist, Slavoj Žižek; paraphrasing Louis Althusser's re-reading of Blaise Pascal's famous statement, he writes: "kneel down and *you shall believe that you knelt because of your belief...*; in short, the 'external' ritual performatively generates its own ideological foundation" (1997: 12–13).[21] It is this latter theoretical position—one in which experiences of interiority are the artifacts of prior institutional situations—that Touna needs to consider adopting to carry out her project, for her idea is that contingent, ancient social conditions (such as the decline of Athenian society brought about by the devastation of its wars with Sparta, among others) made possible new types of social relationships that organized and thereby managed diverse human beings, increasingly free to move between cities, complete with their inevitably diverse interests. Her point is that it was these all too public conditions and relationships (some blindly structural, such as plagues, while others were mixtures of structure and agency, such as wars or individuals experimenting within newfound structural options) that made possible new ways of perceiving one's self in relation to the place of others—made possible the appearance of new sorts of private selves throughout society's various public domains. Keeping in mind that these new ways of perceiving the self—and thereby being either a public, authorized self or a contained, domestic self—were a product of the social will therefore be crucial to the success of her project; relying on Veyne's guidance would therefore not be wise, for he reads a modern, philosophically idealist notion of the individual backwards in time, as if it can shed light on the motives of the ancients.

Or, again, consider another justifiably respected specialist on the ancient world, Jean Pierre Vernant. Sadly, here too we find a similar failure to carry social theory to its logical end by seeing privacy—and, along with it, that most intimate private possession we are said to have: our very selves—as a thoroughly social phenomenon. For, writing on the so-called mystery religions, in an essay entitled "Some Aspects of Personal Identity in Greek Religion," he notes: "Religious life may have taken a more individual character here. A mystery established a community which was not social, but, rather, spiritual, in which each individual would participate of his own free will, through free associations, and regardless of his civic status" (1983: 326). This is a puzzling statement for any social theorist to read, for we now seem to have on our hands three separate domains: the individual, the social, and the spiritual.[22] What's more, the individual, who opts for membership in a so-called voluntary association, is somehow set apart from the social inasmuch as free will seems to be a natural possession of such a socially autonomous actor rather than the name participants give to the taken-for-granted limits of the social norms into which they have been acculturated.[23]

The problem with Vernant's approach to the mystery religions becomes even more evident when we juxtapose it with that of Burkert—who, starting from the position that "Greek religion, bound to the polis, is public religion to an extreme degree,"[24] concludes that "mysteries do not constitute a separate religion outside the public one; [instead,] they represent a special opportunity for dealing with gods within the multifarious framework of polytheistic polis religion. In Crete, we are told, the very rituals which were absolutely secret in Samothrace or Elusis were performed in public" (276, 277). For social theorists, Vernant's sharp, modernist distinction between the personal and the public (not to mention the spiritual) therefore holds far less promise than does Burkert's recognition that the ancient Greek polis, like all societies, was comprised of multiple sub-groups, all integrating members within specific forms and levels of the social, ensuring that even so-called secrets are understood by scholars as publicly traded (though often strictly regulated) goods.

So, to conclude this brief illustration, the problem here is that, with regard to the notion of personal religion, Veyne and Vernant—both admittedly respected and influential scholars of the ancient world—merely reproduce a modern view of the individual, normalized considerably by pitching it backward in time. They therefore present as eternal and thus natural what, once approached differently, turns out to be merely historical and inevitably contingent; to appeal to Smith once again, they simply described their present reality rather than explaining its function and its origins. Their guidance on thinking seriously about social experiments in ancient Greek identity-formation is therefore limited, at best, for they have not followed their fellow countryman and intellectual predecessor's model: "My task," Durkheim wrote on the opening page of his introduction to *The Elementary Forms of Religious Life*, "will not stop at description" (1995: 1).

So, in response to Touna's proposal for using the Hellenistic material to examine such an important topic as the social origins and political effects of the Hellenistic self, I offer a somewhat ironic caution: she may find herself surprisingly alone in carrying out this work, at least when it comes to the body of modern scholarship that usually accompanies those who set out to study ancient material. That is because she has charted a course that runs counter to the rich tradition of the scholarship that has developed in response to the Greek material—or, better put, a tradition that, somewhat like Aphrodite using Phaedra, deftly makes use of the ancient material to advance what turns out to be thoroughly modern arguments. If I am correct, then two things follow: first, those theorists who will accompany her on this intellectual journey will likely come from other fields where formerly timeless identity has lately been historicized so well (e.g., Postmodern Studies, Gender Studies, Race Studies, critical Historiography, and, to a lesser but still significant degree, Religious Studies, etc.); and second, the usual distinction between primary and secondary sources, between historical, source material and subsequent scholarly commentaries, will break down because, just as in the case of Bagg's translation of *Hippolytos*, the common or accepted reading of the ancient material will turn out to be a hindsight creation of later centuries and thus later concerns. The scholars on whom she would normally think to draw upon in supporting her case may therefore end up being but more instances of data in need of analysis—hardly a bad turn of events, come to think of it, for this is to be expected when one begins working on a novel (and precisely because it is original, important) idea.

Drawing on my initial reading of *Hippolytos*, and my own "road to Damascus"-like conversion when hearing Touna's counter-reading—a reading suggested to me with all the moderation and awareness of social place that Hippolytos lacked—my reply is therefore an encouragement for Touna also not to be content with mere description; moreover, I advise her to become a little less solemn in her work and a little more *im*moderate in her approach to the scholarly tradition on which she draws in doing her work (though, *unlike* Hippolytos, remaining strategic and tactful, of course), thereby joining such predecessors as Marx, Durkheim, and Freud in always being a suspicious hermeneut, not too quickly trusting secondary work, and, instead, assuming from the outset that its use of ancient materials is not innocent and thus never merely descriptive. If so, then she may find that her work will end up being as much focused on modern readings of the ancient material as it is in offering her own reading of the ancient material. For the narrative that needs to be problematized may not lie in the distant past but in the more recent past's attempts to guarantee the immortality of its social relations by pitching their images as far back as possible, hoping that in finding them at such distance we would all be persuaded that they can naturally be found everywhere and every time.[25]

Problematizing such a narrative will not come without risks, of course, for it means upsetting a number of long cherished assumptions about the present and the past, the self and the other, and the privileges that come to those who unquestioningly use, and thereby, reinforce them. Like Durkheim and the effect that his unrelenting emphasis on the priority of the group over its member's sense of themselves as individuals has for many who read him today, for her readers Touna might also be seen to be "the bearer of a message they tend to find disagreeable at best and incomprehensible at worst" (Berlinerblau 2005: 214). Though, come to think of it, this is not a bad reaction to elicit for anyone with an original idea who is willing to chart her own course instead of taking the usual short cut of uncritically describing common sense. For one who is patient enough to take the long way around starts from the position that there's nothing all that common about common sense; seeing it instead as a problem to be examined, and thus the object of questions (i.e., common to whom?), is the continual challenge of a serious, scholarly investigator. And I have every confidence that Ms. Touna can manage just such a challenge.

Notes

1. For more information, visit www.studyofreligion.gr and click "Student Events" in the main menu. Oddly, there is no evidence or mention at this website of the first year's conference though the following year's event, in 2010, is indeed listed as the "second annual"—although two of the students from that year continue to be involved as "team members" according to this website.
2. Visit http://www.as.ua.edu/greece for more information on the events from the Spring 2011 semester.
3. In March 2014 the Dean of Arts & Sciences at the University of Alabama brought Dr Spyros Pavlides, the Dean of Sciences at Aristotle University, to lecture at the University of Alabama and, in May of 2014, a nine-person team of faculty from Alabama travelled to Thessaloniki as part of the inaugural research collaborative between the two schools.
4. That Touna has, since then, moved to pursue a PhD program at the University of Alberta, working with Willi Braun as her supervisor, is perhaps the

best example of how agency and structure are intertwined—for although she hardly controlled, say, the conditions that determined the funding decisions that make many international doctoral students' studies possible, no amount of financial assistance would have made her studies possible had she not applied.

5.   The third year of this program is now being planned; see: http://www.as.ua. edu/rel/greece.html. (Ed. Note: on April 27, 2011, about a week before we were to depart on this trip, a major tornado struck Tuscaloosa, killing 53 in the city. My own house was struck, and this prompted me to cancel the trip for 2011. Since then I have not returned to Greece with students.)

6.   A related translation (illustrated by Leonard Baskin) was first published by Bagg in 1969 (Northampton, UK: Gehenna Press). For more information on Bagg, see his web site: http://robertbagg.com/, where a slightly different version of his translation of *Hippylotos* is posted as a Word file (http://robert-bagg.com/events.htm [accessed March 1, 2013]).

7.   McDermott (2000) attempts to identify passages (i.e., allusions) in the existing version "that seem designed to call attention, self-consciously, both to the fact that this play was a revision and to the nature of some of the changes made between the original and its correction" (240). She concludes that the Nurse and Phaedra's roles were likely switched between versions, such that Phaedra's earlier forthright approach to Hippolytos and the Nurse's former discouragement resulted in a revision in which Phaedra resists the urge while her Nurse approaches Hippolytus.

8.   For reasons that I will discuss below, I am citing the Bagg edition for these quotations, noting page numbers instead of traditional line numbers due to the fact that it is rather difficult to provide accurate line number from his edition.

9.   Hippolytos:

>   Damn you! I hate women. I'll never quell
>   that loathing, Some say I'm insatiable hostile—
>   but women are insatiably lewd.
>   Either convert them to chaste decency
>   or allow me to stomp on their sex till I'm dead (Bagg 48).

10.   Quoting the Nurse, "she [i.e., Aphrodite] has destroyed Phaedra, me, and the royal house!" (Euripides 2000: 161, see lines 353–61).

11.   Even Walter Burkert agrees: "Gods cannot give life, but they can destroy it. There is no devil in the ancient religions but each god has his dark and dangerous side… Aphrodite cruelly destroys the unyielding Hippolytus" (1985: 188).

12.   More on personal religion below.

13.   For example, I think here of David Hume's classic portrait (1956) of early humans grappling with their environment: "We are placed in this world as in a great theatre, where the true springs and causes of every event are entirely

concealed from us; nor have we either sufficient wisdom to foresee, or power to prevent those ills, with which we are continually threatened. We hang in perpetual suspense between life and death, health and sickness, plenty and want; which are distributed amongst the human species by secret and unknown causes, whose operation is oft unexpected, and always unaccountable. The *unknown causes*, then, become the constant object of our hope and fear; and while the passions are kept in perpetual alarm by an anxious expectation of events, the imagination is equally employed in forming ideas of those powers, on which we have so entire a dependence" (28–29).

14. For example, when speaking to Socrates he says: "[W]hen I speak in the assembly about matters of religion [eusebia], and tell them in advance what will occur, they laugh at me as if I were a madman, and yet I never have made a prediction that did not come true. But the truth is, they are jealous of all such people as ourselves" (*Euthyphro* 3c; Plato 1987: 181).

15. After identifying himself as the lone person able to pick flowers for a crown for Artemis, in a virginal field "where no shepherd would think it wise to pasture his animals, a perfect field no iron blade has yet cut down," Hippolytos goes on:

> No man alive approaches my good luck—
> To ride with you [i.e., Artemis], to share confidences:
> Your voice is distinct in my ears,
> Though your face I have never seen. (Bagg 20–21)

16. The servant speaks:

> If you believe arrogance offends,
> It's strange that you never
> Speak to one proud and awesome goddess. (Bagg 21)

17. Of significance is that this reading also assists us to understand why the revisions received such a different hearing from the earlier version—if indeed the first version was received as poorly as the ancient sources attest and for the reasons that Euripides scholars agree upon. For now we see that Phaedra's sexual forthrightness in the earlier version, much as Hippolytos's self-preoccupation in the later version, contravened important social values for the public behavior of women at the time. The revised version's Phaedra, fighting to her death against her unaccountable passions, portrays the character in a far more noble and thus acceptable light, especially important inasmuch as the audience knows that she is merely used by Aphrodite as an instrument of her revenge, and thus truly innocent. The character's battle with her own sexual nature, therefore, more effectively manages—to borrow Touna's word—an otherwise unmanageable (at least in the eyes of the festival's judges and Athens's ruling elites of the time) and thus potentially dangerous thing when let lose in public: female eroticism.

18.   It is an approach reminiscent of William James's work on religion, in that it finds the most important unit of analysis to be the lone devotee's private experience which is only later expressed publicly, in words and action, and thus inevitably in some derivative, and thus polluted, fashion (e.g., McCutcheon 2003a: 252–90; McCutcheon 2005c).

19.   I am hardly the first to identify what amounts to the historian's version of the genetic fallacy: just because something happened chronologically earlier does not mean that it exists in a necessary causal or development relationship with that which comes later.

20.   Festugière: "There is no true religion except that which is personal. True religion is, first of all, closeness to God. Every religious ceremony is but empty make-believe if the faithful who participate in it do not feel that thirst for the Absolute, the anxious desire to enter into personal contact with the mysterious Being who is hidden behind appearances... The intensely religious man is wont to withdraw from the world in order to contemplate it at leisure. He appears therefore to be solitary, odd, unsociable" (1, 17). Hippolytos's seemingly personal and thus anti-social relationship with Artemis is, for Festugière, what theologians once might have termed a *praeparatio evangelica*, or at least an early foreshadowing of a modern mystical form of Christian spirituality, obviously advocated by the Dominican, Festugière.

21.   For a classic example of such an approach, consult Durkheim and Mauss's still provocative attempt to offer a social account for origins of classification systems (1963).

22.   Vernant had earlier speculated on "the interlocking of the social and religious spheres" (325), confirming this reading of him as assuming that "the religious" was somehow apart from "the social." It is in this way that a revised notion of *sui generis* religion often re-enters the work of solemn scholars who claim to have left older traditions in our field behind. But for a serious social theory, there is nothing apart from the social.

23.   This is likely the way we should understand, for example, American nationalist claims that the US "is the freest nation in the world," despite the fact that some visitors, accustomed to a very different economy of freedom, conclude that it is a surveillance state.

24.   I recognize here the difficulties in his use of the category "public religion," inasmuch as it has meaning only if distinguished from "private religion." The position I am arguing here would do away with the distinction and, instead, work to develop an analysis that takes into account the many overlapping and potentially competing publics that comprise any social group.

25.   Again, Festugière nicely sums up this troublesome position: "However—and let me stress this point—these forms of personal religion after Alexander do not constitute a novelty in Greece. Nothing changes so completely in the nature of man when deep-seated impulses are in question" (10).

Chapter 15

Introduction

> Not everything that Russell McCutcheon wrote about my article is
> inaccurate or simply false, but much of it is. Bolstered by his mis-
> reading of broad swaths of the article, Professor McCutcheon has
> done little more than insist "No, this is not what I meant at all!"
> Alas, as Michel Foucault (and so many others) has pointed out,
> an author is typically the last to dictate the meaning of his or her
> words. Despite what McCutcheon may think, however, my *JAAR*
> article (2011) was neither about carrying forward his traditional
> nor his authorial intent. (Omer 2012: 1083)

So opens Atalia Omer's curious rejoinder to a brief article of mine (which
comprises this chapter) that I wrote in response to a long essay that she
first published in *JAAR* in 2011—an essay in which I think it fair to say
that she tries to press further some of my earlier work (i.e., to overcome
what she characterizes as my limiting binary between critics and caretakers), to then argue for the need for scholars of religion to become, what
she termed there, critical caretakers who are capable of "imagining ways
to redress abuses, misinterpretations, manipulations, and unjust interpretations of religion vis-à-vis political, cultural, and economic organizations of
social life" (Omer 2011: 485). Her rejoinder to my reply, which closed out
our *JAAR* exchange, is curious for more reasons than this brief introduction can address, of course, but suffice it to say that (as quoted above) citing
Foucault's death of the author in her opening lines, in order to spank me for
my "mis-reading" and for my overt falsification of her text (later called a
"caricature of my original argument" [1083]—linked, no doubt, to what she
names as my reliance on "theoretical sloganeering" [1084]—itself a form
of sloganeering, if you ask me, that cuts its own rather broad swath through
twenty years of my own writing career) *and then* telling readers what she
actually meant in her original essay…—well, it seems to me that the contradiction here is so apparent that I need not dwell on it any further. After all,
she is not the first to use the old one-two punch of inserting a self-beneficial
reading of a text into the newly vacated space created by a blunt postmodernism that dislodged the interpretation with which she disagrees. Remove
one agent—a falsifier, a poor reader, a sloganeering caricature artist—and

insert another who is the better hermeneut inasmuch as she is the original owner of the meaning.

But the truly curious thing to me about this exchange is not the content (i.e., arm wrestling with Omer over who gets to determine the correct meaning of a text and the true intentions of the author) but, instead, the context in which the exchange took place; for while readers can find and read her original essay for themselves, and also her rejoinder as well as the following response to the first of her two papers, what they will *not* find in the archives, no matter how close their close reading of these texts may be, is what lies tangled in the background of these various pieces—that which conjured them into existence in the first place. Disentangling and telling that tale, as best I can, strikes me as worthwhile, for it says some surprising things about what it means to recover agency and voice.

On June 13, 2011, I wrote the editor of *JAAR*, Amir Hussain, an email to express my puzzlement at seeing poetry beginning the second issue of 2011 (a topic to which I have recently in a separate essay [contained in McCutcheon 2014]). I admit that I had not even looked at the contents of the issue that just arrived in the mail, because of how perplexed I was concerning why a uncontextualized poem opened it. But what was more perplexing, perhaps, was that in his reply he noted that, at first, he thought I was emailing to complain about Omer's essay (2011) in that issue, which, it turned out, had been accepted prior to him taking over the journal—an article that, at the time, I had not even seen listed in the table of contents, much less read. (For those keeping score, that means we're talking now about the agency of the prior *JAAR* editor and [presumably] his anonymous outside readers, who accepted the article, and Hussain, for bringing her essay to my attention.) Not long after that, my colleague, Merinda Simmons, messaged me asking if I had read Omer's essay, for she apparently had and she wanted to discuss it. (The agency now goes to Simmons.) So, with two mentions of the same essay in such a short time frame, I decided to read it.

As made plain in the following brief reply to that essay, I found the use to which Omer had put some of my work rather odd, for in trying to go beyond my position Omer had, as I read her, actually provided a piece of data that my earlier position had critiqued. But talking now about the reply that I eventually wrote gets the cart well ahead of the horse. So, returning to my narrative, not long after learning of the essay and then reading it, Simmons and I met to discuss it—notably, the particular sort of identity politics that she thought was evident in Omer's article, whereby a specific political program is advanced as the obvious (apparently to the author, at least) path that scholars ought to be adopting in their studies (a move well known to Simmons from her work in other data domains). We both thought that a reply was in order and agreed to write one together. On June 18, 2011, I alerted the editor of the journal that we intended to co-write a reply to the essay that he had brought to my attention and submit it to him for his consideration—something to which he was very open. But then, on August 31, 2011, after Simmons and I had met again, this time to discuss the first draft that she had agreed to write, for me to then rewrite/revise, it was evident to me that any contributions from me would not be all that helpful. So I wrote to the editor that day:

> I recently read over a draft of what my colleague (Merinda Simmons) wrote as the basis for a reply to Omer's JAAR essay. Struck me not only as quite good (i.e., fair, critical, well-written, etc.) but also as bearing the marks of her own scholarly voice and thus something that will stand far better as her own piece than something co-written with me—I've therefore recommended that she finish the piece and send it directly to *JAAR*. I'm hoping that *JAAR* entertains it as a response.

An encouraging reply from the editor, and a copy of that email to Simmons meant that I was no longer involved and this was, instead, her topic to tackle, in her words and using her own arguments and examples. That Simmons and I happen to agree on some (but hardly all) matters strikes me as no more significant than the fact that, say, Omer happens to agree with a variety of the people whom she cites and whose arguments she builds upon in her work (such as her adoption of my book's terminology)—none of us, after all, think up arguments in a vacuum.

And thus, like Elvis, my agency had now left the building.

At this point the story gets a little more interesting, I think, for by November 30, 2011, not terribly long after Simons had formally submitted her reply to the journal, she let me know that *JAAR* had decided that it was too long (about eight thousand words) and that it therefore needed to be peer reviewed (yet more agency enters our tale, but anonymously so). Deciding not to cut it down to a five to seven page paper, as was suggested to her as one option, Simmons agreed to see what the external readers said. Now, as evident from this very book, I've been involved in a number of response/reply exchanges, certainly not all explicitly linked to papers that were on my own work,[1] and I don't think I have ever had the blind peer review process govern the publication of a piece of writing that was in direct response to something already (and recently) published in a journal. While it is certainly up to the editor to decide whether the journal wishes to publish an unsolicited response, invoking the peer review process to adjudicate an outright reply strikes me as rather puzzling, especially based on the criterion of length; for, lacking the word limit policy for replies that, if memory serves me correctly, *JAAR* once had, this seemed at the time to be an arbitrary criterion at best, especially given the fact that Omer's original essay was itself thirty-eight journal pages in length and over fifteen thousand words long (by my rough count)—suggesting that, if Omer's argument was as substantial as the length of her paper then any well-argued response would itself more than likely also be substantive.

Anyone who has served as an editor of a journal knows that there are a number of factors well beyond the editor's agency, such as the time taken to find external readers to agree to evaluate a submission, let alone to have them do so in not just a timely but also a worthwhile manner. Perhaps for this reason, it was not until July 3, 2012 (about nine months later) that Simmons finally heard back from *JAAR* concerning her direct reply to one of its own articles. As I recall, another journal had learned of her piece in the meantime and was interested in it, so she had been querying *JAAR* periodically for word of its decision (e.g., in May 2012, several months after submitting the response, Simmons let me know that she had emailed the editor but no decision came forward). Although her paper was never formally rejected by *JAAR*, she was finally told on July 3, 2012, after querying the editor again, that, informally, the anonymous external readers found the paper interesting but did not think that it "fit" the journal. How an article written explicitly in direct response to a paper published in the journal the year before did not fit the very same journal was, of course, not explained.

At this point several things happened in pretty short order. 1. Simmons decided to send her response instead to Aaron Hughes at *Method & Theory in the Study of Religion* (a new agent is introduced to the game)—who was then the incoming editor and, as such, was putting in place the contents for 2013, his inaugural year with the journal, and who, in short order, accepted it (Simmons 2013b). Soon after, he sent it to Omer (who now enters my narrative as a player for the first time) for her response (2013); 2. Once Simmons had communicated *JAAR*'s final decision to me, I sent (on July 7, 2012) what I still think was a professional but, yes indeed, a strongly worded email (with the subject line: "An expression of my disappointment in JAAR's review process") to the editor of *JAAR* (and copied it to Simmons, given that the topic was concerned with her work), written in both the voice of a member of JAAR's editorial advisory board and also as someone who had helped to broker Simmons's submission of a direct reply to one of its own articles (after all, the journal invites board members to submit their own work and to help to find material for the journal as well as find possible reviewers for books). In that email I expressed my strong displeasure at the manner in which "fit"—a category that is not tethered to any publicly stated criteria whatsoever and thus one that can neither be supported nor critiqued—was used to reject an article; 3. Thinking about past email exchanges with the editor that took place prior to the notion of co-writing a reply along with Simmons had occurred to me—back when the editor had kindly agreed to entertain a response to Omer written by me—I also notified him that:

> I therefore plan to write a very brief reply to Omer and send it to you in the coming days and I fully expect that, as per our much earlier conversations on this topic, *JAAR* will publish it (with whatever response Omer is or is not invited to write). I ask you to confirm in writing that you will do this.

And finally, 4. I ended my email by making sure that it was understood that my concern was for a wider set of professional issues that, I thought then and still do now, are at stake in this admittedly very minor episode in the untold history of our field. And so I wrote:

> On a side note, I have myself written the introduction to the *MTSR* papers on Aaron Hughes's essay and the responses that Matt Day commissioned while he was editor of *MTSR* [Ed. Note: see McCutcheon 2012]. It has already gone into production and will appear in the last issue for 2012. I will not revise it in light of this unfortunate episode, but the central issue of that introduction is the terribly problematic nature of the institution of peer review. Finding *JAAR* using the notion of "fit"—especially with regard to (in my professional opinion) a well written/argued/documented article directly responding to one of *JAAR*'s own published essays—sadly provides but one more example of this.

Five days later, on July 12, 2012, I completed my brief reply to Omer's original essay and submitted it online to *JAAR*; the editor, who exchanged a couple of frank emails with me subsequent to my forthright message quoted above, agreed to publish it and by early September 2012 it went into production and was published, along with Omer's long rejoinder (whose opening paragraph was quoted at the outset of this introduction) in the last issue for 2012.

But what do I hope readers take away from this tale of agency and voice? First off, reading Omer's reply to Simmons (both of which were eventually published in *MTSR*; pre-publication versions of each were shared with me by Simmons) indicates that, curiously, Simmons herself has been erased from the entire debate, inasmuch as she is, in Omer's estimation, nothing but a "parrot" for myself (after all, Omer's *MTSR* rejoinder to Simmons was originally entitled "Parroting McCutcheon, Policing 'Religion': On Merinda Simmons's Protection of the Critic vs. Caretaker Dichotomy"—in my reading, the rejoinder is oddly more addressed to me than its author, Simmons). For a scholar so interested in issues agency, marginalization, and power, it is fascinating for Omer to so easily dismiss Simmons's voice as an author and critical thinker in her own right and, instead, attribute Simmons's arguments to her senior male colleague (yes, I think the structural constraints known as gender as well as university rank need to enter the discussion here)—a contradiction no less interesting than citing Foucault's death of the author while simultaneously asserting ownership over her original *JAAR* essay's *correct* meaning. (Aside: I fear what Omer would have said in reply to me had I claimed that her agreement with other more senior males cited in her work indicated that she was just an unthinking, passive mouthpiece [i.e., what I take it to mean when one is said to parrot another's words] or had she known the history of my reply and the manner in which it was not the need to defend myself that motivated my response but, rather, a desire to ensure that an alternative voice made it into the journal's pages once Simmons's reply was denied entry.)

Second, given that my *JAAR* reply to Omer, which follows this introduction, is about two thousand words, whereas her rejoinder to me is fifteen journal pages long and over six thousand words (yes; her rejoinder is three times longer than my reply!), I wonder if her piece was sent out for peer review, just as Simmons's was—given how substantial and long it was. I doubt it, of course, since invoking this in Simmons's case struck me as arbitrary, at best; also, the time frame from when Omer would have received my reply from *JAAR* to when the two papers were published was so short that only an extremely prompt and efficient set of external readers could have done the job so quickly. Judging by the eight or nine months it took Simmons to get just a vague, informal reply from her anonymous readers, relayed through the editor via email…, well, for whatever reason, it's unlikely anyone thought Omer's piece needed vetting by external readers. If I am correct in these speculations, then it certainly raises questions concerning the consistency of the editorial processes within the journal—fairness and justice being a major preoccupation of Omer's essays, I can't help but hope that she would support my inquiry into such a seemingly inconsistent and thus unfair double standard. Why was external review necessary in the case of Simmons's critique of Omer but possibly not of Omer's critique of me?

Third, given that Omer's rejoinder repeatedly informs readers that I have falsified and caricatured her work (pretty much the same tactic adopted in her reply *MTSR* to Simmons, by the way—which makes Omer's above-cited critique of me, as if I was protesting "No, this is not what I meant at all!" pretty ironic, no?), it makes me wonder about the standards of *JAAR* in publishing my reply in the first place (i.e., if Omer is *correct* in her assessment of my poor reading skills, then my following paper is absolutely filled with falsehoods and, according to her, mere sloganeering instead of rational argumentation) *or* in agreeing to publish her rejoinder to me (i.e., if she is *incorrect* in her assessment of me and is, instead, defending herself by means of what might be considered by some to be rather outlandish, perhaps even unprofessional, claims that undermine my own hard won reputation as a scholar who offers critiques but does so in a rigorously argued manner). Had external readers been involved to assess both articles prior to acceptance and publication—if making this call was beyond the expertise of the editor, that is—then this regrettable episode in "he said/she said" could have easily been avoided, for one of our two essays likely should *not* have been accepted by the journal. To rephrase, unlike FOX News in the US, *JAAR* is not charged to be "fair and balanced" but, instead, to publish essays that employ arguments that can be contested and debated, much as it ought to be stating reasons for declining to publish something that can equally be contested and debated.

Fourth and finally, this episode provides a wonderful example of not only the sort of argumentation and rhetoric that scholars sometimes use when engaging each other but also an insight—for those new to the game—of what can take place behind the professional curtain. That things can get far more heated and thus interesting when the stakes are even higher (such as deciding whether to hire someone, or tenure them, or how to allocate budgets, or grant scholarships, etc.), should not go unnoticed.

I now find that my introduction to the following chapter is considerably longer than the chapter itself (which is followed by an appendix that seemed directly relevant)—perhaps this is as it should be, in this case, for it is indicative of the complicated social worlds of desires and accidents that are not apparent when one gives a text a "close reading" in an effort to recover the true meaning of its author or the silenced voice of some subject. That the people named in this introduction—Simmons, Omer, Hussain, Hughes, let alone the unnamed outside readers who apparently played so important a role in this story—all undoubtedly have their own versions of the tale, with details entirely unknown to this author, should tell us much about the tangled world we enter when trying to identify, much less redress, the so-called "abuses, misinterpretations, manipulations, and unjust interpretations" of texts or lives.

A Direct Question Deserves a Direct Answer: A Reply to Atalia Omer's "Can a Critic Be a Caretaker too?" (2012)[2]

The refreshingly straightforward question contained in the title of Atalia Omer's essay (2011) affords me the opportunity for an equally direct answer: No.

But because engaging scholarship requires us to offer well-argued reasons for our decisions—I recall here Bruce Lincoln's "show your work" (1999: 208)—I must back up and start anew.

In May of 2012 I was asked by David Robertson—one of the founders and hosts of the web-based The Religious Studies Project—to provide a concluding commentary to a series of short interviews concerning whether scholars of religion should be critics or caretakers.[3] While I certainly do not have any special ownership of either of these two nouns—in fact, I got them from Burton Mack (1989, 2001)—two of the interviewees clearly understood the question as having something to do with the title of my 2001 collection of essays, where these two words figured prominently in a title that rivals Omer's own for directness (though mine was a declarative statement). So what came as a bit of a surprise as I first listened to those responses was that several of the other people did not even have the terms of the debate straight. That is, some of the interviewees understood "critic" (i.e., culture critic) as being either interest-free and thus naively objective or, instead, one who castigates others,[4] thereby prompting them to distance themselves from such an old school or misguided role for the scholar of religion.

What is instructive about this episode, at least to me, is that it makes plain that, even though we all have opinions of other people's work, we do not always read each other very carefully. What's more, claiming that we all have interests and values or vocally disagreeing with the role of critic qua disparager are both a bit of a tabloid move, inasmuch as it implies that anyone who is a critic is either a luddite positivist or somehow out to belittle the people whom they study. Neither, however, have anything to do with how I have used the word critic or critique. I therefore find this sort of scholarship rather lamentable, since the lesson that I learned early on in my own career was that, if you were intent on disagreeing in print with another scholar, then you had better do your homework beforehand and have a pretty good descriptive understanding of his or her argument before offering your own. At least that's incumbent upon those who disagree with the way that our field is usually practiced. For doing anything less makes it all the easier for your interlocutors to dismiss your work. Of course, this can also happen even when critics try to make a rigorous argument; case in point, I recall, early in my career, once being likened in this very journal's pages to a "dog wagging his tail after having learned a new trick" (Griffiths 1998b: 894). It should be obvious how my own work would have been perceived if, over the years, I had adopted this sort of demeaning tone. But those who represent the status quo are afforded such luxuries and—as people on all sorts of social margins have long known—those who do not must play the game even better in order to have whatever place at the table they are given.

But now I find myself in the enviable position of having gained a place at that very table—that is, being kindly offered space in *JAAR* to comment on Atalia Omer's recent use of the critical/caretaker pairing in her essay, "Can a Critic Be a Caretaker too? Religion, Conflict, and Conflict Transformation" (2011). I opened this reply by making reference to The Religious Studies Project since, in Omer's *JAAR* essay, I yet again find someone who, it seems to me, has not read my work very carefully. I say this because, as argued throughout *Critics Not Caretakers*, and indeed throughout pretty much all that I have written, I see the two roles as mutually exclusive. Yet, in a puzzling manner, Omer thinks them complementary, claiming that my work is both *crucial* to her own yet *insufficient* (2011: 462). I am unsure how it is crucial (apart from providing her with the terms around which she organizes her essay). As for the latter judgment, my work is, admittedly, insufficient for all sorts of uses that I can imagine; in her case, it is judged "insufficient for thinking about transforming conflicts and underlying structures of injustice" (2011: 460). This, however, is an understandable lack, making Omer's criticism of me less than compelling; for my work actively argues *against* scholars of religion ever seeing this as a credible role to play. That I should then be critiqued for not enabling it is, to put it mildly, somewhat odd. Of course, Omer is free to argue for such a goal and to develop tools that she believes will help her to accomplish it (though I am unsure why the pages of *JAAR* are the place to publicize this type of research[5]), but why even use my work to help her do that? For, at least as I understand it, the implication of my writings is that we must so dilute the notion of critic if we are to invent some notion of a critical caretaker (her preferred, synthetic term), that we might as well just get rid of the notions of critic and critique altogether. That is, in Omer's essay I find my work being put to use to argue for the very thing that I explicitly argue against, suggesting to me that she should just take these two technical terms and put them to new use (as Arnal and I have done with a title of Mircea Eliade's in our own co-authored book [2013]); for I read her essay—which argues that scholars of religion are particularly well suited to (though sadly absent from efforts to) bring about conflict resolution on the geo-political scene—as but one more example of the type of position against which my work argues.

As but one brief example, consider this, from near the close of her long essay:

> The critical caretaker...think[s] holistically about transforming unjust sociopolitical configurations. To dispel possible confusion: the "critical caretaker" approach does not paternalistically propose telling people how they should think of themselves and their group identity... Rather, this approach suggests an entry point for scholarship in religion to engage creatively and offer relevant expertise to peacebuilding processes in imagining the transformation of relational patterns, especially in contexts where religion, ethnicity, and nationality seem to be conflated with one another. (Omer 2011: 487)

In an essay that takes for granted just what constitutes peace, justice and the whole, one that presupposes that people just ought to recognize the actual, normative distinctions between those domains known as religion, nationality, and ethnicity (otherwise, how else would one *conflate* them?), I find it perplexing that the author would think that there is anything critical going on in this sort of scholarship. In fact, inasmuch as very specific notions of peace and justice are implied, and thus normalized, but are never articulated and defended, I do indeed read this essay as quite paternalistic (sic) inasmuch as it universalizes and thereby naturalizes a very specific and local sort of social formation—one that is, of course, in step with our own liberal democratic/free market interests. Whether I myself would wish to live in such a world is, of course, entirely beside the point—that people agree with you doesn't make your claims persuasive or correct.[6] And this is where we differ rather significantly: the scholar of religion qua critic has no interest in determining which social formation is right or true or just or best and she does not practice conflict management. Instead, she is an equal opportunity historicizer, taking all claims far more seriously than a caretaker might, for she starts from the position that "justice" and "freedom" and "peace" and "holism" are utterly plastic, rhetorical tools used by virtually all social actors, in countless ways, often in pursuit of directly competing goals. After all, I can think of all sorts of social values excluded from being legitimate candidates for inclusion in Omer's whole.

So, returning to the disarmingly simple question of Omer's title, I repeat my direct answer: No. For, as I have argued in a variety of works, I have no idea how to combine "the phenomenological input of the constructive approach with the critical scrutiny advocated by McCutcheon" (Omer 2011: 487) without—as I read Omer herself doing—merely ending with an updated version of Eliade's New Humanism, one in which the scholar of religion uses critique to dislodge one set of normative values only to reinstate his or her own in their place, as if only those with which we disagree have a history. Unlike Omer, I do not think that the scholar of religion is any better placed than anyone else to come up with insights into the proper or most fulfilling ways in which human beings ought to arrange and govern themselves. But, like other scholars who take the historical and thus the contingent seriously (e.g., most recently, in our field, see Nongbri 2012), as culture critics we *are* rather well equipped to point out the devices being used, whether by those whom we study or those whom we know as colleagues, that allow the particular to appear universal, the historical to seem transcendent, the uncommon to be portrayed as common sense, and the mundane to be sanctified.

Having opened by quoting Lincoln, let me now close by citing him once again, this time repeating his final words in an essay that critiques attempts to find complementarity in such contradictory positions: "Really, it is time to do better" (2012: 136).

Appendix

In early March 2013 I was contacted by Michael Kessler, the Associate Director of the Berkley Center for Religion, Peace, and World Affairs at Georgetown University, to write a blog post in response to some questions he had that further examined the topics at the center of my exchanges with Omer in *JAAR*. As described on its website:

> The Berkley Center for Religion, Peace, and World Affairs at Georgetown University, created within the Office of the President in 2006, is dedicated to the interdisciplinary study of religion, ethics, and public life. Through research, teaching, and service, the Center explores global challenges of democracy and human rights; economic and social development; international diplomacy; and interreligious understanding. Two premises guide the Center's work: that a deep examination of faith and values is critical to address these challenges, and that the open engagement of religious and cultural traditions with one another can promote peace. (http://berkleycenter.georgetown.edu/about; accessed April 28, 2013)

The following is the exchange that was posted on their blog; I include it here because it strikes me as elaborating the key issues at stake in the ongoing debate concerning the public role of the scholar of religion.

1) Against Atalia Omer, you pushed back:

> **The scholar of religion qua critic has no interest in determining which social formation is right or true or just or best and she does not practice conflict management. Instead, she is an equal opportunity historicizer, taking all claims far more seriously than a caretaker might, for she starts from the position that "justice" and "freedom" and "peace" and "holism" are utterly plastic, rhetorical tools used by virtually all social actors, in countless ways, often in pursuit of directly competing goals.**

1a) As a preliminary matter, aren't there ways to address some of these concerns: can't a critical scholar develop a theoretically sophisticated account of these concepts and then engage in empirical-material criticism of existing regimes that do not satisfy the conditions of "justice" and "freedom" and "peace"?

Sure, one can do that—Atalia Omer tries to do just that in her essay. But is she successful? If all we're doing is generating "theoretically sophisticated" definitions of justice, or whatever, and then seeing if situations match our definition (i.e., satisfy the conditions), well that's one thing, but if we think we're finding the definitive definition and then judging situations based on it...? Only the latter seems worthwhile given the approach I read such authors as Omer adopting. But in my reading, notions like justice or freedom or peace are never theorized or the assumptions that drive their use are never articulated since some "we" seem to already know what we're talking about—it really is like reading a Platonic dialogue with poor Euthyphro called upon to define what he takes to be a self-evident thing—"What is piety?" Socrates asks and his first answer: "Doing as I do!" And that's my problem with such scholarship—it is unreflectively reproducing a social world conducive to the scholar's contingent, even ad hoc interests.

Now, if such scholarship *did* articulate and then try to defend the assumptions that drive this or that use of "justice," then the notion of a critical caretaker would certainly fall apart, for I think it would become pretty evident pretty quickly that there are all sorts of arguments that are driven by all sorts of assumptions that do not necessarily agree on just what justice or freedom or peace ought to mean. So as soon as one leaves the domain of merely *asserting* these to *arguing for* them then I would hazard a guess that, in that moment, one has lost the edge on being a critical caretaker and one is now a social critic, for I think that one would be hard pressed to—in recognizing that there's nothing self-evidently just about this or that definition/implementation of justice but that it needs argumentation and, at times, let's be brutally honest, coercive violence in order for it to stick and be efficacious— ignore the utter multiplicity of interests driving the variety of definitions. While as a citizen or a husband or a consumer or a son or a public employee or... (I think you get the picture) I may have all sorts of specific interests (some of those surely not necessarily overlapping, by the way, right? What do we do with that?!), but as a scholar of religion I think my role is pretty clear here and it is not to decide which way of living or organizing ourselves into groups is the best, most just, or makes most freedom possible.

1b) Does objectivity require bracketing any concern for theorized justice and advocacy? Why is the scholar limited to "generating critical, scholarly theories about normative discourses"? ..."the scholar of religion as critical rhetor comes not to inform the world of how it ought to work but explains how and why it happens to work as it does?"

I've written on this a fair bit over the years—the key to those who wish to argue for social advocacy is to be able to portray their own interests as normative, as common sense, and the advocacies of others with whom they disagree as irrelevant, aberrant, radical, politicized, whatever. They're play-ing the boundary management game no less than me—I'm clearly involved in that game, however not trying to conserve some notion of objectivity, as the question suggests, but, instead, trying to prompt scholars in my field (1) to identify the professional standards that they think define who we are as—not as humans or not as citizens or not as…, but as *scholars of religion*—and then (2) to rally others to conserve those standards and agree to play by them, encouraging people with interests that fall outside them—as we all do/have—to pursue those interests but without the handy imprimatur of their PhD diploma propelling their claims to the front of the line.

Frankly, it's a classic case of misplaced authority—just because a movie star is famous I'm not sure why I should care about his or her political views and pet issues. Many of us likely agree on that point but when it comes to people with PhD degrees, well, I'm not sure I should be interested in listen-ing to someone with a PhD in, say, molecular biology make speculations on, let's say, the possible motives for the recent bomb attack at the Boston Mara-thon. What's the link between the credentialed expertise and the claim? Sure, the twenty-four cable news cycle just wants someone who looks legitimate saying something provocative, but how does that help the profession of the person who is likely unqualified to be making such claims? When it comes to scholars of religion, especially those operating with an old school notion of religion as deeply personal and deeply meaningful, as linked to transcen-dental values and the realization of some ideal form of personhood—Eliade, Campbell, and so on, not to mention many of the field's current leading writ-ers—then it is likely very tempting to see one's credential in studying ancient texts or one's credential in doing fieldwork in some distant place or one's credential in examining themes in films, whatever, as a license to make grand statements about this thing called "the human condition" (not to mention jus-tice, freedom, peace, fulfillment, you name it). But I don't buy it. My PhD recognizes and thereby grants me specific authority in a very tightly demar-cated area of expertise—mine is on the history of our English-speaking field and its relation to social and political issues of the late nineteenth and twen-tieth centuries, theories of religion, the methodologies scholars use, and so on. Although I have something to say, for instance, on the worldwide field, I've got no credentials to make authorized claims about, say, the history of the South Korean field or the study of religion in Japan; for starters, I don't read either language, so why would someone think my two cents was some-how worth listening to? What's more, if my authority does not even extend to these domains, despite them being so obviously close to my own expertise on the history of the English field, then why would I be considered an expert in how all human beings ought to live and organize themselves?

**2) How do you respond to a critic of your position who would con-
clude that you would relegate the scholar to having no role in social
transformation?**

To be honest, I would say that this person hasn't really read me all that
much—it's like I've written nothing since 1997 (when *Manufacturing Religion* was published) or 2001 (when *Critics Not Caretakers* came out). I'd
also say that they're working very hard to ensure that "social transformation"
only names the changes they support—much as "progressives" and "conser-
vatives" work hard to use those monikers to name only the things that they
support—as if the opposite of a progressive cause is, what, regressive? To
them, maybe, but not to the person who supports those other interests. So
there's social transformation happening all around us, but it seems to me—
linked to my above answer—that the authorized sphere in which I do my
work is the classroom and in published texts, both of which play by the rules
of my profession and, at least in many of our cases in the US, the rules of
the public university. You know, there's all sorts of people working for social
transformation, by the way—consider the movement across the country to
ban gay marriage or get Intelligent Design taught in public high school science classes. Is that social transformation? What of scholars who uses their
doctorates to portray their position on these topics as authoritative, trying to
live a life of praxis and put their deeply held beliefs into practice concerning,
I don't know, the ungodly or inhuman nature of openly gay marriages. Is that
social transformation? Is that person involved in a legitimate scholarly practice? Would your blog invite someone critical of them to elaborate on why
he or she thinks people ought *not* to be using their PhDs to legitimize such
positions? Likely not, because your blog readers might likely just know that
this is just the "wrong" sort of social transformation. No?

**3) Does the religion scholar have a role in promoting "interreligious
understanding"? That is, clarifying misconceptions about religious
communities, ideas, and practices.**

"Misconceptions" is the issue here—according to whom? There's all sorts of
Evangelical Christians who say that Roman Catholics are not Christians—
I've taught many students over the years, in Tennessee, Missouri, Alabama,
who have told me this in all seriousness. What's my job as a scholar of religion—to tell them they're wrong? If so, then I guess that my job, as a scholar
of religion, is to authorize a dominant, theological and politically liberal
position and normalize it by disciplining these students for their "misconceptions"? But if my role is to protect orthodoxies, then which one? For there's

a lot of orthodoxies out there, all competing with one another. For adopting that position and teaching the typical survey of Christian history, one that contextualizes this Evangelical identity debate within some long view history, as if Christianity is some real, overarching thing that just includes all the disputes, is doing just that. In other words, the ideologically loaded nature scholarship that dips into the issue of "clarifying misconceptions" would only be apparent if I adopted those Evangelical students' views (i.e., if I adopted the "wrong" orthodoxy); but if I adopt the "correct" orthodoxy then I'm just recounting historical facts I guess.

So I hope my point is obvious: before even asking about whether we have a role to play in interreligious dialogue and mutual understanding, we've got to ask to whom are we talking and whose interests are we representing. And voilà, we're back to picking winners and losers. I'd prefer not doing that with the things we study and, instead, study the orthodoxy processes themselves. For example, I'd prefer not to study Shi'a and Sunni Islam as two real things (like pretty much every world religions course does, lamentably) but, instead, to study this very distinction itself, its history, the things at stake in the local boundary skirmish over the limits of each. Rather than taking this particular social distinction that is of relevance to specific people for specific reasons for granted and thus as the starting point for our work we could see it as our goal—that is, to figure out how the distinction is created and what purposes it serves. Or consider that Protestant/Roman Catholic/Orthodox do not name stable actual realities but, instead, shifting local identity practices (each with multiple internal competing identities vying for power)—we study those identity practices themselves instead of their products, instead of trying to get people to talk to one another and everyone to just get along. They'll talk if they want—or not. That's up to them. So it doesn't strike me as the scholar of religions' job to set the terms on which they will supposedly agree or agree to disagree.

4) Prior to the 2012 annual meetings, a number of prominent religious studies scholars wrote a letter/petition to the AAR Board of Directors and SBL Board of Directors. Included in that letter was this phrase:

> **As members of the American Academy of Religion and the Society of Biblical Literature, we believe that we have a moral responsibility to promote the just and ethical treatment of workers, and to intervene when powerful individuals or institutions seek to undermine their fundamental rights as workers and as human beings.**

In response, the boards wrote (July 10, 2012):

The AAR Board and the SBL Council, sensitive to our mutual respect for the rights, dignity, and worth of all people, which we understand to include the rights of workers to organize into unions, have met together to decide how to proceed. Canceling our contracts with the Hyatt would be financially prohibitive. Nevertheless, we have worked to ensure that all AAR and SBL members have the right to exercise their conscience in reaction to the boycott. We will alert members of the boycott as a part of the process of making hotel reservations. In addition, if members who have already booked sleeping rooms in one of the Hyatt properties wish to change hotels, we will help accommodate that change....

Third, we want you to know that our response to this situation is not limited to contractual and logistical concerns. Indeed, as scholarly societies that foster critical inquiry, we also want to engage important issues like these from intellectual and policy perspectives. With that in mind, we have formed a committee to begin planning a plenary session at the Chicago Annual Meetings that will consider the ways in which academic and religious communities have related to labor movements in North America

The SBL Council and the AAR Board of Directors

Do you see any role for the guild in making claims of this sort? Under what conditions might the guild take a stand, if ever?

No, I don't actually—and even the AAR/SBL seems ambivalent, since forming a committee likely never brought about much radical social change, right? As people with specific social and political interests the originally quoted letters writers believe that they have certain moral responsibilities. No doubt. I do too. But *as members of the AAR and SBL* I would argue that we all have only professional responsibilities—to cite properly, not to copy someone else's work, not to falsify their research, to treat students and colleagues and the people we study in what our field sees as a proper manner, and so on. Again, we see here the wonderfully instructive slippage outlined above, the way in which many members of our field authorize what are actually contestable social and political interests, an authority that seems to take them out of the realm of opinion and contestable/contingent social interest. Might there be members of the AAR and SBL who think, I don't know, that the backs of unions ought to be broken? Probably. Where is their representation in all this? (Or are they just obviously wrong?) Is not the AAR and SBL leadership responsible to represent them too? I bet there are many openly Marxist members of the organization who have just a little bit of problem with private ownership and the profit motive—what will the leadership do if they band together and, say, write a letter protesting Oxford University Press's right to own the intellectual property that we publish in *JAAR*? Form a committee? Or would this just be judged as, I don't know, silly…? Which moral responsibilities will easily get portrayed as collective professional duties? What's the AAR/SBL's stand on, say, child labor? The international sex trade? Lead levels in paint? The role of vaccinations in possibly causing autism? How to reduce the US trade deficit? The fate of the rain forest? The fate of the family farm…?

So here's the point: in order to be successful, the so-called critical caretaker has to press forward an argument to seek protection within the umbrella afforded by their professional credentials to make claims that extend far beyond their credentialed expertise—claims that are really just one among many others on countless topics that strike people as important and worth their time. The gap between those two domains is sometimes profoundly apparent and yet other times not at all. Ensuring the latter is the task of the good rhetorician. Recognizing the gap and one's own limits is, I'd say, the mark of a good scholar. Too few say "I don't know" (hearkening back to Socrates, intentionally) when they're put in front of the media's bright lights—I think that a few of us miss the days when professional modesty was a social value that we thought worth pursuing.

Before closing, let me add for those who have stuck with me this far: I hope that readers understand that I've got *all sorts of views* on peace and justice and freedom and potable water and poverty and private ownership, and so on—but I've not talked about those issues here since I don't think that my PhD from the University of Toronto in the academic study of religion, and the various accomplishments I've had within the profession (the things that made me, of all people, apparently stand out to be asked to write some things for this blog, right?) authorizes me to have some opinion on these that trumps theirs. We can talk about those views maybe, but not in the pages of an academic journal in my field and not in one of my classes.

Notes

1.   In fact, given that my work has mostly been concerned with examining the methods and theories used by scholars of religion, one could reasonably say that it has largely comprised replies to other scholars (which constitutes merely secondary scholarship, or so the argument as outlined in the Introduction to this book would have it). For example, several of the chapters collected in *Critics Not Caretakers* (e.g., chs. 3, 4, 5, 6, 7, and 10) and *The Discipline of Religion*, (e.g., chs. 2, 4, 9, 10, and 11), though substantive

essays in their own right, were originally unsolicited replies written on the work of other scholars (such as McCutcheon 2006a).

2. My thanks to, among others, my colleague in Alabama, Merinda Simmons, for our many conversations on the scholarly shortcomings of critical caretaking.

3. Apart from myself, the scholars interviewed included: Tim Fitzgerald, Steve Sutcliffe, Linda Woodhead, Grace Davie, Eileen Barker, Benjamin Beit-Hallami, Jolyon Mitchell, and Lisbeth Mikaelsson. As of mid-July 2012 the set of interviews are posted at http://www.religiousstudiesproject.com/. [Ed. Note: the interviews were posted on July 16, 2012 at: http://www.religiousstudiesproject.com/2012/07/16/podcast-should-scholars-of-religion-be-critics-or-caretakers/.]

4. That our colleagues should default so easily to using a non-technical, folk sense of a term that is being used in scholarly discourse is itself worth mulling over.

5. My point is that there are all sorts of people who write about religion, from all across the political and theological spectrum, and who are also envisioning new ways for society to be organized (members of the US Tea Party come to mind, in fact), but whose writings, no matter how rigorous and well-documented, would likely *not* be seen as credible candidates for inclusion in our field's leading journal. So I propose a question of my own: What makes Omer's essay an example of scholarship on religion, as opposed to religiously liberal scholarship?

6. This would be the logical fallacy of argumentum ad populum: assuming an argument is true simply because it is shared by (many) others. For example, just because "four out of five dentists surveyed recommend sugarless gum for their patients who chew gum" does not make sugarless gum any better for you, whether or not it is one of Trident's "four delicious flavors."

Chapter 16

Introduction

Sometime ago I realized that there was important theoretical work signaled by gerunds—those verbs that act an awful lot like nouns; for instance, as I once phrased it, the advantage for a social theorist of the concept "social formation," as opposed to, say, "social forces," "society," "group" or even "institution," was that it "nicely represents not only the ongoing work of bringing an imagined social group into existence but also the sleight of hand in making it appear always to have existed" (McCutcheon 2001a: 25; see also Mack 2000). "Social formation" could name a thing, of course, prefaced by an indefinite article, for example, but, simultaneously, it also names the ongoing process whereby the supposed thing comes into being, repeatedly and continually. Singing a national anthem is therefore an event in the day and life of members of *a* social formation and at the same time a socially formative act, that is, a repetitive act constitutive of the formation of a particular, shared idea of citizenship—one element of a never ending process of citizen*izing* (to coin an awkward term). For if social life is dynamic, always caught in the act of creating and legitimizing itself, then words to name it that tactically convey, like Gertrude Stein's old saying about Oakland, that there is no there there (Stein 1937: 289), would be particularly handy to the astute theorist. Gerunds therefore keep processes on the table (somewhat akin to the way Derrida's overstrike), something that is lost when static nouns take center stage.

This emphasis on processes is evident in the work of Jonathan Z. Smith, the scholar of religion who—at least over the past fifteen years or so—has certainly been most influential of my thinking. Looking at his titles alone it should be clear that the -ing ending of such titles as *Imagining Religion* (1982), *Relating Religion* (2004), and even his most recent edited collection, *On Teaching Religion* (2013)—something that obviously influenced my own *Manufacturing Religion* (1997) and *Studying Religion* (2007)—ensures not just that the notion of process remains at the forefront of our studies, thus prompting us to have an eye toward change and history, but it also keeps our eyes on agency, inasmuch as procedures presuppose actors and their activities. Perhaps this is why I wrote, just above, that Smith's works have been influential of my *thinking* rather than of my *thoughts*—inasmuch as the later portrays as settled what the former represents as an ongoing activity. In fact, when co-editing a *Festschrift* in honor of Smith, Willi Braun and I very much had on our minds his focus on agents, their structured situations, the choices they make within them, and the manner in which these situations make certain sorts of agents possible; that's among the reasons we settled on the title *Introducing Religion* (2008).

In arguing for the importance of gerunds I specifically think of Gustavo Benavides's critique of, as he phrased it, "the tyranny of the gerund" (2002). As he phrases it there:

> But it is also worth considering whether the relentless processual emphasis, embodied in the gerund, is not likely to distract scholars of religion from seeking to identify the building blocks, the constants, the recurrent features of religion. In other words, while it is important not to succumb to reification, it is also necessary to keep in mind that the rejections of hypostases can itself be reified. (as quoted in Tweed 2006: 78)

"If one is to do justice to that elusive cluster called religion," as Benavides argued in a related essay two years earlier, in which he offered a similar critique directed at my first book, "one certainly needs to generate theories; but in order to be able to develop those, it is necessary to have access to more translations, to more old-fashioned philological work, to more historical accounts, to more ethnographies" (2000: 117). The notion of building blocks, of raw materials as he phrased it in that 2000 essay, from which "that elusive cluster called religion" results, is, for me, an indication of someone who has not taken the social theory behind the gerund all that seriously—and for good reason, of course, since it troubles many of our commonplace assumptions about how the world, and our place within it, works. For in reply I might inquire: Translations of what? Philologies of what? Histories of what, starting when, and from whose point of view? And lastly, ethnographies of whom with questions posed from whose point of view? That is, without a definition of religion that I, as a scholar, working within a scholarly tradition, *come to the table with and which is not therefore a naturally occurring artifact already operating outside me, in the world*, I'm not sure which of the many things people write, say, do, or leave behind, *ought* to attract my attention *qua* scholar of religion. I'm therefore not sure where to dig for those coveted raw materials. Instead of a divining rod guiding me, or instead of naturalizing the common sense of my own social group, I have argued (in ways obviously indebted to Jonathan Z. Smith) on a variety of occasions that, as scholars, our choices, our definitions, and the connections that they allow us to make from within a veritably unlimited archive (called "the past") are, instead, actively constitutive of the things that will come to orbit together in that supposedly elusive cluster; in fact, this indicates to me that there is nothing elusive about it whatsoever, for I (that is, my interests, my curiosities, my theories) am the unifying, stipulative force (that is, religion is nothing but the product of the discourse on religion, as so many scholars now uncontroversially claim when it comes to such other cultural items as race or gender or nationality). Attributing elusiveness to the product of my own discursive practices strikes me as ahistorical and obscurantist, that is, an effort to erase my own tracks, as if the object I created somehow got there of its own accord. Taking gerunds seriously means always looking for the fingerprints—even if they are our own.

It is just such a serious emphasis on process and action—along with owning the concretizations that are necessary for all analytic work to take place,[1] rather than presuming them to be the naturally occurring raw materials found in the wild—that constitutes the focus of a small group scholars mentioned twice in earlier notes in this book, a research collaborative that we've called Culture on the Edge, in an effort to rethink presuppositions that cultures are autonomous units of internally coherent signification that do or do not interact with one another. Despite all working in a wide variety of areas, the members of the group—Craig Martin (St Thomas Aquinas College), Monica Miller (Lehigh University), Steven Ramey (University of Alabama), Merinda Simmons (University of Alabama), Leslie Dorrough Smith (Avila University), Vaia Touna (University of Alberta), and myself—are all interested in developing new ways to study identity formation, ways that avoid the problem of assuming it to be a static affectation that is first felt on the inside and only subsequently projected outward (as evidenced in the common, philosophically idealist notion of "*expressing* an identity," "*expressing* our emotions," or simply "*expressing* oneself"). That the members of our research group are all scholars of religion certainly says something about a frustration with the field that, I think it fair to say, is shared by all of us: the common inside/out model of the field, so well represented by William James a hundred years ago but, sadly, still assumed by so many of our colleagues, that is, that the thing in the world that we call religion is first a private feeling or an individual's experience that is only secondarily encoded in sign systems (e.g., language) and, as such, eventually put into faltering words that, by definition, can never really do justice to the nuance of the original sentiment.

If, instead, one started with a far more dynamic, anthropocentric and historically-centered social theory, one that assumed not the priority of the inner, timeless, and unseen world but, instead, started, in a materialist manner, with the public historical world that can be scrutinized, then how would one talk about identity, its formation and changes? For possible models on how to do this the group looked first to work being done outside the study of religion, to those scholars now working on, for example, what is more traditionally called diaspora or, more recently, hybridization and creolization studies, but we were sadly disappointed for, despite the new terminology and the supposed focus movement, that is, on change over time and place, we found there the same individualistic, ahistorical, philosophically idealist social theory, one that presupposed originals (what we might call building blocks or raw materials, perhaps?) followed by derivations—purity leading to mixing and thus pollution coupled with a nostalgia for a long lost past. While this may be the function of nostalgia for social groups who employ the devise in socially formative acts, this did not strike us as the set of presumptions useful in studying how these acts work. As the group's collabortatively written self-description phrases it:

> Case in point: any discussion of an "African diaspora"—a technical designator now commonly used by scholars as referring to empirically observable processes—relies heavily on an assumed continuity and cohesiveness of a category "Africa," despite the many interpretations of what it means to be "African." Nonetheless, scholars will quickly refer to and talk about the so-called African diaspora without paying substantive attention to the problem of imagining a real and original signified to such a complex signifier. Scholarly attention is instead focused on analyses of the diasporic experiences, employing notions like "hybridity" and "creolization," with the hope that these intellectual tools will do the heavy lifting of theorizing the heterogeneity of diasporic communities. While much work has attended to dispelling the idea that an always-existing, *sui generis* nature lies within national identities and heritages (which some scholars of diaspora reference), the implications of understanding national, geographic, or ethnic identity instead as an always fluid, discursive construction often remain unconsidered in such scholarship. Just as with the earlier notion of syncretism, which seemed to advance social theory but, ironically, reinforced conservative notions of identity (inasmuch as the syncretistic social movement was assumed to derive from two previously existing, static origins which had simply been blended), the supposed gains of diaspora studies and creolization discourse turn out to reproduce a theoretically unsophisticated approach to studying identity as an ongoing historical event that is always on the edge (i.e., always under renovation).

Instead, we settled on the work of the French social theorist, Jean-François Bayart, for our model, specifically his important book *The Illusion of*

Cultural Identity (2005—a book Willi Braun first brought to my attention several years ago), and Bayart's insight that there are no identities but only "strategies based on identity" or, as we might phrase it, there are only situationally specific identity claims and their claimants.

"[T]here is no such thing as identity," Bayart provocatively writes, "only operational acts of identification." He continues:

> The identities we talk about so pompously, as if they existed independently of those who express them, are made (and unmade) only through the mediation of such identifactory acts, in short, by their enunciation. (2005: 92)

I find traces of Louis Althusser here and his notion of interpellation, whereby an identity, a specific type of subjectivity that is not so much "adopted by" as "placed upon" an individual—as in being enveloped by and thus subjected to a structure, thereby becoming a certain sort of subject in relation to it—results from a series of public operations among members of groups who each occupy various locations across the social formation's power grid. In his classic example, from his essay "Ideology and Ideological State Apparatuses: Notes Toward an Investigation" (2001: 85–126), Althusser cited the well-known example of the police officer who hails someone on the street: "Hey you there!" In a note (2001: 118, n. 18), Althusser elaborates as follows: "hailing as an everyday practice subject to a precise ritual takes quite a 'special' form in the policeman's practice of 'hailing' which concerns the hailing of 'suspects'." In the moment of being called upon, in the realization of just who has called out to you, a very specific system of power relations encircles the social actor, making possible (or not!) a variety of social relations and opportunities. A subject, with an identity, is operationalized in that very moment from out of the otherwise ambiguous material of social life.

My point? When Captain Louis Renault, at the end of Michael Curtiz's classic film "Casablanca" (1942), says "Round up the usual suspects!" we miss something crucial—as does the late arriving policeman who follows his superior's order and hustles off to find "them"—if we think that identity is a solitary and timeless possession that the careful interpreter can find if we just look closely enough for the trail it leaves behind (akin to a close readings of the text). What we miss are the gerunds—that is, the processes by which mere people become "persons of interest"; we miss what transpired a moment before in the film, when Humphrey Bogart's "Rick" shot the Nazi officer, Major Strasser, as witnessed by Renault himself, who, though corrupt, misdirects the arriving policemen, thereby conspiring with Rick against the Germans. For we, the audience, along with the co-conspirators, know that it is only in light of this strategic misdirection and the authorized criteria of the police Captain, that people somewhere well off stage (minding their own business, for all we know, or plotting some unrelated caper) have just unknowingly become "the usual suspects" who will soon be rounded up, questioned, and perhaps even held accountable for Rick's actions. Overlooking the gerunds means overlooking the human actors, their choices and their collaborations, and the structured situations in which they act and which are reproduced by means of their actions.

This is what lies in the background of this chapter, which is a reply to Ann Taves's very brief response to a review essay of mine, published in the *Journal of the American Academy of Religion*. My original essay used a recent book of hers (2009), on a cognitive science approach to the topic of religious experience, as the opportunity to press the cognitive scientists who study religion, ritual, and so on, a little further than I have so far seen them pressed, concerning the manner in which they naturalize (by placing it in the genes or in the hardwiring of cells) what some of us consider to be a contingent social process (i.e., naming something *as* religion). The following reply, however, focused more tightly on Taves's own book, asking what really is new in her new approach to the study of special things, wondering aloud whether we instead need to be studying the special-izing process itself rather than the things is apparently creates—looking for the gerunds rather than the qualities of the nouns.

Recovering the Human: A Tale of Nouns and Verbs: A Rejoinder to Ann Taves (2012)

Most simply put, are we studying nouns or verbs? That is the question that I pose as a rejoinder to Ann Taves's reply (2012). For I notice a curious grammatical ambivalence in her most recent book, *Religious Experience Reconsidered*—a book that I admit to using too little in my earlier review essay (2010), seeing it merely as the jumping off point for a longer reflection on the (questionable, to my way of thinking) gains of the cognitive science of religion.

The ambivalence that I find in her book I also see elsewhere in the field, inasmuch as, for example, discourse analysis is now widely drawn upon but only to a point, for sooner or later we find scholars talking about the supposedly real things that somehow operate outside of, or prior to, discourse. Elsewhere I've identified the curious manner in which the adjective "religious" miraculously survives when people discard what they now see as the troublesome noun "religion" (as if we could still qualify things as "political" if, for whatever reason, we no longer used the term "politics") as well as how plurals (e.g., religions, Islams, etc.) are now somehow more acceptable than singulars (as if it is completely sensible to talk about "dogs" when, again for whatever reason, we no longer use "dog" to name a distinct biological grouping) (see Arnal and McCutcheon 2013). But here, instead, consider a more recent example: a book review panel at the Society of Biblical Literature held at the recent San Francisco meeting (November 2011) for which I served as a respondent.

Frustrated by the longtime dominance of theological motives and methods in the SBL, the contributors to *Secularism and Biblical Studies* (Boer 2010) offered another model for how to study the bible—what several of them called the work of the secular or atheist exegete. What their reconsiderations failed to recognize, I argued (see McCutcheon 2014: ch. 5), was that their work still conformed to a number of assumptions shared by their so-called theological adversaries, making their own work far less radical than they assumed. After all, despite their so-called secular methods, their object of study was still a thing called the bible, understood as a self-evident text (i.e., noun) containing meaning (i.e., noun), if only read correctly (which was a Marxist hermeneutic in the case of several contributors). Instead of studying such things as how the text is used (i.e., verb) in historically specific

moments of tradition/identity-formation and instead of studying how dis-
parate texts have been collected, copied, maintained, and used together
(i.e., more verbs) *as if* they were a homogenous document (i.e., the act of
canon-formation), these scholars took all of these (all too human) practices
for granted, thereby taking as already settled that a thing called the bible is
something that ought to be studied and something that contains continually
relevant meaning. There is deep irony in such an exegetical approach selling
itself as overcoming theological preoccupations, for the bible understood in
this manner strikes me as a fetish in the classic sense.

I use this illustration to indicate the importance of moving from studying settled nouns to dynamic verbs if we are to do something other than
what participants are already doing for themselves—that is, that we move
from studying the meaning of the Bible (a ritual activity, really) to studying
how meaning is negotiated and managed *by people*, or how the discursive
object "bible" is created, maintained, and used *by people* (and this advice
merely follows Smith's own recommendations in his 2008 SBL Presidential
Address [2009]). *Religious Experience Reconsidered* suggests, in places,
that it has made the move to recover the human interests and practices (and
I could add to that the mundane bio-chemical procedures) that are symbol-
ized in language by verbs, but, I fear, it has not done so consistently or as
thoroughly as some of us may wish.

For the sake of this rejoinder's brevity, consider the evidence in the Preface alone (where authors sometimes disclose more than they might have
intended): Taves states there that her "interest [is] in exploring the process
whereby experiences come to be understood as religious at multiple levels,
from intra personal to intergroup" (xiii), noting that "the book is written for
those interested in taking both perspectives [i.e., humanistic and scientific] to
develop a naturalistic understanding of experiences deemed religious" (xiv).
We are therefore not interested in studying religion or religious experiences,
but, instead, "the process whereby" things "come to be understood as," that
is, classed or deemed as, religious. So far, so good. Those doing the deeming (a gerund) now rightly attract our attention, akin to looking at the person
who is pointing (and thereby seeing their effort to impose [yes, a verb] a
specific set of contingent sensibilities onto others, etc.) rather than passively
following his or her finger to look at the supposedly interesting object (yes,
a noun). But, to my way of reading, Taves then waffles on this important
switch from examining supposedly settled objects to the prior conditions
that made those objects worth observing in the first place. This is signaled
in her disclosure that she has an "interest in and preoccupation with unusual
sorts of experiences" (xv). Here, I think she has left the realm of experiences
deemed (by Taves herself, presumably) unusual and is now simply talking

about plain old unusual experiences, those that are, apparently, overlapping to whatever degree with a whole family of other unusual experiences and which are somehow distinguishable not from experiences *deemed* (again, presumably by Taves) ordinary but, instead, from what I gather are actually ordinary experiences. For, as she concludes, "[t]here is no reason, however, why this bias [i.e., her interest in studying unusual experiences] should preclude using the approaches recommended here to study more ordinary types of experiences" (xv). So, within the space of only two and a half prefatory pages a careful reader is left wondering whether we are studying nouns or verbs—that is, whether we are examining the human pre-conditions that enable us to deem some object *as* special or, instead, simply examining special objects themselves, taking their classificatory status as an identity rather than the result of a choice (whether conscious or not) by social actors. This ambivalence (between objects and the conditions that made the mere white noise of reality into objects of discourse) is evident in a passage that I flagged early on, and which I still see as an odd sort of disclosure to come in a book dedicated to the study of "deeming" rather than identities:

> My own view is that the cultivation of some forms of experience
> that we might want to deem religious or spiritual can enhance our
> well-being and our ability to function in the world, individually
> and collectively. Identifying those forms, however, is not the pur-
> pose of this book. (xiv)

Regardless of how we name them (i.e., regardless what discourse we use to make sense of them or express them), there apparently are some experiences that are just better for us. Here I see the same ambivalence, for on the one hand Taves writes that she wishes to study why people deem this or that *as* religious (or special or whatever word one chooses to name the family of set apart things), presumably having no stake in the actual identity, interrelations, or value of the things so named, yet, on the other, she seems to make an ontological claim about a pre-discursive identity of certain sorts of experiences coupled with a moral/political stand on their value for the individual and society, whether or not we identify them as religious or spiritual. This is rather puzzling, for it seems to me that either we take seriously that we are studying processes or we take the procedures as settled, as of no interest, as happening off stage, whatever, and just get on with talking about things—I cannot see how we can have it both ways. For then it would be as if a legal theorist moved, in the space of one Preface, from talking about studying the conditions that allowed some generic action to be understood as "just" (in which case we are not discussing justice but, instead, historically variable discourses on justice) to then claiming in a *sotto voce* aside that some actions that we may or may not want to call just are simply more equitable and thus better for us—as if "equitability" was an uncomplicated pre-discursive reality. To put it another way, taking her interest in studying deeming seriously, and with an eye toward that long quotation just above, I want to know if Taves's approach can be extended to examining how she herself sets apart such "more ordinary" things as those generic values *deemed* enhanced and those mundane modes of living *deemed* well-being or *deemed* as more or less functional? For unless her readers share her choices and sensibilities, and thereby fails to ask just these sorts of questions, Taves's method finds plenty to study in this one disclosure alone.

It is this ambivalence—moving from studying why we call generic things religious to somehow knowing that there are a variety of worthwhile and inter-connected religion-like things in the world, whether we call them religion or not—that I tried to signal in my earlier review essay, in which I suspected something old amidst the something new. For despite the innovative research that her book draws upon, and her effort to create a big tent of which the phenomenon formerly known as religion is but one instance of singularization, I still see some very traditional things going on, from Wittgenstein's family resemblance definition (i.e., there are many religion-like things in the world, arranged in terms of degree), along with a little dash of Tillich (though we now opt for special, rather than ultimate, to name the sliding scale of value), perhaps some of Bellah's notion of civil religion (in which national parks can also count as data for the scholar of religion) and even a nod toward Eliade's New Humanism, inasmuch as it may be that Departments of Religious Studies are home to those who study the most special things of all (for Taves hazards a guess, in her closing, that "it is quite possible that the more special people consider something to be the more likely they and others are to place it under some religion-like heading" [165]).

I am willing to entertain that I have over-read Taves on such points as these and perhaps she is simply advocating that the study of religion be considered but one more site for studying the generic, species-wide (if not wider) process of signification—inasmuch as calling something religion or magic or unusual or ordinary, and then acting in this or that way toward the signified "it" that our deeming has created, is no more special that deeming anything to have an enduring identity and value (such as not only public lands, historic monuments, state museums, or symbols of office but also certain sounds that are deemed special and called language in distinction from mere noise). If so, then we have in *Religious Experience Reconsidered* a model for how to recover the human when those around us are bent on studying human products as if they were free floating signifiers. In this case perhaps Taves and I share more than I had realized. But given that some singularizations seem to be a little more singular, and some special things are a little more special, I am not yet convinced.

Notes

1.   To quote J. Z. Smith, grant me that, for instance, that society exists or that ritual exists, and allow me "the kind of monomaniacal power or imperialism that a good method has when we're honest about it. Without the experience of riding hell bent for leather on one's presuppositions, one is allowed to feel that methods have really no consequence and no entailments" (2007: 77).

Chapter 17

Introduction

Over the past several years, as part of the growing internet boom which has taken much of the life (i.e., a euphemism for income from subscribers and advertisers) from print journalism, not just online commercials but also a variety of journalism-esque blogs—ranging from fairly well done investigative journalism to editorializing commentary—have sprung up around the topic of not just religion but, of all things, the academic study of religion as well. I have in mind such sites as the non-profit *Religion Dispatches* (http://www.religiondispatches.org/), launched in 2008 and described on its About page as

> a daily online magazine that publishes a mix of expert opinion, in-depth reporting, and provocative updates from the intersection of religion, politics and culture…provid[ing] a forum for journalists, scholars and advocates to share their expertise and inform the conversations that shape our lives and our democracy. Because we're observers (but not necessarily observ*ant*), respectful but not reverent, we tackle stories that others can't, or won't.

With *RD*'s notion of an online forum in mind—one that, to my way of thinking, problematically brings scholars and advocates together—I also think of *The Immanent Frame* (http://blogs.ssrc.org/tif/), subtitled, "Secularism, Religion, and the Public Sphere." Founded in 2007, this site is funded by the Social Science Research Council (SSRC), under the auspices of its Religion and the Public Sphere program,[1] and describes itself, on its About page as:

> publish[ing] interdisciplinary perspectives on secularism, religion, and the public sphere. TIF serves as a forum for ongoing exchanges among leading thinkers across the social sciences and humanities, featuring invited contributions and original essays that have not been previously published in print or online.

Or perhaps consider even the generally pithier items posted at the *Bulletin for the Study of Religion*'s blogging portal (https://www.equinoxpub.com/blog/), where, recently, some items of my own, originally posted on my Department's blog (instituted by my colleague, Steven Ramey, in 2012 and once associated with our the topics of our guest lectures; http://as.ua.edu/ rel/blog/), have been reposted. But generally, despite the enthusiasm with which some in the field have greeted these sites, I have avoided writing much for them—and not because I am a luddite or fail to derive enjoyment from trying out various writing styles (as this chapter may demonstrate).

When, in August of 2001, I arrived at the University of Alabama to Chair its small Department of Religious Studies—a Department that, apart from myself, was then comprised of untenured, early career faculty, was not enrolling nearly enough majors, and was therefore not able to meet the minimum graduate numbers set by the Alabama Commission on Higher Education (ACHE)—I found that, like a number of other Departments at that time, its web presence was in a sad state (see McCutcheon 2004a for more elaboration). Given how important the web was then already becoming as a vehicle to represent a Department positively among a wide constituency (e.g., students, colleagues, administrators, parents, etc.), within a year my colleague at the time, Kurtis Schaeffer (now Department Chair at the University of Virginia) had learned enough HTML code to work with a University-made template to create a new site that (especially when compared to the old one) made us look competent and professional. Because he was very early in his tenure-track period at the time, it made little sense to expect the site to grow much under his direction—for, based on my experience while working in southwest Missouri, where I had witnessed an early-career faculty member maintaining a Department site, web work can be a bottomless pit of time and energy (because there's never any end to a site; that's likely why we so infrequently see those "under construction" web pages anymore, for we have come to understand the web as always being under construction). So I learned enough about HTML code and FTPs to do what I needed to do, and learned to use a well-known web development software called Dreamweaver (that I still use version Dreamweaver 3, which is now *ten* iterations behind the current version, tells you all you need to know about my level of competency); benefiting from the expertise Schaeffer had gained as well as getting some early advice from Herb Berg, my friend and colleague, who also did serious web design on the side, I became our Department's webmaster, which I've been since then (with a brief hiatus a few years back). Within a couple years, and after the Department had paid our University's design people to have a logo made and web template to match, our Department site was well over four hundred pages in size—many of them substantive but always engaging; long before the days of Facebook, it had become a site that our students and graduates would routinely visit for updates and news on Departments events. So I would like to think that, early on, I grasped the importance of the web for both conveying the *impression* of industry and engagement as well as creating *actual* engagement and signifying *real* industry. That impressions and actual states of affairs are not always connected is something it did not take long to learn—not to mention how the former can assist in creating the latter.

But when, in February of 2009, I was approached by Linell Cady to contribute something to *Religion Dispatches* (as I recall, along with Gary Laderman, she was one of the original editors and an early contributor to *RD*, back when, as it was described to me, they offered $250 for an essay of about eight hundred to one thousand words), I never followed up on the invitation, apart from thanking her and, more than likely, indicating that I would think about it. My concern was, and when it comes to blogging still remains, the implications of the sort of simplification necessary when writing for the world wide web's audiences. (Even the *Journal of the American Academy of Religion*—undoubtedly the widest circulating periodical in the field, and one very interested in reaching new readers—is going carefully into the comment world for the articles that it posts online; for while wanting *inclusion* of new voices we of course need a way to *exclude* those who do not play by the "right" rules, no?) Now, writing for an audience larger than just a small group of specialized, scholarly readers is not inherently problematic—with care and skill, I think that that the complexity or nuance of a scholarly argument can effectively be made to a wider reading public (as we try to do at edge.ua.edu, the blog for Culture on the Edge). After all, our field's founders in the late nineteenth-century were writing as much for wide readership as any other audience—at a time when Europeans were rather hungry for details on the practices of the exotic Other, of course. But I find that much in our field that passes for popularizing inevitably ends up reproducing the very set of assumptions about the world that, I think, deserve critical examination (e.g., that religion is different from other elements of culture; that religion is primarily an inner, deeply human[e] experience only subsequently expressed; that religion is divisible into a variety of stable subtypes known as "world religions"; and that religion—if "properly" manifested and expressed—is a beneficial power in the world). As virtually any media theorist post-Marshall McLuhan or Noam Chomsky will tell you, the medium not only *is* the message but the message *conserves* the interests of those who own the medium and who consume it (or are consumed by it). That this applies to scholarly books as well goes without saying of course; but that scholarly books are not trying to reach millions, or hundreds of millions, of readers by somehow providing each of them with a picture of the world conducive to their interests (for why else will they visit your website and not some other?), must also be taken into account.

So, given that my work happens to be interested in questioning the conditions of folk knowledge (that, in many cases, passes for scholarly knowledge) that surrounds the topic of religion, blogging for sites like *Religion Dis-patches* or *The Immanent Frame* has never really struck me as a very produc-tive venue for my writing (though, as I note in places, I've made good use in this book of some content originally posted in abbreviated form on our blog); a long and detailed argument that tries to persuade a reader to rethink basic sets of assumptions about the world generally does not happen in 800 to 1,000 words; concision, Chomksy taught me, is the gatekeeper of the status quo. For example, while I applaud his previously cited post at the *Huffington Post*, the hundreds of, shall we say, spirited comments that followed my col-league, Steven Ramey's, insightful blog, earlier this year, on the discursive creation of the group now commonly known as the Nones (those who report on polls as having no religious affiliation), confirms this for me.[2]

My concerns for the sort of work that, with the advent of online journal-ism in our field, would begin to count as widely accessible, and thus perhaps normative, scholarship on religion, was also confirmed in late November of 2011, when a colleague in Missouri posted a link on my Facebook wall while we were all attending a national conference. The link took me to a newly posted *Religion Dispatches* article entitled "Why the World Needs Religious Studies;" written by Nathan Schneider—a frequent contributor to *Religion Dispatches*, as well as a variety of other online sites, and who has been described on a blurb for his book, as being "[p]art philosophy junkie, part spiritual seeker, all journalist" (see Schneider 2013)—it was based on a talk that he had been invited to give to students at Brown University on the practical benefits of their major in Religious Studies. It was posted on my wall because I was mentioned in the article.

Schneider's online article prompted me to do some writing of my own—an email, sent on November 28, 2011, to Gary Laderman, who, at the time (but now no longer) was still the editor of *Religion Dispatches*; I also posted this email as a public note on my Facebook wall (something I informed Laderman of, of course). After a brief opening, the email said:

> While attending the recent AAR/SBL meeting in San Francisco, a friend on Facebook posted a link to Nathan Schneider's latest *RD* piece, "Why the World Needs Religious Studies."[3] While reading it I was curious to learn that my work comprises a threat to the field. I quote the full paragraph:
>
> > "The Great Idea of religious studies has come under threat on two fronts—from without and within. From without, it's victim to the various budget cuts and legitimation crises that plague the humanities and social sciences generally in the modern research university. Exacerbating these is a common suspicion among scholars outside the field that religion in

any form should've long since been excised from the curriculum. To make matters worse, the field faces critics from within: well-meaning but destabilizing attempts by religion scholars to rethink and reinvent the whole enterprise from the ground up, even to the point of unsettling its foundations. (Timothy Fitzgerald's *The Ideology of Religious Studies* and Russell McCutcheon's *The Discipline of Religion* come to mind.) These are important exercises, but they exact a cost. When religion scholars forget how much the world outside the academy needs them, they can be prone to theorize their own field into oblivion."

As one who has had his own academic writing characterized (in order to dismiss it, presumably) as mere journalism, I am hardly in the position to make accusations about the so-called seriousness of a critique. But early on I was taught that, in order to make a criticism stick, one had to be a generous reader, providing one's interlocutors with little excuse to dismiss your critique as shallow or as evidence that you just hadn't done your homework and were relying, instead, on easy generalizations. As Wayne Proudfoot is often quoted, one's object of study must at least recognize him or herself in your descriptions of his or her position, prior to whatever analysis taking place. That I fail to recognize what I have tried to accomplish so far in my career in this admittedly brief aside is the reason why I am writing to you.

I find this characterization of my work deeply troubling, especially if it is indicative of the level of precision required of *RD* posts. The paternalism of the characterization of my motives as "well-meaning" and the speculation that I have forgotten what this writer thinks is important about the field seems to me to undermine many of the good things that *RD* is trying accomplish by reaching a wider audience for scholarship on religion. Assuming *RD* takes its mission seriously, I suspect you would welcome an opportunity for any of your expert contributors, as your site characterizes them, to acquire a truly in-depth viewpoint, even if it is one that provokes them to reconsider their position. I therefore invite your Associate Editor, through you, to do a little more homework, visit us at the University of Alabama, and speak to any of the students with whom I have worked over the last 19 years, at three different public US institutions. Simply put, I would welcome an in-depth *RD* article on what we have accomplished here in Tuscaloosa over the past decade, the challenges that we faced when reinventing the Department, and those that we continue to face. I believe that drawing on more than easy generalizations will reveal a few interesting things about the work that I have so far tried to accomplish in our field.

I look forward to making the hotel reservations.

Laderman eventually contacted me and we had a very nice series of telephone conversations, but Schneider actually coming to our Department to do some fieldwork, to learn how this apparently destabilizing critic had played a role in reviving a program that, back in 2000, was potentially destined to lose its major, never happened—though I still hold out hope. I know that he "Liked" the public note that appeared on my Facebook wall, but that's all I've ever heard from him—and who knows what clicking the "Like" button even signifies.

But on November 14, 2011, I received an invitation from John Modern and Kathryn Lofton, both in charge of a site called *freq.uenci.es*, described as a genealogy of spirituality, and which is part of the umbrella created by *The Immanent Frame*.[4] Modern said that he had seen a Facebook post of mine about Schneider's article and asked me to write a blog related to the topic. While I did not accept their kind invitation, in March of 2012 Lofton followed up and asked me to assess the site's first 100 posts, as part of a second level of discourse on their efforts. Given that I have little to say about spirituality in any form, but likely much to say about scholars who try to write either traditionally or innovatively on the topic, I gladly accepted. The following article (minus the hyperlinks), written purposefully in a style reminiscent of that which I found in a number of the pieces that I looked at on the site, is what I submitted to them and what was posted at *The Immanent Frame*.[5] As it turned out, my earlier concerns for what a popularized discourse on such topics as religion, faith, and experience, not to mention spirituality, might look like were, once again, confirmed.

Three Dots and a Dash (2012)

"It resists classification…"

Language is a funny thing. Take my epigraph, for example: three words from the fourth paragraph of freq.uenci.es' project statement. I find these three words interesting—worth re-reading, even un-reading, rather than just reading—because of the contradiction that they carry along with them; for they unsay what it is that we think they just said.

Like I said, language is a funny thing.

To begin this project of un-reading, I start off-stage, before the meaning takes place, and note that the removal of these words from a larger context is signaled by those three dots which, when read as a unit, indicate that something is not just passively missing but omitted (as its Greek root, ἔλλειψις, makes plain)—that is, this notation leaves a trace of the agency, the choice, of the one who has done the extraction. For, much like the verbs "remove" or "omit," it makes evident that an strategic operation has taken place; what's more, the 66s and 99s that frame the text inform readers that it had surgical precision, for they allow them to conclude that this is precisely how it is in the absent original—"Go, find it, and compare for yourself," they challenge. "But see here now?" they simultaneously ask, "Something new is happening, right before your eyes."

Ellipsis and quotation marks—marks by which writers make admissions to readers (akin to Bruce Lincoln's sense, in the epilogue to his *Theorizing Myth* [1999], of how footnotes "show your work") and by which readers are reminded that writers fabricate their texts (they don't just happen by themselves, after all), doing so by inserting their own uninvited interests into other people's prior situations, making texts of other contexts, thereby interrupting someone else's work and putting to new use just this one piece of a past. And it is precisely by such an interruption that meaning is created—"This here thing is related to that thing there, but they are not the same." Texts re-signified by their extraction from there and their insertion here; old contexts erased (but yet hinted at). Nothing stands alone, unaccountable.

Our punctuation marks mark our punctuations.

When I consider the form of the text above, that's what I come up with. This structure, evidenced/produced by the punctuation, makes the text's history profoundly apparent, the specified limits and the edges are there to see, and the manner in which meaning-making takes place—as a staged series of past and present relationships among interchangeable parts—remains. "I am doing something here," these marks say, in the voice of the writer, "Watch closely." Because of the punctuation (in both senses of the term: a marking and an interruption), the reader can't erase the agency of the writer—the historically-situated chooser, Roland Barthes's scriptor, the one who has set the table for the reader—any more than readers can erase the sign that there was once another placesetting at which these words and other readers once sat next to each other, accompanied by no trailing dots, framed by no 66s and 99s. Yet the original is hardly original, of course, for it made reference to, deferred to, its own absent ancestors. Turtles—texts/contexts—all the way down.

But let's begin again and ask what happens if I read, instead of un-read, those words—that is, take for granted the setting in which this language game is played, authorize its rules as inevitable and natural, thereby seeing (or better, not seeing) the spot at which I, as a reader, have been seated as invisible and limitless, then what do I make of these three words? What if I see them as having no context? What if I drop my attention to the work being done by the quotation marks and ellipsis and, instead, hear the words speak directly to me, much like being captivated by the wit of the dummy instead of the person so successfully throwing the voice? Well, now there apparently is a thing, an "it" we'll call it, that, like that animated dummy, has an agency of its own (for, we are told, it resists classification); by means of its own huffing and puffing, the absent signifier that goes by its pronoun defies being classed, has no context, and cannot be controlled. Its rugged individualism prevents anything from getting not just too close but close at all, with no one and no thing occupying a neighboring space.

"I can't quite put it into words" presupposes just such an it, haunting our dreams before language gives it shape.

But if knowledge is said to be the result of the way we organize the world, the way we group things together to arrive at our judgments of similar or different, more or less, near or far—Kingdom, Phylum, Class, Order, Family, Genus, Species—then this dearly distant Cousin It remains forever aloof, all covered in hair and a hat, infinitely removed, and thus an utterly unknowable mystery—just as the vague pronoun-of-a-name suggests. After all, "the rejection of classificatory interest is, at the same time, a rejection of thought" (as Jonathan Z. Smith reminds us in the concluding sentence to his essay, "Classification" in *The Guide to the Study of Religion* [Smith 2000b]).

One reader but two readings of a project statement (though one is an un-reading, really): one results in the trace of history while the other is shrouded in mystery. But only one is good to think with.

So just what is freq.uenci.es about then? At the level of reading, its task is to document something that defies knowledge—"spirituality" being the noun formerly known as it. The object of this online archive therefore defies language, since language is nothing but classed specificity—for good or ill, a rock is not a pebble, neither is it a stone and hardly a boulder. For whatever reason, these things matter to us and the way we sort the matter that matters is found in the specifics of language. "Over there" is the unspecified region where we ask someone to put—we wouldn't even say "place," since we don't much care—some thing of little or no consequence. But an item that defies placement, defies relationships of similarity or difference inasmuch as it apparently occupies (of its own volition) a class of its own, is in a space where there are no relations and thus no consequences—a space beyond all places we could possibly set at all dining tables in all possible worlds. It is a space of fantasy, outside of history and thus apart from language (whatever sense it makes to phrase a claim like that within language and within this historical moment; like I said, language is a funny thing).

What is clear is that the results of my reading and un-reading are rather uneasy partners. For on the one hand, we have framed three words and three dots that show the work, that stand for the happenstance, always changing relationship between text and context, writer and reader, how each are always the other too. Meaning historicized. No text stands alone. Yet on the other, we have three words, alone, referring to no writer, no reader, but to the absent, incomparable noun that apparently moves under its own steam. A stand-alone text. *Sui generis* religion by another name.

A contradiction presents itself (or is presented by another?).

For when the reading is judged from the vantage point of the un-reading—and meaning historicized, I would argue, is the only vantage point to be had for those who name themselves historians—then the writer of the project statement (for there is always writer, right?) is implicated in an effort to hide footprints, to sweep clear the evidence, and to leave the scene of the accidents of history. For, much like the passive voice, having set the reader's table with the words of his or her choosing, such a writer then makes a dash for the exit, erasing all evidence of the choices he or she has made, leaving the reader to assume that the table was set by itself. And thus we arrive at a situation comparable to the old dine and dash—a situation where our choices appear free of cost—but only if we get away with it.

Three words—"It resists classification"—followed either by three dots or a dash—between these two options we have a contradiction in styles, at the very heart of freq.uenci.es. Is our object of study incomparable or infinitely comparable?

To be fair, the entire paragraph (one of six, in fact) from which I excised those three words that became my epigraph reads as follows:

> Frequencies seeks to commence a genealogy of spirituality. This
> project approaches spirituality as a cultural technology, as a diverse

reverberation, as a frequency in the ether of experience. We begin in a moment when novelists wonder about the divine, psychological counselors advertise as spiritual advisers, and scholars seek to capture spirituality's ephemeral nature through survey research. Spirituality abounds, even as it is unclear what it is. Whatever it is, it seems hard to capture. Spirituality takes hold beneath the skin and permeates below the radar of statistical surveys. It resists classification even as it classifies its evaluators and its believers as subjects of its sway. Frequencies will focus this profusion into an epic anthology of wide-ranging analysis.[6]

A genealogy of the discursive object "spirituality" is, for me, far different from a genealogy of spirituality—they cannot sit easily beside each other, at the same table. Suggesting that *claims* of spirituality, in fact the very *use* of the term itself, is a cultural technology—a technique, used by someone, a technician perhaps, that does something within culture, within history, I gather—is far from seeing spirituality itself as such a technology. But reading the paragraph I am unsure which we are talking about. I fear that what the site might understand as a productive ambiguity, capable of attracting a multiplicity of views, or layers (to stick with the notion of genealogy), is, for me, a paralyzing cacophony. The trouble? In genealogy the pronouns and the nouns alike—things like justice or marriage or gender or civility or self—refer back to historical practices, habits, institutions, ways of organizing, and the agents who made (and, yes, were made by) these contingent structures. Yet in this paragraph, the source of the Nile too often seems to be the ungenealogized—the un-un-read—noun spirituality; like a rumored and alluring Big Foot marching through the woods, looking back at us, coming in and out of focus, the fabricated object is our target, and not the situated discourse that brought us to the edge of the woods and made us look.

And so, reading that project statement, staring at all those trees, those posts, and thereby missing the structure that the un-reading sees as managing the profusion, visitors to the site likely assume that all of *freq.enci.es'* parts naturally and comfortably fit together—a searchable crazy quilt whose busy mosaic hints at a transcendent whole that's bigger and thus more significant than the sum of its parts. Only in this way would we assume that (to name but three entries) Martin Marty's interest in the "most sustaining and inspiring elements of what we can call post-modern spirituality..."[7] and Lee Gilmore's use of language to point toward some unspeakable thing ("that mysterious 'more'—an ineffable sense of something larger than ourselves")[8] could somehow inhabit the same space as Gabriel Levy's entry in which *freq.enci.es'* main noun appears in ironic quotation marks and , dare I say, is reduced to brainwaves.[9] Only by occupying some god's eye vantage point, where the omniscient narrator sees into the hearts of all those blind monks, groping around that poor elephant, would we think that these three entries had something in common—instead of seeing the former two as data for the third. To rephrase: that we would likely never assume that assorted mediations and lamentations on, say, this or that sense of justice, would appear side-by-side with a genealogical analysis of the discourse on justice itself, yet freely assume such a comfortable fit when it comes to this thing called spirituality is, I think, the problem that requires attention. For, with my earlier reading and un-reading in mind, "a digital compendium in which the ideals of spiritual self-expression and individual flourishing are held in tension with the historicity of those conceits"—to quote from the opening to the project statement's fifth paragraph—is one where the tension is so great as to shatter the archive itself. After all, a house divided against itself cannot stand.

Three words. Three dots. Three examples.

A dash. A tension. A contradiction.

Three dots *and* a dash is, of course, Morse code for the letter V, and V— as every Beethoven fan knows, as does any World War II history buff—also stands for Victory; to have it both ways, to hold both a reading and an un-reading in the space of one epic anthology, would indeed be an victory—a victory over making choices and living with consequences, a victory over History, even Death ("Where is thy sting now, eh? For this very critique will be posted at the same site as its object!"). But the historian in me can't imagine such a totalized scenario, in which we can have our cake and cri-tique it too—leaving a trace of agency and choice while simultaneously obscuring both. No, we have to choose, and live with the consequences.

> "Scott for gods sake write and write truly no matter who or what
> it hurts but do not make these silly compromises" – Letter from
> Ernest Hemingway to F. Scott Fitzgerald (May 28, 1934).[10]

Victory for those unwilling to compromise, those with an eye toward the situation, cognizant of the inevitability of choice, aware that "ineffable" is a word like any other and that "the big picture" is every little picture's ide-ological fantasy, is therefore not three dots *and* a dash; instead, it's three dots *or* a dash—either historicity or a mad dash off the stage of context, of consequence, and of accountability. That's the choice—between the satis-fying closure of Beethoven's long fourth note or the utter indeterminacy of his first three—his three dots, his ellipsis—followed by not just a rest or a pause, but a silence of who knows what length…,

leaving us not sure whether to applaud or…

Notes

1. Apart from *The Immanent Frame*, there are several projects currently underway within this program, such as New Directions in the Study of Prayer and Religion and the United Nations; see http://www.ssrc.org/programs/religion-and-the-public-sphere/ for a full list.
2. "What Happens When We Name the Nones?" posted at: http://www.huffingtonpost.com/steven-ramey/what-happens-when-we-name-the-nones_b_2725169.html (accessed March 4, 2013).
3. The article, published November 20, 2011, can be found at: http://www.religiondispatches.org/archive/culture/4636/why_the_world_needs_religious_studies_/ (accessed March 17, 2013). It is also available as a PDF on the author's own website, The Row Boat, at: http://www.therowboat.com/articles/WorldNeedsReligiousStudies.pdf (accessed March 17, 2013).
4. On a flyer for a program session at the 2011 meeting of the AAR that was devoted to this website, it was described as "an assemblage of texts and images about spirituality from eminent scholars, writers, artists. Conceived as an experiment, Frequencies does not define the terms of spirituality. Rather, it is an attempt to collect parts of a cultural technology with obscure mechanics."
5. The seven responses to the site's first 100 posts are found at: http://blogs.ssrc.org/tif/frequencies/.
6. Ed. Note: see the full project statement at: http://freq.uenci.es/project-statement/ (accessed March 17, 2013).
7. Ed. Note: find Marty's entry at: http://freq.uenci.es/2011/12/06/atomizer/ (accessed March 17, 2013).
8. Ed. Note: find Gilmore's entry at: http://freq.uenci.es/2011/09/27/burning-man/ (accessed March 17, 2013).
9. Ed. Note: find Gabriel Levy's entry at: http://freq.uenci.es/2012/01/13/thought-waves/ (accessed March 17, 2013).
10. Ed. Note: find the letter at http://www.lettersofnote.com/2012/04/forget-your-personal-tragedy.html (accessed March 17, 2013)

Chapter 18

Introduction

In the past decade, or so, there have been quite a few books published on the subcategory of (or, for some, synonym for) modernity that is commonly called secularism—its history and its future. While it certainly didn't start with Charles Taylor's work, of course, his widely read move from studying the history of the modern notion of the self (1989) and then authenticity (1991) to secularism (e.g., based on his Gifford lectures of 1999, published in 2007) seems to have paved the way for a variety of others—an anchoring citation to his work, often placed somewhere in the introduction, now seems almost a requirement of subsequent work on this topic. When it comes to the study of secularism as carried out by scholars of religion I now think of such works as Hent de Vries's thousand page edited volume, *Religion: Beyond a Concept* (2008—just the first of five planned volumes, three of which have appeared), Janet Jakobsen and Ann Pellegrini's edited book, *Secularisms* (2008), Winni Sullivan's work in *The Impossibility of Religious Freedom* (2005) and the collection of papers she recently co-edited (along with Robert Yelle and Mateo Taussig-Rubbo), entitled *After Secular Law* (2011), as well as Marcus Dressler and Arvind-Pal S. Madair's co-edited *Secularism & Religion-Making* (2011), not to mention this being the overarching theme of *The Immanent Frame* website (funded by the independent Social Science Research Council [SSRC] and which began, back in October of 2007, with a review symposium on Taylor's *A Secular Age*[1]), which "publishes interdisciplinary perspectives on secularism, religion, and the public sphere" (http://blogs.ssrc.org/tif/about/).

But despite my own interest in these topics, stretching back to the late 1990s and early 2000s (e.g., see chs. 11 and 12 of McCutcheon 2003a as well as McCutcheon 2005c), I am often disappointed in such studies inasmuch as they often strike me as *naturalizing* some domain called religion or faith or spirituality while *historicizing* another domain called the secular. That is, as suggested in previous chapters, I find a frustrating partial theorizing of our ability to think of religion as a domain of the human and thus the historical (i.e., contingent), because the common narrative among many scholars is that while humans are naturally and eternally religious (e.g., those cave paintings in France are certainly evidence of an ancient artist's religious emotions or people who lived in the Indus River Valley several millennial ago were obviously religious, given the cross-legged pose of figures portrayed in some material evidence that remains), people have only recently (i.e., the past few hundred years, starting in Europe and then spreading from there) cordoned off the naturalness of religion within the so-called wall of separation invented by the secular state, all in an effort to privatize and thereby control the religious dimension. With this widely shared thesis in mind, scholarship on the so-called post-secular therefore speculates on how multiple global religious identities will interact once the limiting, artificial environment of secularism crumbles—and some are confidently predicting that it already is.

For example, I think of Robert Yelle's argument (one that is common to a number of scholars writing in this area) that secularism is actually a recent product of prior religion. He writes:

> Christianity arguably created a separation between the religious and political domains with its distinctions between the "Two Kingdoms (Cities, Swords)" and, even earlier, between Christian "grace"and Jewish "law." The original version of the "Great Separation" was the founding narrative of Christianity, which according to Saint Paul, effected a fundamental break with its own Jewish past. Following Christ's redemptive sacrifice on the Cross, the laws that prescribed sacrifice and other rituals were ineffective as a means of salvation, and were abrogated. Religion was no longer a matter of law but of grace; no longer of the flesh but of spirit…
>
> This present essay traces some of the ways in which what we call "secular law" has been shaped by Christian soteriology and supersessionism… (2011: 24)

In reading this paragraph, a useful thought experiment comes to mind: what would we make of such a text without the thoroughly modern world religions discourse up and running in our heads, whereby (for example) we somehow just know that religion is different from other units of culture (it does not strike me that "Christianity" and "Judaism" here name general socio-political groups) and thus requiring a technical participant language all its own (uppercase C for the word "cross," saints, sacrifices, rituals, salvation, grace, redemption, etc.), that religion is driven by beliefs and theology (which is obviously something other than mere rhetoric or propaganda), and that what might otherwise be seen as historically and geographically distinct social movements are, in fact, just variants on an eternal theme (whereby many different social movements all somehow become part of some grand thing called "Christianity" or "the Christian tradition" that somehow unfolds across history)? Without these assumptions in mind—assumptions I argue are entirely modern in their pedigree—would one even be able to make such statements? To press one simple point to illustrate this little thought experiment: how do we, as scholars, know that Paul *ought* to be called a Saint and portrayed as part of (better put, at the very origins of) some seemingly transcendental thing called "Christianity" and thus quoted extensively when talking about early Christianity? For it is not difficult to imagine a different historian portraying him (or the him we today imagine to have existed then, since all we have are copies of copies of copies of letters) as a relatively minor first-century itinerant Mediterranean political reactionary and propagandist whose writings (and the interpretive traditions that accompany them) have, for later generations, become rhetorically useful in a variety of their own social experiments, with the result that today, in producing their own identity for their own purposes, people call him "Saint" and consider him an "early Christian." To state it another way, had these letters not become useful to divergent subsequent readers, with divergent subsequent interests, would we even know about Saulos of Tarsus today, let alone quote him in the origins myth of some thing called Christianity?

I call this manner of dehistoricizing religion while historicizing the secular a partial theorization (rather than a "re-enchantment," as those who support such work often term it) because, as suggested already in this volume, it strikes me as failing to take seriously how binary systems function—such as sacred/secular, religious/non-religious as well as such related pairings as private/public and even experience/expression. For as I have said elsewhere, I do not think that, prior to the invention of cooking, people somehow just knew that they were eating their food raw. That is, the idea of rawness (or, prior to the development of domestic, indoor dwellings, the ability of earlier humans to conceive of themselves as being "outside"), though it procedurally predates the notion of being cooked (i.e., one can't uncook one's food), nonetheless does not chronologically predate the notion of something being cooked. Instead, inasmuch as the two concepts define themselves only in light of their logically paired other, they necessarily co-arise, and therefore ought to be studied as an historical grouping that, at some point in time, in some specific situation, made it possible for people to arrange the world in a fashion that was seen as beneficial to someone, for whatever reason and whatever ends.

But this is not the approach that I find in the work of most who tackle the project of accounting for secularism's rise or role. For example, consider the following, which I published in *The Discipline of Religion*, when discussing this topic there:

> A step toward just such a project appears to have been made by Peter Harrison in his impressive book, *"Religion" and the*

Religions in the English Enlightenment (1990)... On the opening
page he writes:

> The concepts "religion" and "the religions," as we presently
> understand them, emerged quite late in Western thought,
> during the Enlightenment. Between them, these two notions
> provided a new framework for classifying particular aspects
> of human life. (1990: 1)

Harrison's book is thus an exercise in studying the practical impact
of these socio-cognitive categories during a specific period of European history. Despite his misgivings concerning Cantwell Smith's
preference for "faith" over "religion" (misgivings clearly spelled
out in Harrison's epilogue [174–75]), he nonetheless employs this
traditional distinction, thus undermining what strikes me as the most
promising and provocative part of his study. For example, soon
after we find the above quoted thesis statement, Harrison elaborates
by employing the very interior/exterior, private/public scheme he
appears to historicize: "In the present work I shall be examining in
more detail this process of *the objectification of religious faith*" (2;
emphasis added). Rather than seeing the concept and institution of
"religion" or "faith" as one technique whereby an interior, seemingly apolitical zone is fabricated and named, Harrison...seems to
presume the existence of an inner, purely subjective disposition or
attitude that somehow predates (both chronologically and logically)
its setting, thus being objectified, externalized, expressed, mani-
fested, controlled, or reified by means of the word "religion." Like
many other critics of "religion," then, a traditional realism creeps
back in, despite the appearance of a social constructionist critique.
What such critics take away with one hand, they swiftly give back
with the other. (2003a: 257–58)

As I would phrase it now, the problem here is ontologizing what, as scholars, we likely ought to see as the *discourse on* religion; that is, the issue I
find curious is the undisclosed (folk) information that such scholars draw
upon in order to know that a prior, internal, and thus affective "it" exists, to
which people, at some later point, attach the apparently limiting word "religion." Historicizing the word, which many scholars now do (i.e., seeing
the word religion placed in quotation marks is now *de rigueur* for writers who wish to display their theoretical credentials), leaves the apparently
free-floating concept/referent untouched. (Aside: in this regard de Vries's
title, *Religion: Beyond a Concept*, is not insignificant.) For while the signifier is understood as historical and arbitrary, the signified is presupposed to
be transcendent and thus necessary.

This move strikes me as normalizing the discourse on religion inasmuch as one pole in the binary pair is retrojected into history, as if people have always been religious but not corralled into, and thus controlled by, secular worlds and their limiting labels until fairly recently. Thus, they were religious even before the modern word religion, and the ability to think of religion as a thing, was coined and defined. Or, as I phrased it in the Preface to the German translation of my own *Studying Religion* (2013), when trying to make this point by using as my example the slippage between German *qua* language and German *qua* modern national identity: "think of the discussion one might have of just what counts as 'German literature,' especially given that the modern German nation-state long postdates the language by quite some time—for instance, is Immanuel Kant a 'German writer' or, being born in 1724 in Königsberg, a 'Prussian writer' and, more importantly perhaps, what is at stake in making or overlooking the distinction?" That politicians and citizens actively assist various nationalist projects by taking the nation-state for granted as an eternal, self-evident body makes sense, of course; however, I would assume that the careful historian of nationalism would not wish unknowingly to naturalize what are in fact fairly recent social inventions. Sadly, though, I do not find scholars of secularism being this careful in their approach to religion.

With this critique in mind, the counter-narrative that I would propose is that whether people distant from us in time thought immaterial beings existed or not (if that's one of the markers for what we today mean by religion), it would be a gross error to call them religious unless we decouple that modern word from a host of commonsense conceptual linkages (i.e., what we simply call the discourse on religion) that automatically come with it for us moderns (e.g., the presumption of faith as an inner affectation, seeing belief as a causal force of action, the presumed priority of individuals over social groups and institutions, assumptions concerning the degraded nature of expressions versus the pristine nature of first-hand experiences, and the automatic and essential linkages that we assume to exist between this so-called religious ritual and that so-called religious claim, etc.). For our very ability naturally to link this initiation rite, with this dietary requirement, with that claim about the universe with those expectations of dress and deportment, all of which are grouped together under a banner that somehow segments the entire set from yet other behaviors, requirements, and claims is the thing that ought to attract our attention if we are interested in the discourse on religion and the coextensive relationship between those domains we commonly know as sacred/secular. My argument, then, is that the very ability to think religion into existence, to see these and just these linked items *as* religious, all in distinction from those other things, *is the product of that broad socio-political and economic movement we today call secu-larism.* The height of secularism, its ideological triumph, then, would be a scholar's presumed ability to imagine its end (i.e., post-secularism) while yet continuing to talk about religion, for now the enabling conditions of the discourse on religion have been erased and its product, religion, is seen as a naturally occurring raw material, with no historical strings attached—some-what like the wooden Pinocchio trying to appear as "a real boy."

To provide a more recent example of this I could focus some attention on the now much used "religion in the public sphere" theme, something that is found all throughout *The Immanent Frame* for example, in order to demon-strate the longstanding philosophically idealist assumptions that ensure that within this literature whatever it is that we call religion is *not* understood as a thoroughly social, material, and historical practice but, instead, is still assumed to be a private affection that is somehow "expressed" or "mani-fested" or "realized" in the so-called public sphere. If those in our academic field who use this term were not reproducing, and thereby conserving, very old rhetorics and interests then "religion in the public sphere" would be understood as utterly redundant and thus less than illuminating, for then we would understand that the very designation of something *as* religion (a product of the thoroughly historical, contingent discourse on religion) was and already is a public, political, and thus contestable designation that always comes with practical implications. (Much like an elected body debating what shall constitute privacy—i.e., as argued in the opening to *The Discipline of Religion* [2003a]—there's nothing private about privacy.) But instead, consider the opening to Jakobsen's and Pellegrini's essay collection (which is based on a special issue of the journal *Social Text* that was pub-lished in 2000). To set the stage for the problem the volume addresses—that is, the curious way in which the religious, though apparently banished from the secular, yet persists within its midst—they draw attention in the open-ing lines of their Introduction to the relevance of the timing of the special issue referenced above:

> [T]he year 2000 is anno Domini, the second millennium after the birth of Christ. Thus, at a time when the entire world was sup-posedly focused on the turn in the calendar from 1999 to 2000, we wondered how a particular way of telling time had become so unremarkably universal. What, we asked, were the implications of the fact that the world secular calendar—the calendar of global finance and world politics—was also specifically Christian time. Wasn't secularism supposed to be a discourse of universal influ-ence precisely because it was free of the particularities of religion? (2008: 1)

What strikes me as curious is the manner in which the authors themselves fail to see that qualifying Christianity *as* religious, and the calendar *as* religious, is not a neutral description but the result of *their* classificatory act and *their* social interests. That is, if *we* designate them *as* religious then yes, of course, there appears to be a contradiction at the heart of secularism. But if, instead, we understand "Christian" as a mundane social designation like any other (as, for example, Bill Arnal argues in chapter 8 of Arnal and McCutcheon 2013)—one whose members employ a variety of authorizing techniques, that we also see elsewhere in culture, to provide it (and themselves) with a competitive advantage in what is otherwise a busy and unregulated social economy—then there's nothing all that curious or meaningful about the appearance of "A.D." in the dating system with which we happen to be familiar, for every calendar needs an arbitrary but agreed upon, and thereby legitimized, start.

The editors therefore could just as easily have *not* seen this as a *religious* calendar producing *religious* time (and thus seen no irony at the core of secularism, thereby avoiding this entire problem) if they had, instead, *chosen* to understood the Gregorian Calendar, the Julian Calendar before it, and the Roman Calendar prior to that, and the various Greek lunar calendars before that, and so on, as something other than an externalization of a prior inner belief that was somehow self-evidently set apart from other elements of culture (it's supposedly a religious belief, after all). Case in point, as the story is commonly told, the 1582 revision to the Julian Calendar was motivated by a desire to bring Easter's date in line with the First Council of Nicaea's views back in 325. Thus, beliefs and rituals around the dying and rising of Christ, Pope Gregory XIII (1502–1585, the calendar's namesake), the Councils of Trent and Nicaea long before it, and a papal bull named "Inter gravissimas" all figure prominently in this story of the obviously religious motivations and origins for the revision, making the calendar religious (I think here of Yelle's narrative of the religious beliefs and motivations that apparently first inspired the separations that came to be known as secularism). But what happens if we see the discourse on belief motivating action, the discourse on the distinctiveness of this sort of belief over that sort (e.g., believing in heaven versus believing the free market, talking of salvation versus talking about progress), as our object of study? If so, then the common narrative of the calendrical restoration *will itself become curious to us*, for we will no longer see Easter as a uniquely religious holiday but, instead, as one among many ritualized social occasions where a social group reconfigures identity and membership via an arbitrary but nonetheless rule governed behavioral occasion. For we do this all across culture all the time, making Easter, in this example, hardly unique or set apart.

Or (with a deferential nod to Bill Arnal, who suggested this to me in reading a draft of this introduction), to come at the same point (that religion exists
because we moderns choose for it to exist) but from the opposite direction,
why have the editors been so concerned with the A.D. in the date as evidence
for religion lurking all throughout secularism and not, for example, the creep-
ing influence of old Norse religion inasmuch the days of the week's names
derive from the old gods and holidays. For do many of us not know that, for
example, "Tuesday" derives from proto-Germanic for "god of the sky" and
"Wednesday" is merely the anglicization of Wodin's Day? As Arnal wrote to
me in response to reading the draft, for such writers "somehow a Wednesday
(or Mercredi [i.e., the day of the god Mercury]) is just a Wednesday, but A.D.
2013 is fraught with significance." That our attention, as scholars, ought to
be focused on the choices and interests that regulate this significance, rather
than taking the significant as self-evident, is my simple point.

The irony, then, is that the so-called secular is further supported in these
scholars' continual presumption that religion pre-exists in some set-apart
domain (i.e., that Easter is obviously religious), instead of seeing *all* social
life as amorphously whole, while variously interested social actors (including modern scholars who arrive on the scene armed with the categorical distinction between religion and politics, private and public, faith and works,
etc.) try to draw lines and boundaries so as to focus or distract attention, align
and realign, to thereby attain or withhold privileges and identities. Surely
there were no pre-existent "traffic lanes" prior to the dotted line being drawn
down the road, correct? So would it not be ill-advised to presume that the
line simply managed one side or the other, rather than seeing its very placement as what simultaneously constituted "sides," in opposition to each other?

Sadly, too few scholars of secularism pay attention to the line as itself
being the identifying force but, instead, see it as merely postdating the obviously separate spheres. For example, consider the way Taylor phrases it; on
his Introduction's second page we read the following:

> And if we go back even farther in human history, you come to the
> archaic societies in which the whole set of distinctions we make
> between the religious, political, economic, social, etc., aspects of
> our society ceases to make sense. In these earlier societies, reli-
> gion was "everywhere", was interwoven with everything else, and
> in no sense constituted a separate "sphere" of its own. (2007: 2)

Although this is not precisely the model of secularism that he explores in
the book (he instead focuses on the conditions that made disbelief possible,
examining "the whole context of understanding in which our moral, spiritual or religious experience and search takes place" [3]), Taylor's approach

to "articulating the conditions of experience," as he phrases it, certainly complements this understanding of religion being everywhere in pre-secular settings (after all, the pre-existent spiritual and religious experience seem merely to get expressed in a secular environment). The only problem, however, is in finding something everywhere which, according to his own argument, doesn't even yet exist. That is, taking seriously, as he argues, that the religion/not religion distinction had yet to be invented, it hardly makes sense to then assert that everything was religious. Instead, whatever everything was (if it even makes sense to say that everything is this or that) in this supposedly homogenous bygone social world, it certainly wasn't religious, unless we—positioned as we are in the modern secular world, where we walk around with the commonsense religion/not religion distinction in mind—say that it was. Thus, concluding that secularism is religious in origin by noting that cloistered monks (i.e., members of an order) were once distinguished in Roman Catholicism from what were then called secular clergy (*saecularis*, Latin: of the time, of the world—those priests who worked among lay people) is surprisingly sloppy history writing, for it anachronistically reads the modern notion of religion backward in time to conclude that Roman Catholicism—then the operating environment for thought, law, political order, whose churches were key social sites for order and identity formation, and so on—was religious even before religion was invented as a discursive marker.

My point: our particular way of telling the secularism narrative—one that sees religion as eternal and the secular as recent—is what makes the paradox that we then try to explain (i.e., data is a product of theory—change the theory and we study different "facts"). For calling the Gregorian calendar religious or classifying ancient people as religious is somewhat like identifying Kant as a German writer—it amounts to taking an unacknowledged stand within the very debate that one ought to be studying instead, that is, examining the discursive construction of seemingly homogenous, set-apart, and historically enduring social identities.

It was our frustration with the preeminence of this sort of scholarship on the religious and the secular that prompted Bill Arnal and me to collect together a set of our essays and publish them as the above cited book, *The Sacred is the Profane: The Political Nature of "Religion"* (2013). Not long after it appeared in print, I was contacted by David True (at Wilson College in Philadelphia) who works with the blog associated with the journal *Political Theology*,[2] and asked by him to write a post that summarized the book's argument. In response to his kind invitation, I wrote the following, which takes as its starting point the frustrations with strategically partial theorizing that I've referenced above.

The Sacred *is* the Profane (2013)[3]

In the Spring of 2007 I presented a public lecture on the politics of the category "religion" at the University of Calgary's Department of Religious Studies. Following the lecture, as part of the usual question and answer session, a professor off to my right, seated back against the wall, asked me a seemingly simple question: "What are the truth conditions for your argument?" Sensing a little bit of a trap being laid for me—which, as we all know, is what most questions that follow academic papers are really all about—I replied that there were no such conditions since the paper's topic, and its mode of delivery, were not concerned with truth, whatever that may or may not be; instead, the paper was concerned with utility and, by extension, with social affinity. "The paper was an exercise in persuasive rhetoric," I recall responding, and therefore none of its claims were either true or false. Instead in that lecture I tried to persuade listeners that should they, for whatever reason, be interested in certain sorts of questions about how groups work to recreate themselves over time and place, then the approach that I modeled in my lecture might be of use to them; if so, then we'd have some things in common (e.g., curiosities, hunches, problematics, and tools) and thus we'd have not just some*thing* to talk about but, more importantly, some *way* of talking about things that caught our attention.

I realized at the time that my answer was completely unsatisfactory to this professor, who, I later learned, was a philosopher of religion very much interested in interreligious dialogue (hence the focus upon truth conditions, I assume). His question, therefore, put squarely on the table a dramatic difference in our approaches, for while he was keen to argue over whether what I had said was true or not, I dropped by Calgary—to paraphrase Michael Newbury's song, made famous by Kenny Rogers and the Fifth Edition in 1968—to see what condition our truth conditions were in. That is, I was and remain interested in so-called meta-questions, trying to figure out how groups establish and manage the parameters that enable their members to distinguish true from false, allowable from unallowable, original from subsequent, center from periphery, desirable from undesirable, safe from dangerous, pure from impure, authentic from fake, even sacred from profane, all of which assists them to distinguish and then police the limits of some posited Self, in distinction from Other. Thus, it's not a matter of truth or falsity, for as Emile Durkheim made clear so long ago, religion—or in my case, use of the category "religion" itself—is neither true nor false but, instead, a brute fact of some people's social lives. And looking at it in this way may help shed some light on how it is that groups who use this designator (or any of its attendant tropes) as part of their larger Self/Other folk taxonomy are able to draw and, despite the unpredictability of their contingent historical conditions, apparently maintain the sense of boundaries that make it possible for their members to distinguish such things as true from false and member from non-member.

It should be clear, then, that despite both of us being physically positioned in the same room, employed in the same academic field, the intellectual positions that marked my questioner and myself were quite far apart. The distance between his interest in truth and my own interest in utility is, I think, indicative of how far the field has traveled over the past several decades—a distance nicely represented by three scholars who, despite constituting three different academic generations, all happen to have shared the same institutional setting at the University of Chicago. I have in mind the difference between, on the one hand, Mircea Eliade's influential studies of the sacred, conceived by him to be a universal structure of human consciousness, manifesting itself in the historical world first here and then there, and in the process inserting timeless value and meaning into the otherwise turbulent and meaningless historical world, and, on the other, both Jonathan Z. Smith's far more ethnographically controlled work on such topics as anomaly, incongruence, and choice, all aimed at determining how significance is fabricated in discrete situations, and Bruce Lincoln's equally careful case studies of human contests over authority and legitimacy in settings where it might all be up for grabs. Despite all three being enviably skilled comparativists carrying out much of their most important work at the same institution (though not necessarily in the same unit, of course), there are profound differences between what we might as well call the earlier and the later Chicago school. Although Smith's and Lincoln's work are hardly identical (and for the time being I leave it to others to tease out the differences), and although these two representatives hardly exhaust the sort of scholarship on religion currently being carried out either at that institution or by its more recent graduates, they do share in common an unapologetic emphasis not on the sacred, as with a previous generation of historians of religion hailing from the Windy City, but on people (or at least the artifacts left by people) who are busy working out relationships of similarity and difference (i.e., identity) in specific moments, using a variety of techniques, some of which scholars have assigned the names of myth and ritual. Although I wouldn't want to make them responsible for things that I happen to find interesting, I can at least say that it is because of the work of people like Smith and Lincoln that current scholars can make the shift from studying religion or faith or spirituality or experience (whether pursuing studies of their history, meaning, or cause) to studying the socio-political work being done by the classification "religion" itself.

Working in this alternative tradition in the study of religion, the essays that my friend, Bill Arnal, and I collected together in *The Sacred is the Profane: The Political Nature of "Religion"* (a few published there for the first time) try to chart some of the developments in how we study this slippery designator. I say slippery because the category religion, used everyday by countless human beings either in the Euro-North American world or those peoples impacted by its exported socio-political and economic systems, is widely understood by most to defy definition; and it is precisely this defiance that makes "religion"—an ancient, Latin-based category but one that was retooled beginning in the early modern period—a remarkably resilient conceptual anachronism. Its resiliency results from its ability to assist social actors from all across the political continuum to grapple with the effects of *ad hoc* social conventions, contingency, and unpredictable circumstance, thereby allowing them to get on with the business of actively engineering their social worlds while appearing to be doing nothing but acting out universal self-evidencies that are said to reside deep in the marrow (whether in the head—inasmuch as religion is thought by some to be about rational belief systems—or in the heart—inasmuch as religion is said by still others to be about non-rational feelings, experiences, and sentiments). The category "religion" is therefore a highly effective technique—a versatile little problem solver, I once called it—that we use to collapse the inconvenient gaps that are sometimes so apparent when confronting the proverbial Other, with interests contrary to our own, in the midst of each contingent situation; it's somewhat equivalent to the common linguistic and behavioral conventions that we so easily slip into those awkward silences: lacking specific content, saying "Uh-huh" can create the impression of interest, affinity, and therefore unity. But such devices work because they strategically miss much; just as Ernest Renan once said, in an 1882 public lecture, that the idea of the nation was founded on forgetting, so too such rhetorical devices (whether verbal or behavioral) allow us to overlook the inevitable inconsistencies of historical existence, like the affirmative head-nodding that greets the rhetorical question, "Know what I mean?"—a behavior that can happen despite head-nodders not having had time to decide if they have the foggiest idea about what someone is saying or whether they even care to find out.

Such seemingly mundane socio-rhetorical conventions—and I would place using the category "religion" to name and thereby isolate part of our social world, among these commonplace techniques—nicely gloss over, at countless social sites, such things as our possible misunderstandings, disagreements, competing interests and, at times, our outright boredoms;

they perform the crucial task of greasing the wheels of our inevitably disjointed social worlds, allowing us to represent ourselves, both to ourselves and to others, as a specific sort of self, as a member of a seemingly unified "us," going in a specific direction for a specific purpose—thereby enabling people to experience themselves as inhabiting a particular subject-position, to the exclusion of its many competitors. And, in so doing, it helps us to make it through yet another day spent in close quarters with people we may find either uninteresting or rather bothersome.

Although I don't wish to speak for my co-author (though I did pass a draft of this post by him before sending it off to the site), I think it safe to say that our concern in these essays is therefore with a series of ordinary strategies used to create a sense of group identity over time—whether that group be scholars themselves or the wider social groups that their labors help to make possible (e.g., the nation-state). For if, as I think to be the case, the use of the category "religion," and its attendant concepts (e.g., sacred, experience, belief, origins, faith, etc.), provides one site where a sense of shared identity is continually re-made, then it makes sense to ask about the role played by the person who devotes his or her life to its study. That is, those who, as part of their professional life, use and teach the use of this taxon to name and document distinguishable aspects of human society ought to attract our attention if we're trying to figure out how it is that individuals maintain a sense of homogenous membership in groups. So my recurring preoccupation with examining the routine practices of exemplary scholars of religion therefore strikes me not simply as a sensible but also a necessary focus.

With these routine practices in mind, I think of a quotation from *On Television*, by the late French social theorist, Pierre Bourdieu, that I've used as the epigraph for a previous collection of essays and which, for a time, Bill and I were considering using again in *The Sacred is the Profane*:

> There is nothing more difficult to convey than reality in all its ordinariness. Flaubert was fond of saying that it takes a lot of hard work to portray mediocrity. Sociologists run into this problem all the time: How can we make the ordinary extraordinary and evoke ordinariness in such a way that people will see just how extraordinary it is?

Although I previously used this quotation in my own introductory book, *Studying Religion*, all the while I suspected that to really do justice to Bourdieu's important insight, one would have to do more than just drop this quotation into an essay. Instead, it seemed clear to me that such an insight into the ordinariness of human behavior—including the act of naming something *as* religious, *as* true—ought to be the engine that drove a study of some of the sites where the ordinary is dressed up as extraordinary, where the pro-fane was sacralized, all in the service of helping regular people to reproduce a sense of themselves as members of coherent yet unique groups—groups that, despite appearing to them as timeless and homogenous, nonetheless have a history—a beginning and, like us all, an end. Well, to be honest, they likely have many histories—too many histories, in fact, so the ques-tion is which will become *the* history? It is my hope that the book Bill and I produced, taking some important cues from the work of people like Smith and Lincoln, and working *against* the grain of the still influential work of Eliade—who was their colleague (in the case of Smith) and teacher (in the case of Lincoln)—exhibits some of what can be gained by no longer seeing the sacred and the profane as two separate things but, instead, seeing this binary as but one of the many tools used to set one particular mundane situ-ation apart from its many competitors, as something special when compared to the other moments vying for our attention, our resources, and our energies.

As such, although our book's title carries a deferential nod to Eliade's influential book—*The Sacred and the Profane: On the Nature of Religion*—hopefully our switch from the conjunctive "and" to the identifier "is," the insertion of the word "political," and the quotation marks around the word religion in the subtitle, signifies the distance our field has come over the past fifty years. For we are now able to redescribe so-called sacrality as but one more process by which authority and legitimacy are bestowed on otherwise mundane moments and situations, all vying for our attention. (I could say much the same for the advantages gained by calling but one form of rhetoric or propaganda "theology," but I'll leave that for the time being...) In fact, it is a distance marked by the motto of my own departmental home at the Uni-versity of Alabama—"Studying Religion *in* Culture"—in which the prepo-sition "in" is italicized. We do this to draw attention to the fact that the more common version of this popular phrase—"Religion and Culture"—employs a conjunction and, along with it, a series of often undisclosed assumptions that we hope our students will learn to recognize on their way to becom-ing scholars. Associated with the work of such influential scholars as the German sociologist of religion, Max Weber (1864-1920), and the Protes-tant theologian, Paul Tillich (1886-1965), the phrase "religion *and* culture" is today widely used (confirmed by a quick Google search for the phrase) to name a field that studies the intersection of these two otherwise distinct domains. That is to say, the areas known as religion, on the one hand, and culture, on the other, are assumed to be separate spheres that may or may not interact with each other, that periodically bump and grind—this very site's self description sums this position up nicely: "*Political Theology* is devoted to studying the intersection between religion, politics and culture."

The field known as "religion and culture" therefore names the intellectual pursuit of studying their periodic intersections and influences upon one another, and the supposedly syncretistic offspring they sometimes produce.

Basic to this way of approaching the field is the widely shared assumption that the area of human practice known as religion is somehow removed or set apart from those historical and social influences that commonly go by the name of culture (which includes such things as language, art, types of social organization, and social custom). Upon further examining this assumption it becomes evident that an even more basic assumption is up and running, concerning the popular belief that the area we identify as religion (sometimes called "organized religion") is in fact the public, and therefore observable, expression of what is believed to be a prior, inner experience, feeling, faith, or sentiment that defies adequate expression (William James is but one of the vanguards of this still up-and-running tradition, Wilfred Cantwell Smith another, along with every person who today says they are spiritual and not religious). The term "religion," then, is thought by many to name the public manifestations (in texts, rituals, symbols, institutions, etc.) of an otherwise inner, personal essence or experience—think of Friedrich Schleiermacher's strategic distinction between "that miserable love of systems" and the authentic interiority of piety, feeling, and intuition. Because one cannot get inside other people's heads to study what the philosopher Immanuel Kant would have termed the noumenon—or so the argument goes—this view assumes that scholars of religion are therefore left with studying secondary, public expressions (Kant's empirically observable phenomena), comparing them across cultures in search of the similarities and differences that may help us to make inferences about that unobservable and inexpressible unity which is thought to have inspired the diversity of beliefs, behaviors, and institutions. Much like Eliade's *The Sacred and the Profane*, "Religion *and* Culture," then, names the field which takes as its data the visible shape adopted by what is presumably the inner, transcendental, and distinct essence of religion—a shape taken when piety is not just felt inwardly but expressed publicly in such historical settings as art, architecture, writing, behavior, and so on—that is, in this domain we know as culture. Put simply, drawing on an often found metaphor in the field, we study the branches, which are visible, in order to understand the roots, which are hidden and deep.

Contrary to this approach, to study religion *in* culture—much as seeing the sacred as nothing more or less than the profane—means that one does not begin with the assumption that two distinct domains periodically bump into each other, for the good or ill of either, producing so-called hybrid or blended effects. Instead, the preposition "in" signifies that the area of human behavior we have come to know as "religion" is assumed, from the outset, to be but one element within human cultural systems—systems which are themselves historical products that, because they are public, can be studied. An assumption basic to this approach is that the objects of study for any scholar in any branch of the human sciences are historical creations that had a beginning and that will change over time. Whether these changes are random or regular, and therefore governed by other factors—such as gender, economics, politics, cognition, or even geography and environmental features—is one of the areas that such scholars explore. To study religion *in* culture therefore means that one's object of study is a product of human belief, behavior and social systems. Nothing more and nothing less.

Although it may strike some as a little too subtle, the preposition found in "Studying Religion *in* Culture," much as with dropping the conjunction in Eliade's well-known title, signals an important theoretical shift—one that creates a significant gap between Arnal and me, on the one hand, and the work of many of our intellectual predecessors and even some of our peers, on the other—allowing us to conceptualize one formerly distinct item as but an element of the other. In our book the sacred is therefore conceived as nothing more or less than the profane—they are inevitably coterminous and the impression of their distinction is necessarily the result of specific social actors enacting and policing divisions. Which is none other than what Durkheim argued over one hundred years ago—set apart and forbidden.... By whom? For what reason? By what means?

Whatever else religion may or may not be, for the purposes of our work the very presumption that part of the social domain is religious is at least a fascinating element within wider human cultural systems. And this element is made possible by the widely circulating but ill-defined concept represented by the word "religion" itself. This concept and this word are therefore items that rightly ought to be studied, we think, as part of a folk taxonomy local to our own group, as well as others, and doing so by using the same tools and methods that our peers employ throughout the rest of the university, to study how other cultures are fabricated—seeing their components not as true or false but as ongoing works in progress.

Notes

1.   See Jonathan VanAntwerpen's editorial blog post that started *The Imma-nent Frame* (http://blogs.ssrc.org/tif/2007/10/18/25/) for links to the initial reviews by Robert Bellah, Akeel Bilgrami, Wendy Brown, Elizabeth Shakman Hurd, Colin Jager, and Hent de Vries. Taylor's book is cited extensively in subsequent posts as well.

2.   The first of the two-part post can be found at: http://www.politicaltheology. com/blog/the-sacred-is-the-profane-part-1-russell-mccutcheon/ (accessed April 30, 2013).
3.   Thanks to Bill Arnal for comments on the first draft of this essay.

Afterword

What remains to be said, at the end of a book such as this, after I've not only repeated some of what I've written in the past but after I've also added something new, as an introduction to each past writing, to help make what I once wrote relevant all over again—what more can one add after having had one's rhetorical cake and eating it too?

As I stated in the Preface, my intended reader, both in this book and, as I realized some years ago, throughout much of my career, has been someone near the start of his or her own career—whether an undergrad or grad student or perhaps even an untenured Assistant Professor—someone dissatisfied with the field as it currently is but perhaps unable to imagine how, and in what specific ways, it could be otherwise. As someone who once had—and, as ought to be fully apparent by now, certainly still has—dissatisfactions of his own with the field, and who has tried, at a variety of sites, to imagine and put into practice a different way of being a scholar of religion (from writing a variety of types of books and editing journals, to serving in professional associations and working alongside colleagues to reinvent a small, undergraduate Department in a public university in the US), I think that it is fitting to end the book with a quotation from a writer who rarely makes his way explicitly into my work but whose influence lurks in the background of many on whom I do rely. For in this one quotation I find many of the themes of this book nicely working together—from category formation and the dangers of misplaced concreteness to the place of rhetoric, the historicity of value systems, as well as the inevitability of social change. The last is crucial, by the way, for despite my longtime focus on critique—and the manner in which my work has sometimes been dismissed as "nothing but negative criticism," I think that more generous readers will know that there is more than criticism to being a critic. For those with ears to hear, a creative program has always been outlined, in the midst of the critique.

So I end by leaving the stage to Friedrich Nietzsche's thoughts on new beginnings—though, because it was my choice to put his words here, I've not really left at all, have I?

58. Only as Creators!

This has caused me the greatest trouble and still does always cause me the greatest trouble: to realize that *what things are called* is unspeakably more important than what they are. The reputation, name, and appearance, the worth, the usual measure and weight of a thing—originally almost always something mistaken and arbitrary, thrown over things like a dress and quite foreign to their nature and even to their skin—has, through the belief in it and its growth from generation to generation, slowly grown onto and into the thing and has become its very body: what started as appearance in the end nearly always becomes essence and *effectively acts* as its essence! What kind of a fool would believe that it is enough to point to this origin and this misty shroud of delusion in order to destroy the world that counts as "real," so-called "reality"! Only as creators can we destroy!—But let us also not forget that in the long run it is enough to create new names and valuations and appearances of truth in order to create new "things."

(*The Gay Science*, Book Two [1882])

References

Abeysekara, Ananda (2011). "The Un-translatability of Religion, The Un-translatability of Life: Thinking Talal Asad's Thought Unthought in the Study of Religion." *Method & Theory in the Study of Religion* 23: 257–82.

Ali, Teriq (2002). *The Clash of Fundamentalisms: Crusades, Jihads, and Modernity*. London: Verso.

Allen, Charlotte (1996). "Is Nothing Sacred? Casting Out the Demons from Religious Studies." *Lingua Franca* 6/7: 30–40.

Allen, Douglas (2002). *Myth and Religion in Mircea Eliade*. New York: Routledge.

Althusser, Louis (2001) [1971]. *Lenin and Philosophy and Other Essays*. New York: Monthly Review Press.

Alton, Bruce (1986). "Method and Reduction in the Study of Religion." *Studies in Religion* 15: 153–64.

—(1989). "Before Method: Cognitive Aims in the Study of Religion." *Studies in Religion* 18/4: 415–25.

Ankersmit, F. R. (2005). *Sublime Historical Experience*. Stanford, CA: Stanford University Press.

Anonymous (1998). Review of *Manufacturing Religion*. *Christian Century* 115/5: 187.

Arnal, William E. (1998). "What if I Don't Want to Play Tennis?: A Rejoinder to Russell McCutcheon on Postmodernism and Theory of Religion." *Studies in Religion* 27/1: 61–66.

—(2005). *The Symbolic Jesus: Historical Scholarship, Judaism and the Construction of Contemporary Identity*. London: Equinox Publishing Ltd.

—(2010). "The Laboratory of Ancient Religions: A Response to Athanasios Koutoupas." *Bulletin for the Study of Religion* 39/2: 30–33.

Arnal, William, and Willi Braun (2012). "The Irony of Religion." In William Arnal, Willi Braun, and Russell T. McCutcheon (eds.), *Failure and Nerve in the Academic Study of Religion: Essays in Honor of Donald Wiebe*, 231–38. Sheffield: Equinox Publishing Ltd.

Arnal, William E., Willi Braun, and Russell T. McCutcheon (eds.) (2012). *Failure and Nerve in the Academic Study of Religion: Essays in Honors of Donald Wiebe*. Sheffield: Equinox Publishing Ltd.

Arnal, William E., and Russell T. McCutcheon (2013). *The Sacred is the Profane: The Political Nature of "Religion."* New York: Oxford University Press.

Atwood, Margaret (1972a). *Surfacing*. Toronto: McClelland and Stewart.

—(1972b). *Survival: A Thematic Guide to Canadian Literature*. Toronto: Anansi.

Barthes, Roland (1973). *Mythologies*. London: Paladin.

Baudrillard, Jean (1995) [1991]. *The Gulf War Did Not Take Place*. Bloomington, IN: University of Indiana Press.

Bayart, Jean-François (2005).*The Illusion of Cultural Identity*. Steven Rendall, Janet Roitman, Cynthia Schoch, and Jonathan Derrick (trans.). Chicago: University of Chicago Press.

Bell, Catherine (1992). *Ritual Theory, Ritual Practice.* New York: Oxford University Press.

—(1997). *Ritual: Perspectives and Dimensions.* New York: Oxford University Press.

Benavides, Gustavo (2000). "What Raw Materials Are Used in the Manufacture of Religion?" *Culture and Religion* 1/1: 113–22.

— (2002). "The Tyranny of the Gerund in the Study of Religion." In Giulia Sfameni Gasparro (ed.), *Themes and Problems in the History of Religions in Contemporary Europe* [*Temi e problem della Storia delle Religioni nell'Europa contemporanea*], 53–66. Cosenza, Italy: Lionello Giordano.

Berger, Adriana (1989). "Fascism and Religion in Romania." *Annals of Scholarship* 6: 455–65.

—(1994). "Mircea Eliade: Romanian Fascism and the History of Religions in the United States." In Nancy Harrowitz (ed.), *Tainted Greatness: Antisemitism and Cultural Heroes*, 51–74. Philadelphia: Temple University Press.

Berlinerblau, Jacques (2005). "Durkheim's Theory of Misrecognition: In Praise of Arrogant Social Theory." In Terry Godlove (ed.), *Teaching Durkheim*, 213–33. New York: Oxford University Press.

Bianchi, Ugo (ed.) (1994). *The Notion of "Religion" in Comparative Research: Selected Proceedings of the XVIth Congress of the International Association for the History of Religions, Rome, 3rd–8th September, 1990.* In cooperation with Fabio Mora and Lorenzo Bianchi. Rome: "L'Erma" di Bretschneider.

Birk, Sandow (2012). "Artist's Statement: American Qur'an." *Journal of the American Academy of Religion* 80/3: 581–86.

Bivins, Jason C. (2012). "Ubiquity Scored: Belief's Strange Survivals." *Method & Theory in the Study of Religion* 24/1: 55–63.

Bleeker, C. J. (1960). "The Future Task of the History of Religions." *Numen* 7: 221–34.

Bloch, Maurice (2008). "Why Religion is Nothing Special but is Central." *Philosophical Transactions of the Royal Society* B 363: 2055–61.

Boer, Roland (ed.) (2010). *Secularism and Biblical Studies.* London: Equinox Publishing Ltd.

Borges, Jorge Luis (1999). "John Wilkins' Analytic Language." In Eliot Weinberger (ed.) and Esther Allen, Suzanne Jill Levine, and Eliot Weinberger (trans.), *Selected Non-Fictions*, 229–32. New York: Viking.

Bourdieu, Pierre (1988) [1984]. *Homo Academicus.* Peter Collier (trans.). Stanford, CA: Stanford University Press.

—(1992). *The Logic of Practice.* Richard Nice (trans.). Stanford, CA: Stanford University Press.

Braudy, Dorothy (2013). "Artist's Statement: Sacred Los Angeles." *Journal of the American Academy of Religion* 81/1: 1–5.

Braun, Willi (1999a). "Amnesia in the Production of (Christian) History." *Bulletin of the Council of Societies for the Study of Religion* 28/1: 3–8.

—(1999b). "Sociology, Christian Growth, and the Obscurum of Christianity's Imperial Formation in Rodney Stark's *The Rise of Christianity.*" *Religious Studies Review* 25/2: 128–32.

—(2007). "The Study of Religion and the Mischief of Curiosity." In Panayotis Pachis, Petros Vasiliadis, and Dimitris Kaimakis (eds.), *Friendship and Society: Festschrift in Honor of Professor Gregorios D. Ziakas*, 63–77. Thessaloniki, Greece: Vanias Publishers.

—(2010). "Introduction: Greco-Roman Religions in Focus." *Bulletin for the Study of Religion* 39/2: 26.

Braun, Willi, and Russell T. McCutcheon (eds.) (2000). *Guide to the Study of Religion*. London: Continuum.

—(2008). *Introducing Religion: Essays in Honor of Jonathan Z. Smith*. London: Equinox Publishing Ltd.

Brown, Peter (2003). *A Life of Learning*. American Council of Learned Societies Occasional Paper Series, no. 55. New York: ACLS.

Burkert, Walter (1985) [1977]. *Greek Religion*. Cambridge, MA: Harvard University Press.

Burnett, D. Graham (2007). *Trying Leviathan: The Nineteenth-Century New York Court Case That Put the Whale on Trial and Challenged the Order of Nature*. Princeton, NJ: Princeton University Press.

Burris, John (2001). *Exhibiting Religion: Colonialism and Spectacle at International Expositions 1851–1893*. Charlottesville: University Press of Virginia.

—(2003). "Text and Context in the Study of Religion." *Method & Theory in the Study of Religion* 15: 28–47.

Cameron, Ron, and Merrill P. Miller (eds.) (2004). *Redescribing Christian Origins*. Atlanta: Society of Biblical Literature.

Campany, Robert Ford (2012). "Chinese History and Writing about 'Religion(s)': Reflections at a Crossroads." In Volkhard Krech and Marion Steinicke (eds.), *Dynamics in the History of Religions Between Asia and Europe: Encounters, Notions, and Comparative Perspectives*, 273–94. Leiden: E. J. Brill.

Capps, Walter H. (1995). *Religious Studies: The Making of A Discipline*. Minneapolis: Fortress Press.

Carrette, Jeremy (ed.) (1999). *Religion and Culture, Michel Foucault*. New York: Routledge.

—(2000). *Foucault and Religion: Spiritual Corporality and Political Spirituality*. New York: Routledge.

Chabon, Michael (1995). *Wonder Boys*. New York: Picador.

Chidester, David (1996). *Savage Systems: Colonialism and Comparative Religion in Southern Africa*. Charlottesville: University Press of Virginia.

Clarkson, Shannon (1989). "Language about God." *Studies in Religion* 18/1: 37–49.

—(1991). "God-Talk: By What Name Do We Call God?" *Method & Theory in the Study of Religion* 3/1: 121–26.

Darnton, Robert (2003). *George Washington's False Teeth: An Unconventional Guide to the Eighteenth Century*. New York and London: Norton.

Davidson, Robert (2012). "Artist's Statement." *Journal of the American Academy of Religion* 80/4: 852–25.

Davis, Charles (1974). "The Reconvergence of Theology and Religious Studies." *Studies in Religion* 4: 205–21.

—(1984). "Wherein There is No Ecstasy." *Studies in Religion* 13: 393–400.

—(1986). "The Immanence of Knowledge and the Ecstasy of Faith." *Studies in Religion* 15: 191–96.

Dawson, Lorne L. (1986). "Neither Nerve nor Ecstasy: Comment on the Wiebe-Davis Exchange." *Studies in Religion* 15: 145–51.

Denby, David (2003). "Dead Reckoning." *The New Yorker* (October 13): 112–13.

Dennett, Daniel (1995). *Darwin's Dangerous Idea: Evolution and the Meanings of Life*. New York: Simon & Schuster.

—(2006). *Breaking the Spell: Religion as a Natural Phenomenon.* New York and London: Viking.

Detweiler, Robert (1998). "Literary Echoes of Postmodernism." *Journal of the American Academy of Religion* 66/4: 737–46.

Didion, Joan (2001). *Political Fictions.* New York: Alfred A. Knopf.

Douglas, Mary (1992) [1966]. *Purity and Danger: An Analysis of the Concepts of Pollution and Taboo.* London: Routldge.

Dourley, John P. (2001). "Jung, Mysticism, and Myth in the Making." *Studies in Religion* 30/1: 65–78.

Dressler, Marcus, and Arvind-Pal S. Madair (eds.) (2011). *Secularism & Religion-Making.* New York: Oxford University Press.

Dubuisson, Daniel (2003). Trans. William Sayers. *The Western Construction of Religion: Myths, Knowledge, and Ideology.* Baltimore and London: The Johns Hopkins University Press.

Durkheim, Emile (1995) [1912]. Karen E. Fields (intro. and trans.), *The Elementary Forms of Religious Life.* New York: The New Press.

Durkheim, Emile, and Marcel Mauss (1963) [1903]. Rodney Needham (intro. and trans.), *Primitive Classification.* Chicago: University of Chicago Press.

Eagleton, Terry (1991). *Ideology: An Introduction.* New York: Verso.

Eastman, Roger (ed.) (1993). *The Ways of Religion: An Introduction to the Major Traditions.* 2nd edn. New York: Oxford University Press.

Ebersole, Gary L. (1989). "Letter to the Editor." *Method & Theory in the Study of Religion* 1/2: 238–40.

Ehrman, Bart (2012). *Did Jesus Exist? The Historical Argument for Jesus of Nazareth.* New York: HarperCollins.

Eliade, Mircea (1959) [1957]. *The Sacred and the Profane: The Nature of Religion.* New York: Harcourt, Brace & World, Inc.

—(1996) [1958]. Rosemary Sheed (trans.), *Patterns in Comparative Religion.* Trans. Lincoln and Londong: University of Nebraska Press.

—(1990). Mac Linscott Ricketts (trans.), *Journal IV, 1979–1985.* Chicago: University of Chicago Press.

Eliade, Mircea, and Joseph M. Kitagawa (1959). *The History of Religions: Essays in Methodology.* Chicago: University of Chicago Press.

Elliott, Scott (2013). *Reinventing Religious Studies: Key Writings in the History of a Discipline.* Durham, UK: Acumen.

Ellwood, Robert (1999). *The Politics of Myth: A Study of C. G. Jung, Mircea Eliade, and Joseph Campbell.* Albany, NY: State University of New York Press.

Esposito, John L., Darrell J. Fasching, and Todd Lewis (2002). *World Religions Today.* New York: Oxford University Press.

Euripides (1964). W. S. Barrett (trans.), *Hippolytus.* Oxford: Clarendon Press.

—(1992) [1973]. Robert Bragg (intro. and trans.), *Hippolytos.* Oxford: Oxford University Press.

—(2000) [1995]. David Kovacs (ed. and trans.), *Children of Heracles, Hippolytus, Andromache, Hecuba.* Loeb Classical Library, Vol. 484. Cambridge, MA: Harvard University Press.

Fasolt, Constantin (2004). *The Limits of History.* Chicago: University of Chicago Press.

Fernando, Mayanthi (2012). "Belief and/in the Law." *Method & Theory in the Study of Religion* 24/1: 71–80.

260   *Entanglements*

Festugière, André-Jean (1960) [1954]. *Personal Religion among the Greeks*. Berkeley and Los Angleses: University of California Press.

Fisher, Mary Pat (2003). *Living Religions*. 5th edn. New York: Prentice Hall.

Fitzgerald, Tim (1997). "A Critique of the Concept of Religion." *Method & Theory in the Study of Religion* 9/2: 91–110.

—(2000a). "Experience." In Willi Braun and Russell T. McCutcheon (eds.), *Guide to the Study of Religion*, 125–39. London: Continuum.

—(2000b). *The Ideology of Religious Studies*. New York: Oxford University Press.

—(2000c). "Russell T. McCutcheon's *Manufacturing Religion*." *Culture and Religion* 1/1: 99–104.

—(2007a). *Discourse on Civility and Barbarity: A Critical History of Religion and Related Categories*. New York: Oxford University Press.

—(ed.) (2007b). *Religion and the Secular: Historical and Colonial Formations*. London: Equinox Publishing Ltd.

Foucault, Michel (1973) [1966]. *The Order of Things: An Archaeology of the Human Sciences*. New York: Random House.

Freud, Sigmund. (1964) [1959]. "Obsessive Actions and Religious Practices." In James Strachey (ed. and trans.), *The Standard Edition of the Complete Psychological Works of Sigmund Freud*, Vol. 9: 117–27. London: Hogarth.

—(1989) [1927]. James Strachey (trans.) and Peter Gay (intro.), *The Future of an Illusion*. New York: Norton.

—(2012) [1927]. Todd Dufresne (ed.) and Gregory C. Richter (trans.), *The Future of an Illusion*. London: Broadview Press.

Geertz, Armin W. (1999). Review of *Manufacturing Religion*, *Journal of Religion* 79/3: 508–509.

Geertz, Armin W., and Russell T. McCutcheon (eds.) (2000). *Perspectives on Method and Theory in the Study of Religion: Adjunct Proceedings of the XVIIth Congress of the International Association for the History of Religions, Mexico City, 1995*. Leiden: E. J. Brill. (Reprinted from *Method & Theory in the Study of Religion* 12/1 and 12/2 [2000]).

Gellner, Ernest (1974). *The Legitimation of Belief*. Cambridge: Cambridge University Press.

Goldschmidt, Henry (2004). "More Things in Heaven and Earth: Idealism and Materialism in Russell McCutcheon's *The Discipline of Religion*." *Bulletin of the Council of Societies for the Study of Religion* 33/3 and 33/4: 81–83.

Goodenough, E. R. (1959). "Religionswissenchaft." *Numen* 6: 77–95.

Green, Garrett (1995). "Challenging the Religious Studies Canon: Karl Barth's Theory of Religion." *Journal of Religion* 75: 473–86.

Griffiths, Paul J. (1998a). Review of *Manufacturing Religion*, *First Things: A Monthly Journal of Religion and Public Life* 81 (March): 44–48.

—(1998b). "Some Confusions about Critical Intelligence: A Response to Russell T. McCutcheon." *Journal of the American Academy of Religion* 66/4: 893–95.

Harrison, Peter (1990). *"Religion" and the Religions in the English Enlightenment*. Cambridge: Cambridge University Press.

Henaut, Barry W. (1986). "Empty Tomb or Empty Argument: A Failure of Nerve in Recent Studies of Mark 16?" *Studies in Religion* 15: 177–90.

Henking, Susan (1999). Review of *Manufacturing Religion*. *Religious Studies Review* 25/1: 501.

Hick, John (1989). *An Interpretation of Religion: Human Responses to the Transcendent*. New Haven: Yale University Press.

Hinnells, John R. (ed.). (1984). *The Penguin Dictionary of Religions*. New York: Penguin.

Hirsch, E. D. (1988). *Cultural Literacy: What Every American Needs to Know*. New York: Vintage.

Hopfe, Lewis (1994). *Religions of the World*. 6th edn. New York: Macmillan.

Hoy, David (1978). *The Critical Circle: Literature, History, and Philosophical Hermeneutics*. Berkeley, CA: University of California Press.

Hughes, Aaron (2008). *Situating Islam: The Past and Future of an Academy Discipline*. London: Equinox Publishing Ltd.

—(2012a). *Abrahamic Religions: On the Uses and Abuses of History*. New York: Oxford University Press.

—(2012b). *Theorizing Islam: Disciplinary Deconstruction and Construction*. London: Equinox Publishing Ltd.

—(2013a). "Editorial." *Method & Theory in the Study of Religion* 25/1: 1–3.

Hughes, Aaron (ed.) (2013b). *Method & Theory in Religion: Twenty Five Years On*. Leiden: E. J. Brill.

Hume, David (1956) [1757]. H. E. Root (ed.), *The Natural History of Religion*. Stanford, CA: Stanford University Press.

Hussain, Amir (2011). "Editor's Note." *Journal of the American Academy of Religion* 79/1: 1–3.

—(2012a). "Editor's Note: Something Observed." *Journal of the American Academy of Religion* 80/1: 1–2.

—(2012b). "Editor's Note: Robert Davidson, Haida Artist." *Journal of the American Academy of Religion* 80/4: 848–51.

Jakobsen, Janet R., and Ann Pellegrini (eds.) (2008). *Secularisms*. Durham, NC: Duke University Press.

Josephson, Jason Ānanda (2012). *The Invention of Religion in Japan*. Chicago: University of Chicago Press.

Jung, Carl G. (1966) [1938]. *Psychology and Religion*. New Haven: Yale University Press.

—(1968). "Conscious, Unconscious, and Individuation." In *Collected Works of C. G. Jung*, vol. 9, part 1: 275–89. 2nd edn. Princeton, NJ: Princeton University Press.

Jurgensmeyer, Mark (2001). *Terror in the Mind of God: The Global Rise of Religious Violence*. Updated Edition with a New Preface. Berkeley, CA: University of California Press.

Kimball, Charles (2002). *When Religion Becomes Evil*. HarperSanFrancisco.

King, Richard (1999). *Orientalism and Religion: Post-Colonial Theory, India, and "the Mystic East"*. London and New York: Routledge.

King, Ursula (1984). "Historical and Phenomenological Approaches to the Study of Religion." In Frank Whaling (ed.), *Contemporary Approaches to the Study of Religion, Vol. 1 The Humanities*, 29–164. New York: Mouton Publishers.

Kitagawa, Joseph M. (ed.) (1985). *The History of Religions: Retrospect and Prospect*. New York: Macmillan.

Koutoupas, Athanasios (2010). "Religion and Politics under the Ptolemies (300–215)." *Bulletin for the Study of Religion* 39/2: 27–29.

Krakauer, Jon (2003). *Under the Banner of Heaven: A Story of Violent Faith*. New York: Doubleday.

Krech, Volkhard (2012). "Dynamics in the History of Religions: Preliminary Considerations on Aspects of a Research Programme." In Volkhard Krech and

Marion Steinicke (eds.), *Dynamics in the History of Religions between Asia and Europe: Encounters, Notions, and Comparative Perspectives*, 15–70. Leiden: E. J. Brill.

Kristensen, W. Brede (1954). *Religionshistorisk studium*. Oslo: Olaf Norlis Forlag.

Küng, Hans (1986). *Christianity and the World's Religions*. Garden City: Doubleday.

La Capra, Dominick (1983). "Rethinking Intellectual History and Reading Texts." In *Rethinking Intellectual History: Texts, Contexts, Language*, 23–71. Ithaca, NY: Cornell University Press.

Landy, Francis (1990). "On The Gender of God and the Feminist Enterprise: A Response to Shannon Clarkson." *Studies in Religion* 19/4: 485–87.

Latour, Bruno (2010). *On the Modern Cult of the Factish Gods*. Durham, NC: Duke University Press.

Lease, Gary (1994). "The History of 'Religious' Consciousness and the Diffusion of Culture." *Historical Reflections/Réflexions Historiques* 20: 453–79.

LeMaire, André (2002). "Burial Box of James the Brother of Jesus: Earliest Archaeological Evidence of Jesus Found in Jerusalem." *Biblical Archaeology Review* 28/6 (November/December): 24–33, 70.

Lentricchia, Frank (1985). *Criticism and Social Change*. Chicago: University of Chicago Press.

Leuba, James H. (1912). *A Psychological Study of Religion: Its Origin, Function, and Future*. New York: The MacMillan Co.

Lincoln, Bruce (1989). *Discourse and the Construction of Society: Comparative Studies of Myth, Ritual, and Classification*. New York: Oxford University Press.

—(1996). "Theses on Method." *Method & Theory in the Study of Religion* 8: 225–27.

—(1999). *Theorizing Myth: Narrative, Ideology, Scholarship*. Chicago: University of Chicago Press.

—(2012). *Gods and Demons, Priests and Scholars: Critical Explorations in the History of Religions*. Chicago: University of Chicago Press.

Lofton, Kathryn (2012). "Introduction to the Yale Roundtable on Belief." *Method & Theory in the Study of Religion* 24/1: 51–54.

Lopez, Donald S. (1998). "Belief." In Mark C. Taylor (ed.), *Critical Terms for Religious Studies*, 21–35. Chicago, IL: University of Chicago Press.

Ludwig, Theodore (1998). Review of *Manufacturing Religion, The Cresset Trinity* 34–36.

Lyden, John (ed.). (1995). *Enduring Issues in Religion*. San Diego, CA: Greenhaven.

Mack, Burton (1989). "Caretakers and Critics: On the Social Role of Scholars Who Study Religion." Unpublished paper presented to the Seminar on Religion in Society, Wesleyan University.

—(1999). "Many Movements, Many Myths. Redescribing the Attractions of Early Christianities: Toward a Conversation with Rodney Stark." *Religious Studies Review* 25/2: 132–36.

—(2000). "Social Formation." In Willi Braun and Russell T. McCutcheon (eds.), *Guide to the Study of Religion*, 283–96. London: Continuum.

—(2001). "Caretakers and Critics: On the Social Role of Scholars Who Study Religion." *Bulletin of the Council of Societies for the Study of Religion* 30: 32–38.

MacKendrick, Kenneth G. (1999). "The Aporetics of a Tennis-Playing Brontosaurus, or a Critical Theory of Religion: A Rejoinder to Russell T. McCutcheon and William E. Arnal." *Studies in Religion/Sciences Religieuses* 28/1: 77–83/

Martin, Craig, and Russell T. McCutcheon (eds.) (2012). *Religious Experience: A Reader*. With Leslie Dorrough Smith. Durham, UK: Acumen.

Martin, Luther H. (1996). "Introduction: The Post-Eliadean Study of Religion: The New Comparativism." *Method & Theory in the Study of Religion* 8/1: 1–3.

—(2000). "Introduction: Review Symposium on Russell T. McCutcheon's *Manufacturing Religion: The Discourse on Sui Generis Religion and the Politics of Nostalgia*." *Culture and Religion* 1/1: 95–97.

—(2009). "The Mithraic Mind: Olympia Panagiotidou's 'Cognitive Approach to the Worldview of Mithraism'." Unpublished.

Martin, Luther, and Donald Wiebe (2004). "Establishing a Beachhead: NAASR, Twenty Years Later." Available at: http://naasr.com/Establishingabeachhead.pdf (accessed March 20, 2013).

—(2012). "Religious Studies as a Scientific Discipline: The Persistence of a Delusion." *Journal of the American Academy of Religion* 80/3: 587–97.

Masa-Bains, Amalia (2012). "Artist's Statement." *Journal of the American Academy of Religion* 80/1: 3–6.

Masuzawa, Tomoko (2000a). "Origin." In Willi Braun and Russell T. McCutcheon (eds.), *Guide to the Study of Religion*, 209–24. London: Continuum.

—(2000b). "The Production of Religion and the Task of the Scholar: Russell McCutcheon among the Smiths." *Culture and Religion* 1/1: 123–30.

—(2005a). *The Invention of World Religions, or How the Idea of European Hegemony Came to be Expressed in the Language of Pluralism and Diversity*. Chicago: University of Chicago Press.

—(2005b). "World Religions." In Lindsay Jones (ed.), *Encyclopedia of Religion*. 2nd edn, vol. 14: 9800–804. New York: Macmillan.

McCauley, Robert N. (2011). *Why Religion is Natural and Science is Not*. New York: Oxford University Press.

McCutcheon, Russell T. (1993). "The Myth of the Apolitical Scholar: The Life and Works of Mircea Eliade." *Queen's Quarterly* 100/3: 642–63.

—(1995). "The Category 'Religion' in Recent Publications: A Critical Survey." *Numen* 42/3: 284–309. Revised and reprinted as McCutcheon 1997b: ch. 5.

—(1997a). "A Default of Critical Intelligence: The Scholar of Religion as Public Intellectual." *Journal of the American Academy of Religion* 65/2: 443–68. Revised and reprinted as McCutcheon 2001a: 125–44.

—(1997b). *Manufacturing Religion: The Discourse on Sui Generis Religion and the Politics of Nostalgia*. New York: Oxford University Press.

—(1997c). "My Theory of the Brontosaurus: Postmodernism and 'Theory' of Religion." *Studies in Religion/Sciences Religieuses* 26/1: 3–23. Revised and reprinted as McCutcheon 2001a: ch. 7.

—(1998a). "Redescribing 'Religion' as Social Formation: Toward a Social Theory of Religion." In Thomas A. Idinopulos and Brian C. Wilson (eds.), *What is Religion? Origins, Definitions, and Explanations*, 51–71. Leiden: E. J. Brill. Revised and reprinted as McCutcheon 2001a: ch. 2.

—(1998b). "Returning the Volley to William E. Arnal." *Studies in Religion/Sciences Religieuses* 27/1: 67–68. See Chapter 3 in this volume.

—(1998c). Review of Bryan Rennie, *Reconstructing Eliade*. *Religion* 28/1: 92–97.

—(1998d). "Talking Past Each Other—Public Intellectuals Revisited: Rejoinder to Paul J. Griffiths and June O'Connor." *Journal of the American Academy of Religion* 66/4: 911–17. Revised and reprinted as McCutcheon 2001a: ch. 9.

—(1999a). "Forum: Of Strawmen and Humanists: Response to Bryan Rennie," *Religion* 29 (1999): 91–92. See Chapter 4 in this volume.

—(ed.) (1999b). *The Insider/Outside Problem in the Study of Religion: A Reader.* London: Continuum.

—(1999c). Review of Walter Capps, *Religious Studies: The Making of a Discipline.* *Zygon* 34: 527–30.

—(2000a). "Myth." In Willi Braun and Russell T. McCutcheon (eds.), *Guide to the Study of Religion*, 190–208. London: Continuum.

—(2000b). "Taming Ethnocentrism and Trans-Cultural Understandings." In Armin W. Geertz and Russell T. McCutcheon (eds.), *Perspectives on Method & Theory in the Study of Religion. Adjunct Proceedings of the XVIIth Congress of the International Association for the History of Religions, Mexico City, 1995*, 298–306. Leiden: E. J. Brill. Revised and reprinted as McCutcheon 2001a: ch. 5.

—(2001a). *Critics Not Caretakers: Redescribing the Public Study of Religion.* Albany: State University of New York Press.

—(2001b). "Methods, Theories, and the Terrors of History: Closing the Eliadean Era With Some Dignity." In Bryan S. Rennie (ed.), *Reconsidering Eliade: The Meaning and End of Mircea Eliade*, 11–23. Albany, NY: State University of New York Press. Revised and reprinted as McCutcheon 2003a: ch. 9.

—(2003a). *The Discipline of Religion: Structure, Meaning, Rhetoric.* London and New York: Routledge.

—(2003b). "Dispatches from the Wars of 'Religion'." In Timothy Light and Brian Wilson (eds.), *Religion as a Human Capacity: A Festschrift in Honor of E. Thomas Lawson*, 161–89. Leiden: E. J. Brill.

—(2003c) "The Ideology of Closure and the Problem of the Insider/Outsider Problem in the Study of Religion." *Studies in Religion* 32/3: 361–76.

—(2003d). Dimitris Xygalatas (trans.), *Kataskeuazontas ti Threskeia.* [Greek translation of *Manufacturing Religion* (1997b)]. Thessaloniki, Greece: Vanias Editions.

—(2004a). "Reinventing the Study of Religion in Alabama: A Symposium." *Bulletin of the Council of Societies for the Study of Religion* 33/2: 27–29.

—(2004b). "Religion, Ire, and Dangerous Things." *Journal of the American Academy of Religion* 72/1: 173–93.

—(2004c). "'Religion' and the Problem of the Governable Self, or, How to Live in a Less than Perfect Nation." *Method & Theory in the Study of Religion* 16/2: 164–81.

—(2005a). "A Few Words on the Temptation to Defend the Honor of a Text." *Bulletin of the Council of Societies for the Study of Religion* 33/3 and 33/4: 90–91. See Chapter 8 in this volume.

—(2005b). "The Perils of Having Ones Cake and Eating it Too: Some Thoughts in Response." *Religious Studies Review* 31/1 and 31/2: 32–66. See Chapter 10 in this volume.

—(2005c). *"Religion" and the Domestication of Dissent, or How to Live in a Less than Perfect Nation.* London: Equinox Publishing Ltd.

—(2006a). "'It's a Lie. There's No Truth in it! It's a Sin!': On the Limits of the

Humanistic Study of Religion and the Costs of Saving Others from Themselves." *Journal of the American Academy of Religion* 74/3: 720–50.

—(2013). *Religionswissenschaft: Einführung und Grundlagen. Steffen Führding and Elija Lutze* (trans.). Frankfurt, Germany: Peter Lang.

—(2006b). "The Resiliency of Conceptual Anachronisms." *Religion* 36/3: 154–65.

—(2007). *Studying Religion: An Introduction.* London: Equinox Publishing Ltd.

—(2010). "Will Your Cognitive Anchor Hold in the Storms of Culture?" *Journal of the American Academy of Religion* 78/4: 1182–93.

—(2012). "The State of Islamic Studies in the Study of Religion: An Introduction." *Method & Theory in the Study of Religion* 24/4-5: 309–13.

— (2014). *A Modest Proposal on Method: Essaying the Study of Religion.* Leiden: Brill.

McDermott, Emily A. (2000). "Euripides's Second Thoughts." *Transactions of the American Philological Association* 130: 239–59.

McMullin, Neil (1989a). "*The Encyclopedia of Religion*: A Critique from the Perspective of the History of Japanese Religious Traditions." *Method & Theory in the Study of Religion* 1/1: 80–96.

—(1989b). "Response To G. L. Ebersole's Criticism of my Critique of *The Encyclopedia of Religion.*" *Method & Theory in the Study of Religion* 1/2: 243–51.

Merod, Jim (1987). *The Political Responsibility of the Critic.* Ithaca, NY: Cornell University Press.

Milne, Pamela (1989). "Women and Words: The Use of Non-sexist, Inclusive Language in the Academy." *Studies in Religion* 18/1: 25–35.

—(1991). "Naming the Unnameable." *Method & Theory in the Study of Religion* 3/1: 127–33.

Morris, Brian (1987). *Anthropological Studies of Religion: An Introductory Text.* Cambridge: Cambridge University Press.

Nietzsche, Friedrich (1984) [1833–35]. R. J. Hollingdale (intro. and trans.), *Thus Spoke Zarathustra: A Book for Everyone and No One.* New York: Penguin.

—(2001) [1882]. Bernard Williams (ed.), Josefine Nauckhoff and Adrian Del Caro (trans.), *The Gay Science. With a Prelude in German Rhymes and an Appendix in Songs.* Cambridge, UK: Cambridge University Press.

Nongbri, Brent (2012). *Before Religion: A History of a Modern Concept.* New Haven, CT: Yale University Press.

Olupona, Jacob (2011). "Introduction to the Discussion of *A Primal Perspective on the Philosophy of Religion.*" *Journal of the American Academy of Religion* 79/4: 789–94.

Omer, Atalia (2011). "Can a Critic Be a Caretaker too? Religion, Conflict, and Conflict Transformation." *Journal of the American Academy of Religion* 79/2: 459–96.

—(2012). "Rejoinder: On Professor McCutcheon's (Un)Critical Caretaking." *Journal of the American Academy of Religion* 80/4: 1083–97.

—(2013). "In the Critic vs. Caretaker Dichotomy a Magic Dwells: Parroting McCutcheon, Policing 'Religion' (a Rejoinder to Merinda Simmons)." *Method & Theory in the Study of Religion* 25/4-5: 382–402.

Orsi, Robert. (2004a). "Fair Game." *Bulletin of the Council of Societies for the Study of Religion* 33/3-4: 87–89.

—(2004b). "A New Beginning, Again." *Journal of the American Academy of Religion* 72/3: 587–602.

—(2005) *Between Heaven and Earth: The Religious Worlds People Make and the Scholars Who Study Them.* Princeton: Princeton University Press.

—(2012a). "Introduction." In Robert A. Orsi (ed.), *The Cambridge Companion to Religious Studies,* 1–14. New York: Cambridge University Press.

—(2012b). "The Problem of the Holy." In Robert A. Orsi (ed.), *The Cambridge Companion to Religious Studies,* 84–106. New York: Cambridge University Press.

Otto, Rudolf (1950) [1923]. John W. Harvey (trans.), *The Idea of the Holy: An Inquiry into the Non-rational Factor in the Idea of the Divine and Its Relation to the Rational.* London: Oxford University Press.

Oxtoby, Willard G. (1968). "*Religionswissenschaft* Revisited." In Jacob Neusner (ed.), *Religions in Antiquity: Essays in Memory of Erwin Ramsdell Goodenough,* 591–608. Leiden: E. J. Brill.

Paden, William (1992). *Religious Worlds.* Boston: Beacon.

—(2000). "World." In Willi Braun and Russell T. McCutcheon (eds.), *Guide to the Study of Religion,* 334–47. London: Continuum.

Pals, Daniel (1986). "Reductionism and Belief: An Appraisal of Recent Attacks on the Doctrine of Irreducible Religion." *Journal of Religion* 6: 18–36.

—(1987). "Is Religion a Sui Generis Phenomenon?" *Journal of the American Academy of Religion* 55/2: 259–84.

Panagiotidou, Olympia (2009). "Cognitive Approach to the Worldview of Mithraism." Unpublished.

—(2011). "Transformation of the Initiates' Identities after their Initiation into the Mysteries of Mithras." *Bulletin for the Study of Religion* 40/1: 52–61.

Penner, Hans (1986a). "Criticism and the Development of a Science of Religion." *Studies in Religion* 15/2: 165–75.

—(1986b). "Structure and Religion." *History of Religions* 25/3: 236–54.

—(1989). *Impasse and Resolution: A Critique of the Study of Religion.* New York: Peter Lang.

—(1998). "Letter to the Editors." *Method & Theory in the Study of Religion* 10/1: 79–83.

—(1999). Review of *Manufacturing Religion. Teaching Theology and Religious Studies* 2/1: 56–57.

Perkins, Judith (1995). *The Suffering Self: Pain and Narrative Representation in the Early Christian Era.* New York: Routledge.

Plato (1993) [1954]. Hugh Tredennick and Harold Tarrant (trans.) and Harold Tarrant (intro.), *The Last Days of Socrates: Euthyprho, Apology, Crito, Phaedo.* London and New York: Penguin.

—(1987) [1961]. *Euthyphro.* In Edith Hamilton and Huntington Cairns (eds.), Lane Cooper (trans.), *The Collected Dialogues, including the Letters.* Princeton, NJ: Princeton University Press.

Popper, Karl R. (1962). *Conjectures and Refutations: The Growth of Scientific Knowledge.* New York: Basic Books.

Preus, J. Samuel (1987). *Explaining Religion: Criticism and Theory from Bodin to Freud.* New Haven: Yale University Press.

Prothero, Stephen (2007). *Religious Literacy: What Every American Needs to Know—and Doesn't.* New York: HarperCollins.

Proudfoot, Wayne (1985). *Religious Experience.* Berkeley, CA: University of California Press.

Rahmani, L. Y. (1994). *A Catalogue of Jewish Ossuaries in the Collection of the State of Israel.* Jerusalem: Israel Academy of Sciences and Humanities.

Ramey, Steven (2013). "Accidental Favorites: The Implicit in the Study of Religions." Presidential Address to the Southeastern Region of the American Academy of Religion (March 16, 2013). Posted at: http://vimeo.com/64419019 (accessed April 4, 2013).

Rennie, Bryan S. (1992). "The Diplomatic Career of Mircea Eliade: A Response to Adriana Berger." *Religion* 22/4: 375–92.

—(1996). *Reconstructing Eliade: Making Sense of Religion.* Mac Linscott Ricketts (foreword). Albany: State University of New York Press.

—(1998). "Manufacturing the *Sui Generis* Discourse: A Response to Russell McCutcheon." *Religion* 28/4: 413–14.

—(2000). "Manufacturing McCutcheon: The Failure of Understanding in the Academic Study of Religion," *Culture and Religion* 1/1: 105–12.

Riley, Philip Boo (1984). "Theology and/or Religious Studies: A Case Study of *Studies in Religion/Sciences Religieuses*, 1971–1981." *Studies in Religion* 13/4: 423–44.

Robbins, Bruce (ed.) (1990). *Intellectuals, Aesthetics, Politics, Academics.* Minneapolis: University of Minnesota Press.

Roberts, Richard H. (1995). "Globalized Religion? The "Parliament of World's Religions" (Chicago 1993) in Theoretical Perspective." *Journal of Contemporary Religion* 10: 121–37.

—(1998). "The Dialectics of Globalised Spirituality: Some Further Observations." *Journal of Contemporary Religion* 13/1: 65–71.

Rubenstein, Mary-Jane (2012). "The Twilight of the *Doxai*: Or, How to Philosophize with a Whac-a-Mole™ Mallet." *Method & Theory in the Study of Religion* 24/1: 64–70.

Rudolph, Kurt (1985). "The History of Religions and the Critique of Ideologies." *Historical Fundamentals and the Study of Religions*, 61–77. New York: Macmillan.

—(2000). "Some Reflections on Approaches and Methodologies in the Study of Religion." In Tim Jensen and Mikael Rothstein (eds.), *Secular Theories of Religion: Current Perspectives*, 231–47. Copenhagen: Museum Tusculanum.

Rybczynski, Witold (1990). *The Most Beautiful House in the World.* New York: Penguin.

Safi, Omid (2006). *The Politics of Knowledge in Premodern Islam.* Chapel Hill, NC: University of North Carolina Press.

Said, Edward (1994). *Culture and Imperialism.* New York: Random House.

Saler, Benson (1993). *Conceptualizing Religion: Immanent Anthropologists, Transcendent Natives, and Unbounded Categories.* Leiden: E. J. Brill.

Salter, Richard C. (1999). Review of *Manufacturing Religion. Journal for the Scientific Study of Religion* 38/4: 573–74.

Sanchez, Stephen H. (2002). "James was Not a Midget!: Observations on a Visit to the James Ossuary Exhibit at the Royal Ontario Museum," posted at http://bible.org/article/james-was-not-midget-observations-visit-james-ossuary-exhibit-royal-ontario-museum (accessed May 11, 2013).

Schimmel, Annemarie (1960). "Summary of Discussion," *Numen* 7: 235–39.

Schleiermacher, Friedrich (1996) [1799]. Richard Crouter (ed.), *On Religion:*

Speeches to its Cultured Despisers. 2nd edn. Cambridge: Cambridge University Press.

Schneider, Nathan (2013). *God in Proof: The Story of a Search from the Ancients to the Internet*. Berkeley, CA: University of California Press.

Scott, Joan Wallach (1991). "The Evidence of Experience." *Critical Inquiry* 17: 773–97.

Seeley, John Robert (1971) [1883]. J. Gross (ed.), *The Expansion of England: Two Courses of Lectures*. Chicago: University of Chicago Press.

Sexton, John (2013). *Baseball as a Road to God: Seeing Beyond the Game*. New York: Gotham Books.

Segal, Robert A. (2005). "The Function of 'Religion' and 'Myth': A Response to Russell McCutcheon." *Journal of the American Academy of Religion* 73/1: 209–13.

Segal, Robert A., and Donald Wiebe (1989). "Axioms and Dogmas in the Study of Religion." *Journal of the American Academy of Religion* 57/3: 591–605.

Seuss, Dr. (1961). *The Sneetches and Other Stories*. New York: Random House.

Shanks, Hershel (2003a). "Cracks in James Bone Box Repaired: Crowds Flock to Toronto Exhibit." *Biblical Archaeology Review* 29/1 (January/February): 20–25.

—(2003b). "The 2002 Annual Meeting: Horsing Around in Toronto." *Biblical Archaeology Review* 29/2 (March/April): 50–59.

Shanks, Hershel, and Ben Witherington (2003). *The Brother of Jesus: The Dramatic Story and Meaning of the First Archaeological Link to Jesus and his Family*. San Francisco: HarperSanFrancisco.

Sharf, Robert H. (1998). "Experience." In Mark C. Taylor (ed.), *Critical Terms in Religious Studies*, 94–116. Chicago: University of Chicago Press.

Sharpe, Eric (1986) [1975]. *Comparative Religion: A History*. London: Duckworth.

Simmons, K. Merinda (2013a). "Protective Parroting: A Rejoinder to Atalia Omer." *Method & Theory in the Study of Religion* 25/4-5: 403–407.

—(2013b). "Regulating Identities: The Silences of Critical Caretaking." *Method & Theory in the Study of Religion* 25/4-5: 362–81.

Slater, Peter (2005) [1987]. "Hope." In Lindsay Jones (ed.), *Encyclopedia of Religion*, 2nd edn. Vol. 6: 4125–27. Detroit and New York: Thomson Gale.

Smart, Ninian (1973). *The Phenomenon of Religion*. London: MacMillan.

Smith, Huston (1959) [1958]. *The Religions of Man*. New York: The New American Library (Mentor Books).

Smith, Jonathan Z. (1975). "The Social Description of Early Christianity." *Religious Studies Review* 1/1: 19–25.

—(1982). *Imagining Religion: From Babylon to Jonestown*. Chicago: University of Chicago Press.

—(1988). "'Narratives into Problems': The College Introductory Course and the Study of Religion." *Journal of the American Academy of Religion* 56: 727–39.

—(1990). *Drudgery Divine: On Comparison of Early Christianities and the Religions of Late Antiquity*. School of Oriental and African Studies: University of London.

—(gen. ed.) (1995a). *The Harper Collins Dictionary of Religion*. HarperSanFrancisco: San Francisco.

—(1995b). "Religious Studies" Whither (Wither) and Why." *Method & Theory in the Study of Religion* 7/4: 407–14.

—(1996). "A Matter of Class: Taxonomies of Religion." *Harvard Theological Review* 89/4: 387–403.

—(1998). "Religion, Religions, Religious." In Mark C. Taylor (ed.), *Critical Terms for Religious Studies*, 269–84. Chicago: University of Chicago Press.

—(2000a). "Bible and Religion." *Bulletin of the Council of Societies for the Study of Religion* 29: 87–93.

—(2000b). "Classification." In Willi Braun and Russell T. McCutcheon (eds.), *Guide to the Study of Religion*, 35–43. London: Continuum.

—(2000c). "Bible and Religion." *Bulletin of the Council of Societies for the Study of Religion* 29: 87–93.

—(2004). *Relating Religion: Essays in the Study of Religion*. Chicago: University of Chicago Press.

—(2007). "The Necessary Lie: Duplicity in the Disciplines." In Russell T. McCutcheon, *Studying Religion: An Introduction*, 74–80. London: Equinox Publishing Ltd.

—(2009). "Religion and Bible." *Journal of Biblical Literature* 128/1: 5–27.

—(2013). Christopher Lehrich (ed.), *On Teaching Religion*. New York: Oxford University Press.

Smith, Wilfred Cantwell (1959). "Comparative Religion: Whither—and Why?" In Mircea Eliade and Joseph Kitagawa (eds.), *The History of Religions: Essays in Methodology*, 31–58. Chicago: University of Chicago Press.

—(1993). *What is Scripture?: A Comparative Approach*. Minneapolis: Fortress Press.

—(1998) [1962]. *Patterns of Faith around the World*. Oxford: Oneworld.

Smith, William Robertson (2002) [1889]. Robert A. Segal (intro.), *Religion of the Semites*. Piscataway, NJ: Transaction Publishers.

Staal, Frits (1979). "The Meaninglessness of Ritual." *Numen* 26: 2–22.

Stamotoulakis, Klearhos (2008). "Magic in Ancient Greece and Modern Izmir: A Comparison." Unpublished.

Stein, Gertrude (1937). *Everybody's Autobiography*. New York: Random House.

Steinicke, Marion (2012). "Introduction." In Volkhard Krech and Marion Steinicke (eds.), *Dynamics in the History of Religions Between Asia and Europe: Encounters, Notions, and Comparative Perspectives*, 1–13. Leiden: E. J. Brill.

Stern, Jessica (2003). *Terror in the Name of God: Why Religious Militants Kill*. New York: Harper Collins.

Strenski, Ivan (1987). *Four Theories of Myth in Twentieth-Century History*. Iowa City: University of Iowa Press.

—(1998). "On 'Religion' and its Despisers." In Thomas A. Idinopolus and Brian C. Wilson (eds.), *What is Religion? Origins, Definitions, and Explanations*, 113–32. Leiden: E. J. Brill.

—(2002). Review of R. McCutcheon, *Critics Not Caretakers. Journal of the American Academy of Religion* 70: 427–30.

Styers, Randall (2009). "A Reply to Klearhos Stamotoulakis's 'Magic in Ancient Greece and Modern Izmir: A Comparison'." Unpublished.

Sullivan, Winnifred Fallers (2005). *The Impossibility of Religious Freedom*. Princeton NJ: Princeton University Press.

Sullivan, Winnifred Fallers, Robert A. Yelle, and Mateo Taussig-Rubbo (eds.) (2011). *After Secular Law*. Stanford, CA: Stanford University Press.

Sutcliffe, Steven (1999). Review of *Manufacturing Religion. Bulletin of the British Association for the Study of Religions* 86 (March): 29–31.

Swift, Jonathan (2009) [1729]. "A Modest Proposal." In Carole Fabricant (ed. and intro.), *A Modest Proposal and Other Writings*, 230–39. London: Penguin.

Taira, Teemu (2012). "Making Space for Discursive Study in Religious Studies." *Religion* 43/1: 26–45.

Taves, Ann (2009). *Religious Experience Reconsidered: A Building Block Approach to the Study of Religion and Other Special Things*. Princeton, NJ: Princeton University Press.

—(2012). "Response to Russell T. McCutcheon's Review Essay: "Will Your Cognitive Anchor Hold in the Storms of Culture?" 78/4: 1182–93." *Journal of the American Academy of Religion* 80/1: 233–35.

Taylor, Charles (1989). *Sources of the Self: The Making of the Modern Identity*. Cambridge, MA: Harvard University Press.

—(1991). *The Ethics of Authenticity*. Cambridge, MA: Harvard University Press.

—(2007). *A Secular Age*. Cambridge, MA: Harvard University Press.

Thompson, E. P. (1991) [1963]. *The Making of the English Working Class*. New York: Penguin.

Thompson, Thomas L. (1999). *The Mythic Past: Biblical Archaeology and the Myth of Israel*. New York: Basic Books.

Thursby, Gene (1998). Review of *Manufacturing Religion, Choice* 35/6: 429.

Touna, Vaia (2008). *Μηδέν Ἄγαν: Η τραγικότητα του Ανθρώπου στον Υπόλυτο του Ευριπίδη* (*Meden Agan: The Tragedy of Man in Euripides's Hippolytus*). Thesis Submitted for the Degree of MA, Faculty of Theology, Aristotle University (Thessaloniki, Greece).

—(2010). "The Manageable Self in the Early Hellenistic Era." *Bulletin for the Study of Religion* 39/2: 34–36.

Tweed, Thomas (2006). *Crossing and Dwelling: A Theory of Religion*. Cambridge, MA: Harvard University Press.

Vásquez, Manuel A. (2010). *More than Belief: A Materialist Theory of Religion*. New York: Oxford University Press.

Vernant, Jean Pierre (1983) [1965]. *Myth and Thought among the Greeks*. London: Routledge.

Veyne, Paul (1988) [1983]. Paula Wissing (trans.), *Did the Greeks Believe in their Myths? An Essay on the Constitutive Imagination*. Chicago: The University of Chicago Press.

—(ed.) (1987). Arthur Goldhammer (trans.), *A History of Private Life. Vol. 1. From Pagan Rome to Byzantium*. Cambridge, MA: Harvard University Press.

Vries, Hent, de (2008). *Religion: Beyond a Concept*. New York: Fordham University Press.

Waardenburg, Jacques (1973). *Classical Approaches to the Study of Religion: Vol. 1. Aims, Methods, and Theories of Research*. The Hague: Mouton.

—(1974). *Classical Approaches to the Study of Religion: Vol. 2. Bibliography*. The Hague: Mouton.

Waghorne, Joanne Punzo (2004). "*The Discipline of Religion* and the Problem of the Empirical." *Bulletin of the Council of Societies for the Study of Religion* 33/3 and 33/4: 85–87.

Wagner, Roy (1981) [1975]. *The Invention of Culture*. Chicago: University of Chicago Press.

Weber, Max (1993) [1922]. *The Sociology of Religion*. Talcott Parsons (intro.), Ann Swidler (intro), and Ephraim Fischoff (trans). Boston: Beacon Press.

Werblowsky, R. J. Zwi (1960). "Marburg—and After?" *Numen* 7: 215–20.

White, Carol Wayne (2004). "Artful, All too Artful: Re-Inscripting 'Religion'." *Bulletin of the Council of Societies for the Study of Religion* 33/3 and 33/4: 81–91.

—(2005). "Religious Scriptors of Human Possibilities and Cultural Transformations." *Iowa Journal of Cultural Studies* 7: 46–62.

Wiebe, Donald (1983). "Theory in the Study of Religion." *Religion* 13: 283–309.

—(1984). "The Failure of Nerve in the Academic Study of Religion." *Studies in Religion* 13: 401–22. Reprinted in Arnal *et al.* 2012: 6–31.

—(1986). "The Academic Naturalization of Religious Studies: Intent or Pretence?" *Studies in Religion* 15: 197–203.

—(1989). "Is Science Really an Implicit Religion?" *Studies in Religion* 18/2: 171–83.

—(1990a). "History or Mythistory in the Study of Religion? The Problem of Demarcation." In Pye (ed.), *Marburg Revisited: Institutions and Strategies in the Study of Religion*, 31–46. Michael Marburg: Diagonal Verlag.

—(1991). *The Irony of Theology and the Nature of Religious Thought*. Montreal and Kingston: McGill-Queen's University Press.

—(1994). *Beyond Legitimation: Essays on the Problem of Religious Knowledge*. Basingstoke, UK: Palgrave MacMillan.

—(1999). *The Politics of Religious Studies*. New York: St Martin's Press.

—(2004). "The Reinvention or Degradation of Religious Studies? Tales from the Tuscaloosa Woods." *Reviews in Religion & Theology* 11/1: 3–14.

—(2005). "The Politics of Wishful Thinking? Disentangling the Role of the Scholar-Scientist from that of the Public Intellectual in the Modern Academic Study of Religion." *Temenos* 41/1: 7–38.

—(2006). "An Eternal Return All Over Again: The Religious Conversation Endures." *Journal of the American Academy of Religion* 74/3: 674–96.

Yelle, Robert A. (2011). "Moses' Veil: Secularization as Christian Myth." In Winnifred Fallers Sullivan, Robert A. Yelle, and Mateo Taussig-Rubbo (eds.), *After Secular Law*, 23–42. Stanford, CA: Stanford University Press.

Žižek, Slavoj (1997) [1994]. "Introduction: The Spectre of Ideology." In Slavoj Žižek (ed.), *Mapping Ideology*, 1–33. London: Verso.

Index

see secondary source
primitive, rhetoric of 164
private or private/public binary 47,
    53, 71 n. 12, 86, 113, 133, 187,
    189, 216, 238–40, 242, 244
private ownership 212
privilege 4, 133
professionalization 156 ff., 179
    modesty 212
    peer-to-peer 137
    pre-professionalization 158
profit motive 212
Prometheus 154
propaganda vs. free speech 134
propriety 127 n. 9
prototype 172
Proudfoot, Wayne 133, 229
psychology 23, 39
public intellectual 69 n. 2, 151
public sphere, rhetoric of 225
    see also private/public binary
public university 57
purity 217, 246
    see also authenticity,
        hybridization, pollution

race 92–93, 114 n. 3, 216
    studies 190
radicalism, rhetoric of 164, 208
Raj, Selva 147 n. 1
Ramey, Steven 14, 139, 147, 175 n.
    6, 180, 216, 228, 236 n. 2
rationalism 130
Read, Kay A. 147 n. 1
reader/reading 59, 94, 96, 99, 104,
    233
    close reading 52, 92, 107, 130,
        201, 222
    intended xi
    misreading 195
    unreading 231 ff.
realism 48, 70 n. 8
    realist notion of history 103
    traditional 240
redescription 56, 66, 122, 250

reduction (reductionism) xi, 11 n. 3,
    22, 42 n. 10, 119, 123, 128–29
    descriptive 133
    explanatory 133
    metaphysical 25
    methodological 57
    naturalistic 25
    ontological 57
    religious 23–25,
reification 6, 171, 174, 215
relics 6, 90
religion
    adjective 144, 174, 194 n. 20, 220
    ahistorical 134
    archaic 140, 142
    building blocks of 215, 217
    category of 2, 4, 30, 130, 168
    civil 223
    cultural *a priori* 128, 130
    definition of 176 n. 11, 215
    dehistoricized 239
    discourse on
        contingent 242
        defined 241
        historicized 173, 240
    diversity 22, 164 ff.
    embodied 8, 92–93
    established 188
    folk conception of 173
    handy analytic 165
    individualist approach to the study
        of 186
    lived 8
    material 8
    motivations 243
    mystery 189
    national 142
    noun (plural vs. singular) 171,
        174, 220
    on the ground 8
    organized 251
    personal (private) 184, 187, 189,
        194 nn. 20 and 24–25
    plural 146, 220, 240
    primal 140, 142

Lightning Source UK Ltd.
Milton Keynes UK
UKOW04f0206250814

237470UK00001B/12/P